D1785122

A SHORT HISTORY OF MODERN CHINESE LITERATURE

A SHORT HISTORY OF MODERN CHINESE LITERATURE

TING YI

KENNIKAT PRESS
Port Washington, N. Y./London

Publisher's Note

The manuscript of this book was originally used by the author as teaching material in his lectures at many universities in China. In 1954 he was invited to teach at Moscow University. He died there before he had time to revise the manuscript to bring it to final form. As it stands, however, it provides a clear factual analysis of the history of modern Chinese literature. In the present edition for foreign readers, the editor has condensed the original text and added some material on later developments.

This book has been translated from Chinese by Chang Hsing-lien (Chapters 1, 2, 3 and 5), Chang Su-chu (Chapter 4), Chou Chia-tsan (Chapter 6), Wang Cheng-chung (Chapters 7, 8 and 9), Liang Liang-hsing (Chapter 10) and Fang Chen-ya (Chapters 11 and 12).

A SHORT HISTORY OF MODERN CHINESE LITERATURE

First published in 1959
Reissued in 1970 by Kennikat Press
Library of Congress Catalog Card No: 76-103236
SBN 8046-0872-5

Manufactured by Taylor Publishing Company Dallas, Texas

CONTENTS

CHAPTER ONE

THE MAY 4 MOVEMENT AND THE RISE AND GROWTH OF THE MODERN LITERARY REVOLUTION IN CHINA. THE CONTRIBUTIONS OF LU HSUN

Section 1. The May 4 Movement and the Spread of Communist Ideas as the Causes for the Modern Literary Revolution in China

During World War I, when the European imperialist powers were occupied with war and temporarily relaxed their aggressive activities in China, Chinese national capitalism, weak though it was, enjoyed a period of expansion. While its development was limited in scope, being still dependent upon imperialism, the Chinese working class grew rapidly. Industrial workers were then estimated to be around three million. In 1917 the October Socialist Revolution in Russia won its momentous victory. The Soviet Government set up by the proletariat and supported by all the working people proclaimed the abrogation of all unequal treaties concluded by tsarist Russia with China and renounced all privileges without compensation. These friendly measures deeply moved the Chinese working people and progressive intellectuals and stimulated the confidence and militancy of the

Chinese proletariat. Subsequently, Marxism-Leninism was introduced into China and well received by a great number of progressive intellectuals. The confluence of all these streams gradually formed a mighty current.

In April 1919, when the news reached China that at the Paris Peace Conference the capitalist powers had recognized Japan's right to succeed to the former German privileges in Shantung, a great patriotic movement against imperialism broke out. This was the May 4 Movement. It gathered way, and by the time of the June 3 Movement,[1] when the proletariat joined in, it had become a nation-wide anti-imperialist and anti-feudal revolutionary movement. Thereafter, the Chinese revolutionary movement became a new-democratic revolution and part of the world proletarian socialist revolution.

In his *On New Democracy*, Mao Tse-tung drew a scientific summary of the conditions in the Chinese cultural circles prior to May 4, 1919. He wrote:

> The studies in the modern school or new learning or Western learning of that time consisted basically (we say basically, because they still retained some poisonous vestiges of Chinese feudalism) in the natural sciences and the bourgeois social and political theories,

---

[1] This marked a new stage in the patriotic movement launched on May 4, 1919. On June 3, students in Peking held public meetings and made speeches in defiance of persecution and repression by the army and police. Following the lead of the students, the workers and business men in Shanghai, Nanking, Tientsin, Hangchow, Wuhan, Kiukiang and in the provinces of Shantung and Anhwei went on strike. In this manner the May 4 Movement developed into a broad mass movement with the participation of the proletariat, the urban petty bourgeoisie and the national bourgeoisie.

all of which are needed by the representatives of the bourgeoisie. At that time the ideology of the new learning played the revolutionary role of fighting the Chinese feudal ideology, and was in the service of the bourgeois-democratic revolution of the old period. However, as a result of the flabbiness of the Chinese bourgeoisie and the advent of the era of imperialism in the world, such bourgeois ideology was defeated in only a few rounds by the reactionary alliance of the slave ideology of foreign imperialism and the Chinese feudal ideology of going back to the ancients; as soon as this reactionary ideological alliance started a small counter-offensive the new learning folded up its banners, muffled its drums and beat a retreat, losing its soul and retaining only its carcass. The old bourgeois-democratic culture had decayed and become enervated in the era of imperialism: its failure was inevitable.[1]

The period of the May 4 Movement brought entirely different conditions. A brand-new cultural force then appeared in China. The communist ideas guided by the Chinese Communists — based on the communist world outlook and communist theory of social revolution — began to spread.

Back in 1917 there appeared in the *New Youth* magazine (Vol. II, No. 5, Readers' Column), an influential progressive magazine, published a letter advocating socialism, evidencing the effectiveness of the preliminary dissemination of socialist ideas.

---

[1] Mao Tse-tung, *Selected Works*, Lawrence and Wishart, London, 1954, Vol. III, p. 143.

The strong and widespread influence of these ideas can be attributed to the efforts of Li Ta-chao,[1] a communist intellectual and outstanding thinker of that time.

In an article entitled "Youth," published in *New Youth* in 1916, Li Ta-chao called upon the young people to "break the meshes of past history, destroy the prison of old ideas."[2]

With the victory of the October Socialist Revolution in Russia in 1917, Marxism was introduced into China. In November 1918 Li Ta-chao wrote two articles, "The Victory of the Common People" and "The Victory of Bolshevism" (*New Youth*, Vol. V, No. 5). In the first, he pointed to two results of World War I. Politically, he said, it had resulted in a victory of democracy over autocracy and, socially, in a victory of labour over capital. He concluded by saying: "The Russian revolution of 1917 is the harbinger of the world revolution of the twentieth century," and "the world of the future will be the world of the working people." In the second, he made even more profound remarks: "This is a victory for socialism, for Bolshevism, for the Red Flag, for the world's working class, for the new current of the twentieth century!"

After the May 4 Movement, the Chinese proletariat gathered strength and its political consciousness grew. The movement itself helped to spread Marxism-Leninism, a source of great enlightenment. Publications

---

[1] Li Ta-chao (1888-1927) from Loting, Hopei Province, was the earliest popularizer of Marxism-Leninism in China and one of the founders of the Chinese Communist Party. He was killed by warlords on April 28, 1927.

[2] Li Ta-chao, "Spring," *Chinese Literature*, No. 5, 1959, p. 17.

mushroomed: *New Youth* edited by Li Ta-chao and Chen Tu-hsiu,[1] *Hsiangchiang Review* edited by Mao Tse-tung, and other periodicals such as *Weekly Review* and *Chekiang Tide* — all propagating the science of socialism. In 1919, *New Youth* published a special number on the study of Marxism. Subsequently the *Manifesto of the Communist Party* by Marx and Engels was translated into Chinese; its publication exerted a great influence on Chinese thought.

In his *On New Democracy*, Mao Tse-tung said:

> The May 4 Movement was in the beginning a revolutionary movement of the united front of three sections of people — the communist intelligentsia, the revolutionary petty-bourgeois intelligentsia and the bourgeois intelligentsia (the last forming the right wing of the movement at that time).[2]

Communist ideas in fact formed the main stream of thought among the cultural circles and serious thinkers of the day. Allying with and influenced by this main stream were some ideas representing the revolutionary petty bourgeoisie and bourgeoisie.

Editor's note:

After the May 4 Movement, particularly after 1921, some of the bourgeois deserted the movement and went over to the reactionary

---

[1] Chen Tu-hsiu (1879-1942) from Huaining, Anhwei Province, was a professor in Peking University and the editor of *New Youth* at the time of the May 4 Movement. He was one of the founders of the Chinese Communist Party. But later he lost his faith in the future of the revolution and took a liquidationist stand. He was expelled from the Party in 1929.

[2] Mao Tse-tung, *op. cit.*, p. 146.

side; among them Hu Shih was the most conspicuous example. This marked the beginning of the struggle between two diametrically opposed roads in art and literature. It is out of the constant struggle between the proletarian and bourgeois outlooks in art and literature that socialist literature emerged. In China, however, the struggle was marked by a special feature. The Chinese bourgeoisie was weak in its social base and the bourgeois literati were in no position to wage battle against proletarian literature as their European and American counterparts had done. They did make some attempts. First there were Hu Shih and his followers, then the Modern Review clique with Chen Hsi-ying as leader, later the Crescent clique, the "third category,"[1] the "nationalist"[2] literary school, and so on. They openly raised their banner against communism and against the people. But they were never able to muster enough forces and were beaten after a few rounds. On this subject more will be said later.

Section 2. The Rise of the Literary Revolution and Its Theoretical Foundation

(1) What Did the Literary Revolution Sponsor?

The May 4 Movement and the spread of communist ideas were the two basic causes for the rise of the revolutionary movement in modern Chinese literature. On account of these causes, the role this literary movement was destined to play, as soon as it rose, was anti-imperialist and anti-feudal. As to its class foundation,

[1] This was the name by which a handful of reactionary writers like Su Wen styled themselves. They claimed that they belonged neither to the proletariat nor the bourgeoisie, and were above classes and politics.

[2] See p. 52.

it was a united front led by the proletariat. It came in answer to the demands of the people.

As a new form had to be used to suit the new content, the literary revolution began by sponsoring the vernacular style of writing. It would be a serious mistake, however, to regard the literary revolution simply as a movement for the vernacular style of writing. This was merely the form decided by the basic content of the literature. Nevertheless, there were other reasons for advocating the use of the vernacular at that time.

There was the question of historical tradition. In China's feudal society culture had long been the exclusive privilege of the ruling class. The ordinary people, under oppression, developed a rich culture of their own — a literature that passed from mouth to mouth, folk arts and a large number of stories, novels and plays in the vernacular from the Tang and Sung dynasties down. The ruling class despised these works and even attempted to suppress them. But as the people liked them, they became popular and were widely circulated. The adoption of the vernacular style of writing in the literary revolution was, therefore, based on historical tradition and it had a mass foundation.

In the circumstances of the new-democratic revolution, Lu Hsun, Chen Tu-hsiu, Chien Hsuan-tung,[1] Hu Shih and others wrote articles in *New Youth* on the literary revolution. The new literary works produced by Lu Hsun, the most outstanding among them, bore the clear imprint of the impact of this literary renaissance. As these men expressed the pressing demands of the bulk

---

[1] Chien Hsuan-tung (1887-1938) from Wuhsing, Chekiang Province, was a phonologist.

of the intellectuals, the reactions from all quarters were tremendous. When the editorial board of *New Youth* was reorganized in January 1918, the magazine became the first to use the vernacular throughout its issues. Soon afterwards appeared *Weekly Review*, edited by Li Ta-chao, and *New Tide*, edited by students of Peking University. The literary revolution was in full swing.

(2) Lu Hsun's Contributions to the Theories of the Literary Revolution

From the outset of the literary revolution, Lu Hsun began to lay a sound foundation in literary theories and the practice of writing. Under the influence of communist ideas he had clearly seen that literature must be subordinate to revolutionary politics and must play an active role in the struggle against feudalism. A profound understanding of the role of literature was not Lu Hsun's only attribute. More important was his ability to apply his theories to his writing. His short story "A Madman's Diary"[1] published in *New Youth* in May 1918 was a militant declaration against the feudal system. It was also the first work of fiction in modern Chinese literature.

With the unfolding of the literary revolution a number of China's old realistic novels came under discussion. *Water Margin*,[2] *The Dream of the Red Chamber*,[3] *Chin*

[1] This is included in *Selected Works of Lu Hsun*, Foreign Languages Press, Peking, 1956, Vol. I.

[2] A well-known novel about a peasant war in the Sung dynasty, said to have been written by Shih Nai-an in the 14th century.

[3] A long realistic novel of the Ching dynasty, written by Tsao Hsueh-chin (1715?-1763).

Ping Mei,[1] *Romance of the Three Kingdoms*,[2] *Pilgrimage to the West*[3] and *The Scholars*[4] were given high appraisal and accepted as a part of the orthodox literature. This effective blow on the traditional feudal concept was a great historic achievement. It is to be admitted, however, that some advocates lacked a profound understanding of these great literary works and a true understanding of their realism and their affinity to the people. Some (of whom Hu Shih was one) became such advocates on the grounds that these works were written in the vernacular. Yet they slandered the ideas expressed in these works, and took up an absolutely negative attitude towards them. Others, while appreciating the political significance of these old novels to a certain extent, failed to make a deep study of them. Chien Hsuan-tung was one such example.

It remained for Lu Hsun to make a penetrating study and a systematic analysis of this great literary legacy. During this period he wrote *A Brief History of Chinese Fiction*[5] — the first of its kind.

---

[1] A well-known Chinese novel by an unknown author in the latter part of the 16th century on the theme of the life of the townspeople.

[2] A renowned historical novel of the 14th century, reputedly written by Lo Kuan-chung.

[3] A famous legendary tale of the 16th century attributed to Wu Cheng-en (about 1500-1580).

[4] A well-known satirical novel written by Wu Ching-tzu (1701-1754). It was translated and published in English by the Foreign Languages Press of Peking in 1957.

[5] Translated and published in English by the Foreign Languages Press of Peking in 1959.

(3) The Progress of the Literary Revolution and Its Shortcomings

The foregoing discussions on the theories of literary revolution concerned, by and large, the conditions prior to the May 4 Movement and they were carried on among a few people. After that movement, the literary revolution gained a mass basis and made tremendous headway. It was estimated that in 1919 alone at least four hundred newspapers appeared in the vernacular together with a number of periodicals, like *Hsiangchiang Review, Young China, Sunday Review, Liberation and Remoulding, Construction,* and newspaper supplements, like Peking's *Morning Press Supplement, Awakening* of Shanghai's *Minkuo Daily* and *Study Lantern* of Shanghai's *Shih Shih Hsin Pao.* While these periodicals and supplements took different political stands and some of them included other than purely literary material, they all published new literary works, promoted the new cultural movement and used the vernacular. Consequently they hastened the progress of the literary revolution. In the wake of the surging tide of the new-democratic revolution the literary revolution assumed the proportions of a nation-wide movement.

The spread of the literary revolution propelled, and in turn was propelled by, the further progress in the campaign for *kuo yu* (national spoken language), the translation of famous Western literary works and the collection and compilation of folk-lore and songs.

While the literary revolution during the period of the May 4 Movement achieved much to its credit, it was not without shortcomings. The most serious of these was some people's blind worship for Western bourgeois culture and absolute repudiation of their own national literary heritage. They one-sidedly stressed the feudal and backward features of this national heritage and overlooked the fact that it comprised a rich spiritual treasury of a great nation in which were preserved splendid, valuable realistic works of the people. For a considerable period of time, these views exerted an adverse influence on the subsequent literary development.

Section 3. The Development of the Theories of the Literary Revolution

(1) The Founding of the Chinese Communist Party and the Surging Revolutionary Movement Under Its Leadership as Reflected in the Literary Movement

After the Chinese Communist Party was founded on July 1, 1921, it concentrated its efforts on leading the working-class movement. The Hongkong seamen's strike[1] in 1922, the Peking-Hankow railwaymen's strike in 1923 (the February 7 Strike)[2] and the May 30 Movement[3] in

[1] The Hongkong seamen's strike broke out in the beginning of 1922 and lasted for eight weeks, forcing the British imperialist authorities to agree to increase wages, restore the original trade unions, release the arrested workers and compensate the families of those who were killed.

[2] Sometimes known as the "February 7 Massacre." The strike itself broke out on February 4, 1923 for the right to organize trade unions. On February 7, the strikers were brutally shot down by the northern warlords Wu Pei-fu and Hsiao Yao-nan with the support of the British imperialists.

[3] The anti-imperialist movement which swept China in protest

1925, brought about a steady growth in the working-class movement and led to a nation-wide revolutionary upheaval. In 1923 the Chinese Communist Party, at its Third National Congress in Canton, discussed the question of forming a united front with the Kuomintang led by Sun Yat-sen. In the following year Dr. Sun reorganized the Kuomintang at the suggestion of the Communist Party and announced the Three Cardinal Policies: alliance with Soviet Russia, co-operation with the Communist Party and help to the workers and peasants. The Communist Party also gave suggestions, guidance and support to the establishment of the Revolutionary Government at Canton. A popular movement was launched throughout the country for the convocation of a national assembly and the abolition of the unequal treaties forced upon the country by imperialist powers. The workers' and peasants' movements expanded day by day—paving the way for the Northern Expedition in 1926, a punitive campaign against the imperialist-backed warlords.

This revolutionary situation led to the beginning of the first split in the united front in the cultural field after the May 4 Movement. As Lu Hsun said about the New Youth group: "Some of its members rose to high positions, some went into retirement, some moved forward."[1]

Having gone through the May 4 Movement, communist intellectuals like Li Ta-chao turned to practical revolutionary work. When *New Youth* moved to Shanghai in 1920 and became a purely political publication, it could

---

against the action of the British police in firing upon demonstrators in Shanghai on May 30, 1935.

[1] Lu Hsun, *Selected Works*, Peking, 1959, Vol. III, p. 173.

no longer devote itself simultaneously to concrete questions of the literary revolution.

Hu Shih, who represented the right-wing bourgeois intellectuals, began to take alarm and waver as he saw the increasing political consciousness of the great masses of people and the widespread of Marxism-Leninism. In 1919 he had written an article in *Weekly Review* under the title of "More Study of Problems and Less Talk About Isms" in an attempt to prevent the propagation of Marxism-Leninism. Now he was no longer interested in the literary revolution. He not only turned from reality himself but endeavoured to lead others from reality by advocating the bourgeois pragmatic method in what he himself called the "systematization of the old learning of China."

Of the other fighters in the literary revolution, like Chien Hsuan-tung and Liu Pan-nung,[1] some became reticent while others left the ranks. Their fighting enthusiasm died down quickly.

Now only Lu Hsun and a group of young revolutionary petty-bourgeois intellectuals who had emerged after the May 4 Movement were left to carry on the literary revolution. They fought relentlessly against the reactionary feudal forces — old and new. The most outstanding of all was Lu Hsun, who battled with increasing vigour and wielded a great influence.

---

[1] Liu Pan-nung (1891-1934) came from Chiangyin, Kiangsu Province. He took part in the revolutionary cultural movement sponsored by *New Youth* and was a professor of Peking University, the head of the Girls' College affiliated to Peiping University and the editor of *World Daily* supplement.

(2) Lu Hsun's Leading Role in the Literary Revolution of This Period and the Viewpoints of the Literary Research Society and the Creation Society

Encouraged by Lu Hsun there appeared in North China some literary associations of which the more influential and more closely associated with Lu Hsun were the Tatler Society and the Wilderness Society. The Tatler Society was founded in 1924 and moved to Shanghai in 1927. It published *Tatler Weekly* which later became a fortnightly. For some time Lu Hsun was its editor. After he had left it, it eventually folded up. Describing the members of the Tatler Society, he said:

> They talked freely, without scruples, tried to expedite the birth of the new, and made strong attacks on all old things which might endanger the new. What kind of new things should be brought into being, though, they never explained very clearly.[1]

In common with the members of the other principal contemporary literary societies, they had an intense hatred for feudalism but a lack of understanding of the prospects of the revolution and the strength of the proletariat. This was, in general, true of the revolutionary petty bourgeoisie as a whole at that time. Most of the leaders of the Tatler Society had previously been members of the New Youth group — Lu Hsun, Chien Hsuan-tung, Chou Tso-jen, Lin Yu-tang and others. Since they held different views, they went different ways after the May 30 Movement: Lu Hsun joined the camp of revolutionary literature, while Lin Yu-tang served foreign

---

[1] Lu Hsun, *op. cit.*, p. 58.

interests like a comprador and Chou Tso-jen turned traitor and collaborated with the Japanese invaders.

The Wilderness Society was established under the guidance of Lu Hsun in 1925, in answer to the demand of a group of young people interested in literature. It published *Wilderness Weekly* which later became a fortnightly. These young intellectuals had a strong revolutionary urge to fight the old society by means of literary writing. They demanded that literature should become a weapon in this struggle. It was the time, however, when the revolutionary wave was sweeping through the whole country. A literature which merely attacked the old society without a new orientation failed to satisfy the desires of the revolutionary youth. With Lu Hsun's departure from Peking in 1926 the Wilderness Society stopped functioning for lack of leadership.

Between 1921 and 1925, apart from the group of young intellectuals in Peking led by Lu Hsun, who persisted in the struggle on the literary front, there appeared in the South, chiefly in Shanghai, many literary associations which put forward their views on literature. The most influential of them were the Literary Research Society and the Creation Society.

The Literary Research Society was sponsored by twelve people including Shen Yen-ping (Mao Tun), Cheng Chen-to, Keng Chi-chih, Wang Tung-chao, Yeh Shao-chun and Hsu Ti-shan. It was founded in Peking in January 1921 and later moved to Shanghai. Its inauguration declaration stated: "The time is past when literature is taken as an amusement when a man is successful and happy, and a consolation when he suffers a reverse." Later, Mao Tun explained that the declaration implied that literature should reflect social phenomena, and discuss and mirror problems of life in general. Obviously this was a realistic view. But what social phenomena should it reflect? Literature should mirror life, but the life of what class? From what standpoint should it reflect and mirror? These questions were not touched upon.

The Creation Society was founded about 1920 by a group of Chinese students studying in Japan including Kuo Mo-jo, Yu Ta-fu, Cheng Fang-wu, Tien Han and Cheng Po-chi. It became known to the public in 1922 when the *Creation Quarterly* was published.

The postscript to the *Creation Quarterly* No. 2 stated: "It is only because we obey our common inner desire that we engage in literary activities." It was, in fact, a tendency towards romanticism, an expression of an inner desire without stressing the importance of reflecting objective realities. This, however, was only one aspect of their viewpoint and not the principal aspect, which was that they advocated that literature should "serve society and life." For example, in his article entitled "The Tasks of New Literature" Cheng Fang-wu, one of the founders of the Creation Society, while holding that in literature "all utilitarian considerations should be abandoned," at the same time he stressed the current tasks of literature. In another article "Realism and Philistinism," he came out more definitely as an advocate of realism.

Thus the literary view held by the Creation Society was essentially realistic though not without romanticist tendency. With this background, its subsequent stand for revolutionary literature is understandable.

The Creation Society issued five journals in all — *Creation Quarterly, Creation Weekly, Creation Daily, Torrent* (which appeared in 1925), and *Creation Monthly* (which appeared in 1926). In 1929 the society was banned by the Kuomintang reactionary government. The following year, it declared itself dissolved when the China League of the Left-Wing Writers was established.

In short, with a large number of young revolutionary intellectuals taking part, the literary revolution in this period grew in scope. Prior to 1921 there were neither independent art and literary organizations nor purely art and literary publications, and very few books on new literature were published. Between 1921 and the May 30 Movement in 1925, available statistics show that there were about 130 art and literary associations, 100 journals and about 1,000 new literary works and translations. The new literature camp was growing very fast indeed.

(3) The Prelude to the Theories of Revolutionary Literature

After the May 4 Movement, although the revolutionary petty-bourgeois intellectuals in general demanded revolution, they could not find the correct road. Therefore they were perplexed and despondent. Inevitably, however, they came under the influence and inspiration of the growing Communist-led revolutionary movement and the ideas of Marxism-Leninism which were rapidly gaining ground. This found expression in contemporary literature in the form of essays which initiated analytical discussions on the social and class bases of literature. They became the prelude to the "revolutionary literature" sponsored after the First Revolutionary Civil War (1924-27).

In an article entitled "The New Movement in Our Literature," published in *Creation Weekly* (No. 3) in May 1923, Kuo Mo-jo sounded a call for a "revolutionary literature." Subsequently, Chiang Kuang-tzu wrote several articles on revolutionary literature. In 1923 the *Chinese Youth* magazine published a few articles on literature, some of which presented progressive theories. Among the contributors of the latter were Yun Tai-ying,[1] who advocated that the new literature "should stimulate the people to work for national independence and democratic revolution," and should oppose useless writing like the "eight-legged essay," a stereotyped old form of essay; Chiu Shih, who suggested that writers should go among the masses of the workers and said that "it is a disgrace to the literati not to have writers going into the coal pits"; Teng Chung-hsia,[2] who advanced the view that a new poet should "first, produce more works manifesting the great national spirit; secondly, write more to portray the real life of the society around him; and thirdly, do practical work for the revolution."

These views were more specific and practical than those of Kuo Mo-jo. Their publication prepared the way for the later movement for revolutionary literature which developed and spread all over the country and became the main stream of China's new literature after the First Revolutionary Civil War.

---

[1] Yun Tai-ying (1895-1930) was a leader and propagandist in the early youth movement initiated by the Chinese Communist Party. Arrested and killed by the Kuomintang reactionary government in Shanghai in the spring of 1930.

[2] Teng Chung-hsia (1897-1933) was one of the outstanding figures in the early working-class movement led by the Chinese Communist Party. He was arrested in Shanghai in 1933 and killed in Nanking the same year.

Section 4. The Struggle of the Literary Revolutionary Camp Headed by Lu Hsun Against Feudal and Right-Wing Bourgeois Literature

(1) The Struggle Against Feudal Literature

The struggle began with a fierce attack on feudal literature. Of all the fighters at that time Lu Hsun was the most daring and thoroughgoing, dealing feudal literature mortal blows. In 1918 he wrote "Random Thoughts" which were first published in *New Youth* and later compiled into *Hot Air*. All these essays were aimed at feudal culture and feudal literature. Striking at the "national characteristics" group, he wrote: "Some say that China's characteristics are both distinctive and good. How is it then that we are in such a mess, with radicals shaking their heads while die-hards sigh?" He added: "Certainly self-preservation comes first. All we ask is whether a thing has the power to preserve us, not whether it is characteristic or not."[1]

In attacking those who opposed the use of the vernacular. Lu Hsun wrote:

> Not content to be mortals, they want to be immortal. Living on earth, they want to go up to heaven. Modern men, breathing modern air, they want to ram moribund Confucian morality and a dead language down people's throats — what an insult to the present! These are "murderers of the present." And by murdering the present, they are murdering the future too.

---

[1] Lu Hsun, *op. cit.*, Vol. II, p. 29.

But the future belongs to our descendants.[1]

Leading the counter-attack, Lin Shu may be taken as a representative of the feudal, classical writers. His two essays entitled "The Classical Style of Writing Should Not Be Abolished," and "The Rise and Fall of the Classical and Vernacular Styles of Writing" and his letter to Tsai Yuan-pei, Chancellor of Peking University, all voiced support for the feudal ethics and opposition to the use of the vernacular. He was unable to put forward any good reasons, however, and could only make a loud clamour.

After the May 4 Movement, as the imperialists resumed their aggressive activities and warlord rule entrenched itself, feudal literature launched a new offensive against the literary revolution. This was carried out by the contributors to the *Criterion* and *Chia Yin* magazines.

In answer to this move for a revival of the feudal literature and a return to the past, those in the ranks of the literary revolution fought back. Again it was Lu Hsun who delivered the sharpest, strongest and deadliest blows.

(2) The Struggle Against Right-Wing Bourgeois Literature

After the May 4 Movement, Hu Shih, as a representative of the right-wing bourgeoisie, began to show his politically reactionary character. He edited *Endeavour Weekly* and *Study Magazine* and advocated "government by good men" and "systematization of the old learning." In 1925 he edited and published *Modern Review*. At

---

[1] *Ibid.*, p. 43.

CHAPTER TWO

THE LEFT-WING LITERARY MOVEMENT— ACTIVITIES OF THE CHINA LEAGUE OF LEFT-WING WRITERS LED BY LU HSUN AND THE DEVELOPMENT OF AND STRUGGLES AROUND THE THEORIES ON REVOLUTIONARY LITERATURE

Section 1. The First Revolutionary Civil War and the Formation of a New Front in the Literary Movement

In 1924 began the First Revolutionary Civil War,[1] in which the Chinese Communist Party played the leading role. With the support of the workers, peasants and revolutionary intellectuals and the assistance of the

[1] The First Revolutionary Civil War (1924-1927) was initiated and organized by the Chinese Communist Party against the northern warlord government. With the participation of the Communists, the Kuomintang convened its First National Congress in January 1924 at which it issued the Three Cardinal Policies—alliance with Soviet Russia, co-operation with the Communist Party and assistance to the workers and peasants—which formed the basis of a national united front between itself, the Com-

the time when the revolutionary movement led by the Chinese Communist Party surged forward, the group of people around *Modern Review* headed by Hu Shih, Chen Hsi-ying and Hsu Chih-mo openly supported the reactionary warlord government under Tuan Chi-jui, opposed the student movement and opposed the Chinese Communist Party.

The reactionary character of the Modern Review group was fundamentally different from that of the Lin Shu, Criterion and Chia Yin groups. As Chu Chiu-pai said:

> This was no longer a rupture between retrogression and the new culture, but a split within the ranks of the new culture. On the one side was the camp of workers, peasants and the common people, on the other the bourgeoisie hand in glove with the remnants of feudalism. These new reactionaries posed as having Europeanized ideas or as belonging to the May 4 Movement.[1]

Lu Hsun wrote many articles mercilessly attacking the Modern Review group. These articles, later compiled into *Bad Luck* and *More Bad Luck,* appeared to be striking at certain individual Europeanized gentlemen but in fact these individuals can be taken as standing for certain social types.

---

[1] Chu Chiu-pai, "Writing for a Great Cause" (Preface to the *Selected Essays of Lu Hsun), Chinese Literature,* No. 5, 1959, pp. 52-3.

Soviet Union, the war proceeded triumphantly. At the point of success in 1927, however, the reactionary clique of the Kuomintang and the big bourgeoisie — then an ally of the Communists — betrayed the revolution which subsequently suffered defeat.

The changes in the revolutionary ranks after the First Revolutionary Civil War were not only reflected in the political field. They were also reflected in the field of new literature where a serious split had likewise occurred. The bourgeois intellectuals who had taken part in the united literary front followed the bourgeoisie over to the counter-revolutionary camp. The proletarian intellectuals and petty-bourgeois revolutionary intellectuals remained. It was left to the Communist Party alone to lead this literary movement forward.

These two groups of intellectuals who had formed the Creation Society and the Sun Society were the first to issue the call for a revolutionary literature.

The Creation Society began to turn towards the revolution about the time of the May 30 Movement in 1925. Its founders, like Kuo Mo-jo and Cheng Fang-wu, took part in the First Revolutionary Civil War. After the failure of the revolution, they returned to Shanghai to resume their literary activities. They were reinforced by fresh strength in the persons of Li Chu-li, Feng Nai-

---

munist Party and people of various circles. When the Northern Expedition was launched in 1926 the National Revolutionary Army succeeded in occupying the greater part of the Yangtse and Yellow River valleys and defeating the northern warlord government. Later, because of the betrayal by Chiang Kai-shek, who headed the reactionary bloc of the Kuomintang and the capitulationist line of Chen Tu-hsiu, who dominated the Chinese Communist Party at that time, the revolution suffered defeat.

chao, Peng Kang and others — intellectuals who had retired from the revolutionary war front and had accepted proletarian ideas. In addition to *Torrent*, which appeared in 1925, and *Creation Monthly*, which appeared in 1926, they published *Cultural Review*.

The Sun Society was formed by Chiang Kuang-tzu and others who had taken part in the revolutionary movement and had accepted proletarian ideas. They published *Sun Monthly* in January 1928.

These publications provided a forum for enthusiastic discussions on revolutionary literature.

Section 2. The Establishment of the China League of Left-Wing Writers and Its Struggle Against Reactionary Politics

(1) The Success of the Agrarian Revolution and the Beginning of the Japanese Aggression of Northeast China

After the failure of the First Revolutionary Civil War, Mao Tse-tung led the revolutionary movement in the rural areas, where he set up revolutionary bases, mobilized the masses and carried out guerrilla war. Between 1930 and 1933 Chiang Kai-shek launched four attacks against the revolutionary bases, but they were all smashed.

In the areas controlled by Chiang's counter-revolutionary forces, savage rule was instituted, the democratic movement suppressed and over a million Communists and revolutionary people were slaughtered.

While the strength of the Workers' and Peasants' Red Army continued to grow and while Chiang Kai-shek conducted his fascist reign of terror, the Japanese imperialists began to carry out their plot to seize China for themselves, starting with the "Mukden Incident"[1] on September 18, 1931. As Chiang Kai-shek persisted in his traitorous policy of non-resistance to Japan while relying on imperialist support to wage civil war against the Workers' and Peasants' Red Army, the Japanese forces quickly occupied the whole of the Northeast. In January 1932 the Japanese attacked Shanghai. In 1933, they occupied Jehol and northern Chahar and in 1935, eastern Hopei.

When the Japanese invasion began, the Chinese Communist Party was the first to call for armed resistance. The Communists led or took an active part in the people's anti-Japanese movement all over the country as well as the anti-Japanese guerrilla war waged by the people in the Northeast. They represented the demands of the Chinese people as a whole and had their full support.

In short, as Mao Tse-tung pointed out:

> This period was on the one hand a period of counter-revolutionary campaigns of "encirclement and annihilation," and on the other a period of the deepening of the revolutionary movement. There were then two kinds of campaigns of "encirclement and annihilation":

---

[1] The surprise attack launched by the Japanese forces on the Chinese army stationed in Shenyang (Mukden), which became known as the Mukden Incident. Because of Chiang Kai-shek's policy of "absolute non-resistance," the Japanese troops were able to extend their aggression and quickly occupied the whole of China's Northeast.

military "encirclement and annihilation" and cultural "encirclement and annihilation." There was also the deepening of two kinds of revolution: the deepening of the agrarian revolution and the deepening of the cultural revolution.[1]

(2) The Formation of the China League of Left-Wing Writers

One form of the "deepening of the cultural revolution" as stated by Mao Tse-tung lay in the founding of the China League of Left-Wing Writers and its revolutionary literary activities headed by Lu Hsun and under the political leadership of the Chinese Communist Party.

The primary factor in bringing into being the League of Left-Wing Writers was that the successes of the revolutionary movement — the continuous expansion of the revolutionary bases, the successive smashing of Chiang Kai-shek's attacks by the Workers' and Peasants' Red Army, and the establishment of the Workers' and Peasants' Democratic Government — had strengthened the determination and inspired the confidence of the people in the revolution all over the country. Secondly, the introduction into China since 1928 of the science theories of Marxism-Leninism and the Soviet theories on art and literature, as well as the discussions on revolutionary literature about that time, had prepared a theoretical background for the formation of the league. Thirdly, the discussions on revolutionary literature had helped to reorganize the literary ranks and define their revolu-

---

[1] Mao Tse-tung, *op. cit.,* Vol. III, p. 149.

tionary strategy. All felt the urgent need to closely unite together under a common aim to fight the common enemy.

In the winter of 1929 a group of revolutionary writers headed by Lu Hsun gathered at Shanghai to discuss the organization of a left-wing league. Preparatory work began in February 1930 and on March 2 it was formally set up with fifty or so members including Lu Hsun, Mao Tun, Yu Ta-fu, Shen Tuan-hsien, Chiang Kuang-tzu, Feng Nai-chao, Tien Han and Jou Shih. At the inaugural meeting, a theoretical programme was adopted. Its full text was as follows:

> In a period of social change art cannot remain stagnant to become a conservative element and a tool of support for the die-hard rule. It must veer boldly towards progress and become a weapon in a war of liberation. Only by keeping pace with the march of history can art spread its brilliant rays.
>
> If a poet is to be a prophet or an artist a leader of humankind, he cannot but stand at the forefront of history and take up the tasks of waging a liberation war for the progress of mankind and eradication of the ignorant and die-hard conservative forces.
>
> Our attitude towards the facts of historical progress and social development, however, is not one of mere abstract appreciation. We know that the capitalist system of the imperialist countries has become a fetter on human progress, and that its "grave-diggers" — the proletariat — have taken up the historic task of waging mankind's last war — class war — in this "realm of necessity" to secure the complete emancipation of mankind.

The logical conclusion is, therefore, that we must stand in the front line in the proletariat's struggle for liberation, destroy all reactionary and conservative elements and develop all oppressed and progressive elements.

We cannot but dedicate our art and literature to a sanguinary struggle for "victory or death."

If we take man's joys and sorrows as the content of art and literature, then our art and literature must take as its content the feelings of the proletariat in this dark and "mediaeval" class society.

Our art and literature are, therefore, opposed to the feudal class and the bourgeoisie. They also combat the tendencies of the petty bourgeois "who has lost his social position." We must render support to and work for the emergence of a proletarian art and literature.

Our theories should point out the correct direction of the movement and help it grow. We should raise new questions from time to time and solve them. We should produce more critical reviews on specific works without neglecting academic studies, write more critiques on the art and literature of the past, introduce the achievements of proletarian art and literature from abroad, and build up theories on art and literature.

Our attitude towards social reality is that we must take part in the liberation movement of the world's proletariat and struggle against the reactionary forces of the world that are opposing the proletariat.

Annexed to this programme were a programme for action and guiding principles for work. The essential points of the former were:

a. The aim of our literary movement is to secure the emancipation of the rising class;

b. We oppose all kinds of oppression of our movement.

The guiding principles were:

a. To assimilate the experience of the new literature in other countries, expand our movement and set up various research organizations;

b. To help new writers gain a literary education and the opportunity to practise and promote worker and peasant writers;

c. To affirm Marxist theories on art and on criticism;

d. To publish magazines, serial books and booklets in the name of the league; and

e. To produce literary works of the rising class.

The meeting elected a standing committee and adopted seventeen resolutions including those on the setting up of a Research Society of Marxist Art and Literary Theories, an International Cultural Research Society and a Research Society for the Popularization of Art and Literature; the establishment of contacts with left-wing art and literary circles abroad; the promotion of a great league of left-wing art; and a plan for publishing left-wing magazines.

Lu Hsun addressed the meeting. In a speech of historical significance entitled "Thoughts on the League of Left-Wing Writers," he called the attention of the league to the following points:

> First, we must battle doggedly and continuously against the old order and old forces, and make the best use of our strength. The roots of the old society go deep, and we cannot shake it unless our new movement is even stronger. Besides, the old society has

good means of making our new forces compromise, although it will never compromise itself. . . .

Secondly, I think we should broaden our battle front. . . .

Thirdly, we ought to bring up a host of new fighters. . . .

. . . .

Last of all, I think it essential for a united front that we have a common aim. . . . If all of us wanted to serve the workers and peasants, our battle front would naturally be united.[1]

The league began its work after its formation under the direction of the Communist-led General Union of China Left-Wing Culture. The league was one among several progressive cultural organizations affiliated to the General Union, like the League of Social Science Writers, the League of Journalists, the League of Cinema Workers and so on. But thanks to Lu Hsun's leadership, the League of Left-Wing Writers wielded greater influence. With branches in important areas, it became the main force of the General Union.

(3) The Growth of the League of Left-Wing Writers and Its Fight Against Repression

With its own organization and programme and under the Party's leadership, the League of Left-Wing Writers became a link in the revolutionary movement as a whole. Like the other revolutionary organizations at that time, it waged a resolute and merciless struggle against the

[1] Lu Hsun, *op. cit.,* pp. 95-8.

Kuomintang reactionary rule. Headed by Lu Hsun, the league persisted in its fight against increasingly brutal repression and gathered strength.

The Kuomintang regime co-ordinated its repression of the League of Left-Wing Writers with its military campaign of "encirclement and annihilation" against the Communists. First, it imposed various restrictions on the publications of progressive books and periodicals on art and literature, framed reactionary "regulations governing publications," and set up the "Books and Periodicals Censorship Committee" which banned the publication of progressive literature or freely deleted or changed its content.

Secondly, it banned the circulation of progressive books and periodicals. The organs of the league, such as *Sprout, Reclaimer, Literature Monthly* and *The Dipper,* were successively compelled to stop publication. By February 1934, 149 literary works in Shanghai alone, including those of Lu Hsun, Kuo Mo-jo, Mao Tun and Pa Chin, were banned by the Kuomintang.

Thirdly, it sabotaged the progressive cultural organizations. In November 1933 the Yihua Films Company at Shanghai was wrecked by Kuomintang agents. Subsequently, many bookshops publishing new literature were also wrecked. All cinemas, theatres, bookshops and newspaper offices in Shanghai received threatening letters from the Kuomintang secret police.

Finally, it had cultural workers arrested and murdered. In 1930, Tsung Hui, a member of the League of Left-Wing Dramatists, was murdered in Nanking. In February 1931, well-known Communist writers Jou Shih, Yin Fu, Hu Yeh-pin, Li Wei-sen and Feng Keng were secretly shot in Lunghua, Shanghai. In the autumn of

1932, armed thugs broke into the headquarters of the Anti-Imperialist League of Shanghai[1] and all those who were attending a meeting there were shot. In the summer of 1933, 150 people who had taken part in an anti-fascist mass meeting were taken to Nanking and killed. In May of the same year, the author Pan Tse-nien was kidnapped in Shanghai and sent to prison in Nanking while another author Ying Hsiu-jen who resisted his kidnappers was shot and killed on the spot. In July the author Hung Ling-fei, a Communist, was arrested in Peking and later murdered, and Pan Mo-hua, a poet, was killed in Tientsin. In June 1935, Chu Chiu-pai, a Communist, one of China's revolutionary leaders, outstanding literary theorist and leader of the movement for revolutionary literature, was killed in Fukien. The secret police threatened Lu Hsun and tried by all means to murder him and even a warrant for his arrest was issued. In the last years of his life Lu Hsun was constantly shadowed by Chiang Kai-shek's flunkeys. Not until his death in 1936 was his name removed from their black list.

The League of Left-Wing Writers answered the frenzied repression of the Kuomintang regime by persistent and uncompromising struggle. As Lu Hsun said:

> Our proletarian literature will continue to grow, however, because it belongs to the great ranks of the revolutionary toilers; and as long as the people exist and gain in strength, so long will this revolutionary literature grow. Our comrades' blood testifies that

---

[1] An organization affiliated to the World Anti-Imperialist Committee, led and supported by the underground Chinese Communist Party in Shanghai.

> the revolutionary literature of the working class suffers the same oppression and terror as the toiling masses, that it is fighting the same battles and shares the same destiny, for it is the literature of the revolutionary toilers.[1]

Such was the result of the cultural "encirclement and annihilation" campaign of the Kuomintang government.

Section 3. The Contributions of Lu Hsun and Chu Chiu-pai

From 1930 to 1936 under the Chinese Communist Party's leadership and with the support of the people, Lu Hsun nursed and cared for the League of Left-Wing Writers. He led the league in its determined struggles against the reactionaries on both the political and cultural fronts and its constructive work on Marxist-Leninist literary theories. He played the leading role in many important literary movements and struggles of the left-wing league, like the movement for popular art and literature, the movement for a common spoken language and the translation and introduction of the literary theories and works of Soviet scholars, as well as the struggles against the Crescent clique, the fascist "nationalist" literature and that of the "third category." His leadership and brilliant, militant pen won significant victories for these movements and struggles.

---

[1] Lu Hsun, *op. cit.*, p. 108.

In this period while stubbornly fighting against wrong and reactionary literary ideas, Lu Hsun made some very special contributions to the building up of the ideas of revolutionary literature in China. Constantly he instilled proletarian ideas into the minds of the progressive writers and young people, and stressed the harmful effects of petty-bourgeois ideas on revolutionary literature and the importance to revolutionary writers of taking part in actual struggles and getting into close touch with the realities of life.

In the early period of the revolutionary literary movement, Lu Hsun had detected and criticized the serious shortcomings of the petty bourgeoisie. Now he again stressed this question. In his talk "Thoughts on the League of Left-Wing Writers" given at the inaugural meeting of the league, his principal target was the tendency of the revolutionary petty bourgeoisie to lose contact with the realities of life and to consider themselves exceptional. Profoundly he pointed out:

> In my view, it is very easy for "left-wing" writers today to turn into "right-wing" writers. First of all, if you simply shut yourself up behind glass windows to write or study instead of keeping in touch with actual social conflicts, it is easy for you to be extremely radical or "left." But the moment you come up against reality all your ideas are shattered. . . . It is most artistic and refined to sit discussing socialism —with no idea of bringing it into being. Socialists like this are quite unreliable. . . .
>
> Secondly, it is easy to become "right-wing" if you do not understand the actual nature of revolution. Revolution is a bitter thing, mixed with filth and blood,

not as lovely or perfect as poets think. It is eminently down-to-earth, involving many humble, tiresome tasks, not as romantic as the poets think. Of course there is destruction in a revolution, but construction is even more necessary to it; and while destruction is simple, construction is troublesome. So it is easy for all who have romantic dreams about revolution to become disillusioned on closer acquaintance, when a revolution is actually carried out.[1]

In criticizing an author who considered himself exceptional, Lu Hsun said:

> Another mistaken view is this notion that poets or writers are superior beings and their work nobler than any other work. . . . some still believe that the poets and writers who support the workers' revolution today will be richly rewarded by the working class when the revolution is accomplished, enjoying special treatment, riding in special cars, and eating special food. The workers may even offer them fine bread and butter,[2] saying: "Eat this, because you are our poets!" This is another illusion.[3]

These views of Lu Hsun still hold significance for us today.

Speaking on the approach of a writer to his work, Lu Hsun emphasized to the writers of that time the great need to take part in actual revolutionary struggle. "Revolutionary writers must at least share in the life of the revolution," he said, "or keep their fingers closely

---

1 *Ibid.*, pp. 93-4.

2 Foreign bread, eaten with butter, was a luxury in China—*Tr.*

3 Lu Hsun, *op. cit.*, pp. 94-5.

on its pulse."[1] The reason for the dearth of good proletarian literature, he explained, was because the revolutionary writers were not going deeply among the workers, and so were unfamiliar with their lives. He said:

> But can the left-wing writers who remain write good proletarian literature? I think it is very hard. For all our left-wing writers today are still educated people — intellectuals — hence it is difficult for them to write the truth about the revolution. . . . But to my mind, an author can understand all these things (thieves, illicit love, and so on) because, living in the old society, he is acquainted with the things and people in it. He cannot do this, though, in connection with the working class and characters with which he has had no contact, or he will paint a wrong picture.[2]

Here Lu Hsun was already touching upon the need for a writer to remould his old ideas and feelings. As to the dearth of good proletarian literature, he was not pessimistic. He said:

> . . . To my mind a fighter who wants to understand the revolution and the enemy should make the closest analysis of the foe confronting him. The same applies to literature. Not only must we know the facts about revolution; we need a thorough knowledge of the enemy and all aspects of the situation today before we can foresee the future of the revolution. The sole hope of development for our literature lies in understanding the old and seeing the new, in comprehend-

---

[1] *Ibid.*, p. 124.

[2] *Ibid.*

ing the past and deducing the future. I believe it is possible for writers in present-day conditions to do this, if they will make the effort.[1]

These valuable opinions of Lu Hsun exerted a great influence on the revolutionary literary movement and the revolutionary artists and writers of the day, and promoted the development of socialist realism in Chinese literature.

Like Lu Hsun, Chu Chiu-pai[2] was one of the leaders of the League of Left-Wing Writers, who played a decisive role in its activities. He began to play a leading role in the summer of 1931 and soon became one of Lu Hsun's close friends. He wrote many essays and articles and systematically introduced Marxist-Leninist theories on literature and Soviet literary works into China. His articles exerted a decisive influence on the popular literary movement and on the struggle against the literature of the "third category." His essays, like those of Lu Hsun, dealt fierce blows to the enemy. As he and Lu Hsun cherished the same ideals and fought together for the liberation of the Chinese people and for

---

[1] *Ibid.*, p. 125.

[2] Chu Chiu-pai (1899-1935) born in Changchou, Kiangsu Province. He was one of the earliest members and leaders of the Chinese Communist Party, and a member of the Central Committee of the Party and of the presidium of the Comintern. From 1931 to 1933 he worked together with Lu Hsun in the revolutionary cultural movement in Shanghai. In 1933 he went to the revolutionary base in Kiangsi Province and became Commissioner of Education in the Central Government of the Soviet Republic of China. In March 1935 he was arrested by the Chiang Kai-shek gang while fighting a guerrilla war in Fukien Province and was killed on June 18.

the cause of communism, it did not take long for them to become close comrades-in-arms. In a letter to Lu Hsun some time later, Chu Chiu-pai said: "We are close to each other; in fact, we were so before we met."

The two worked closely together in guiding the left-wing league. During the two and half years up to January 1934, when he left Shanghai for the Central Revolutionary Base in Kiangsi Province, Chu Chiu-pai's work and leadership exercised almost as great an influence on the left-wing league and the revolutionary literary movement as that of Lu Hsun himself.

The movement for the popularization of literature during the period when the League of Left-Wing Writers existed was also jointly led by Lu Hsun and Chu Chiu-pai.

The question of the popularization of literature was first touched upon in 1928 in connection with the question of literature serving the workers and peasants, in the course of the discussions on revolutionary literature held at that time. With the establishment of the left-wing league, it became a paramount question, and one that the league focussed its attention upon. Taking the actual conditions of Chinese society as a point of departure, Lu Hsun said:

> In the present society when there is still unequal opportunity for education, there is a need for various kinds of art and literature — some easy, others more difficult to grasp — for readers of different levels. However, there's a need for a great number of writers who, considering the interests of the masses, try their best to produce works simple and easy to understand

for everybody to read and enjoy and much of the old rubbish can be done away with.[1]

About the same time, Shen Tuan-hsien, Feng Nai-chao and a few others put forward their views in a number of articles. They pointed out that the aim of the popularization of literature was to enable literature to reach the masses and heighten their fighting spirit and enthusiasm. In form, they said, popular literature might make use of the old ones which were familiar to all while from time to time developing new ones to replace the old.

In 1931 Chu Chiu-pai published his article "The Realistic Question of Popular Art and Literature." It was much richer in content than the discussions in 1930, treating the question systematically and proposing concrete measures and a programme. In 1932 another article of his, "The Question of Popular Art and Literature," appeared in the first issue of *Literature Monthly*, and this was followed by a series of articles by many others. The movement for popular literature was on.

The principal points of discussion may be stated as follows:

First, it was stressed that popularization was an important task on the literary front of the current revolutionary movement, one that should be put forth as the basic line and direction for creative writing in the present art and literary movement. The aim of popularization should be to raise the cultural level of the masses and, through popular revolutionary art and literature, to help organize the masses politically.

---

[1] Lu Hsun, *Collected Works*, Chinese ed., Peking, 1958, Vol. VII, p. 579.

Secondly, that the essence of the question of popular literature lay in the character of its content. The prevailing views were that the writings should include:

a. Those which were agitational — to be considered as a measure to oppose all kinds of arbitrary counter-revolutionary propaganda during a sudden turn of events;
b. Those for the purpose of organizing struggles, which should take as their main theme the class struggle in general and specific class struggles on day-to-day issues; and
c. Those for the purpose of understanding life. It was necessary to understand life from the proletarian viewpoint, to clearly unfold the significance of life's realities and to be able to interpret the ideal of the proletariat (socialism).

To handle such content well, the writers should learn from the masses and live the way the masses live.

Thirdly, what form should popular literature take? The prevailing view was that in its initial period the popular revolutionary art and literature should make use of all that was good in the old forms, but that this should not mean blind imitation. On the contrary, it was necessary to create new forms on the basis of the old and to study the question of form in world proletarian literature in order to fight the traditional, reactionary popular art and literature.

Fourthly, what was the artistic value, if any, of popular literature? Would the popularization of literature have an adverse effect on literature's artistic values? In an article "On the Popularization of Literature," Chou Yang wrote:

> To disregard the low cultural level of the toiling masses in present-day China and only engage in high-sounding talk about raising the level of the masses to appreciate true, great art is in fact to refuse to serve the masses. It is a kind of liquidationism. For the time being, therefore, we should make use of the old forms like folk songs, opera scripts and story-telling which are rooted in the art and literary life of the masses to organize and arouse them as expeditiously as possible. At the same time we should help them raise their educational and cultural level so that the toiling masses may gradually approach true, great art. . . .
>
> Therefore, instead of dragging literature down, popularization will raise it; in other words it will heighten the militancy and class character of literature.

At that time Lu Hsun gave his valuable opinion on popular literature, particularly on the question of making use of the old forms. He pointed out sharply that this was not a matter of "filling an old bottle with new wine"; it was rather one of "weeding out the old to let the new emerge." He said: "When adopting the old forms, we have to eliminate something in them. When eliminating something, we have to add something. The result is the appearance of new forms. This is innovation."[1]

Such a dialectical view as uniting the adoption of old forms with the creation of new forms was something none of Lu Hsun's contemporaries had yet been able to advance in the course of discussions. In other articles —

---

[1] *Ibid.*, Vol. VI, p. 20.

"On Reprinting of Woodcuts," "On the 'Third Category,'" "Trifling Talks on Picture-Books," and "Amateurish Literary Discussions," Lu Hsun also discussed the questions of the forms of popular art and literature, the language to be used in popular literature, and popularization and elevation. All his views have been proved correct and borne out by present-day practice.

During the discussions on popular literature, it was felt that the question of language as the basic element in literature's form must be solved before further progress could be made in creating new forms for popular literature. Consequently in 1934 discussions began on the question of a popular spoken language.

The discussions were enthusiastic but they were mainly about the "latinization" of the Chinese language. Some of those who took part in the discussions made the mistake of completely repudiating the Han (Chinese) characters. The Chinese characters have their merits as well as defects. They should be reformed under certain conditions. But it was wrong to repudiate them completely.

On the question of language there was a mistaken conception. Some of the participants claimed that language had a "class character." They did not know that language is not a part of the superstructure of society, changing with the economic basis. It has no class character and there is no such thing as a class language.

In order that the old theories on art and literature might be cleared out and the theories and works of revolutionary literature might enjoy a healthy growth, the need for systematically studying Marxist-Leninist theories of art and literature and the socialist realist method of writing was keenly felt. Lu Hsun and Chu Chiu-pai made the greatest contributions towards introducing the large amount of Marxist-Leninist theories on art and literature into China. In the two years from 1929 to 1930 Lu Hsün translated *The Theory of Art* by Plekhanov, *The Theory of Art, Literature and Criticism* by Lunacharsky and *The Soviet Policy on Art and Literature.* Chu Chiu-pai translated many literary articles by Lenin and Gorky. In spite of certain shortcomings in the theories of art and literature of Plekhanov and Lunacharsky, these books solved the basic questions of Marxist-Leninist theories of art and literature. Therefore they had great influence on the literary movement in China. As Lu Hsun said: "They enabled us to study them and become firmer and stronger."[1]

In the same period many literary works of the Soviet Union were translated into Chinese. Here again Lu Hsun and Chu Chiu-pai played a pioneering role. Lu Hsun had been interested in Soviet fiction before the movement for revolutionary literature began. Later he encouraged other people to read and translate it. He translated Fadeyev's novel *The Nineteen* and Yakovlev's *October.* Chu Chiu-pai translated a number of novels by Gorky. Later a great many Soviet literary works were introduced, including Gorky's *Mother, The Three, Childhood* and other short stories, Serafimovitch's *Iron Stream,* Sholokhov's *And Quiet Flows the Don,* and poems, novels, and plays by other authors. These works inspired tremendous revolutionary enthusiasm and confidence in the Chinese writers, pointed out the correct road in methods of writing and stood as concrete examples of a socialist realist literature. They also exerted a deep and beneficial influence on young people who were studying or practising art and literature.

---

[1] Lu Hsun, *Selected Works,* English ed., Vol. III, p. 123.

Section 4. The Art and Literary Movement in the Soviet Areas[1]

(1) Decisions of the Kutien Conference on Art and Literary Work

In 1929, there was a Party conference held at Kutien, in Fukien Province. Among the decisions reached at this conference were a number on art and literary work which could be put into practice under the conditions then prevailing. These were adopted from proposals made by Mao Tse-tung in the light of the need to educate the soldiers of the Red Army, arouse mass struggles and win over the masses in the enemy-controlled areas. It was provided that the textbooks for the soldiers should be written with artistic taste — taking the stories of the revolution, folk songs, pictures and newspaper articles as teaching material — and that activities such as drum dances, theatrical performances, games and the writing of wall newspapers should be promoted. Propaganda should be an important instrument of the Red Army and the reorganization and training of the propaganda teams should be one of the tasks to which the Party should devote greater efforts. It was also decided that the art section of the Red Army should be strengthened; that lithographic and mimeographic pictorials should be published; that the propaganda teams should perform topical skits under the direction of the propaganda section; that the soldiers' societies should

[1] Liberated areas at that time were called Soviet areas.

set up clubs; and that the political departments of the Red Army should be responsible for collecting and composing revolutionary songs expressing the sentiment of the masses.

Mao Tse-tung's practical guidance gave impetus to the art and literary work in the Workers' and Peasants' Red Army. From that time on, art and literary work became an essential part of the Red Army's political work. Officers and men took part in extensive art and literary activities which were often linked to the regular work or fighting tasks of the troops.

Mao Tse-tung's attention and guidance were not confined to the art and literary work in the Red Army but extended to that of the rural areas. Take Changkang Township, Hsingkuo County, Kiangsi Province, for an example. In 1933 there was one club in each of the four villages. Every club had its committee for sports, wall newspapers and evening entertainments. Every village had its own wall newspapers posted in the Lenin Primary School. From time to time new performances were staged by the clubs.

Take another example. In 1933 Upper Tsaichi, in Tsaichi Township, Shanghang County, Fukien Province, had a club with some fifty people taking part in its activities. Thirty or so used to stage new plays. Wall newspapers were posted in four places, one in each village. In Lower Tsaichi some fifty people were active in the club. Wall newspapers were posted in five places.

These examples show how extensively art and literary activities were carried on in the rural areas at that time.

(2) The Policy of the Workers' and Peasants' Democratic Government on Art and Literature

The Workers' and Peasants' Democratic Government under the correct leadership of Mao Tse-tung attached special importance to art and literary work. Chu Chiu-pai, then Minister of Education, was concurrently in charge of the Bureau of Art under the ministry. He rendered valuable and significant services to art and literature. Li Po-chao in an article "People's Art and Literature," published in the *Renmin Ribao* (People's Daily) on June 18, 1950, recalled the conditions of those days as follows:

> The centre of art and literary activities for the masses in the Soviet Area was then in the Red Army College of which Yeh Chien-ying and Liu Po-cheng were successively the commandant. They attached importance to art and literary work as supplement to education. A few people interested in art and literature who had come from other provinces, together with the top cadres in the Red Army, sponsored the organization of worker-peasant dramatic societies which soon spread to the provincial and county levels, with branch societies even at district level. The scope of work was expanded and more cadres for such work were needed. In the Central Soviet Area the first drama school was opened. Comrade Chu Chiu-pai suggested that the school be named after Gorky.

As people's dramatic societies appeared in every county and every district, Chu Chiu-pai planned to further develop them, in quantity and quality. He proposed to call together the heads of the worker-peasant dramatic societies from Yunchi District in Juichin County, Changting County, the Central Printing Works, and various other districts for six months' training. He said: "Without a nucleus for dramatic work, there can be no movement for a worker-peasant drama."

This movement was given special attention because drama was a form of art which could most easily make contact with and be accepted by the masses. The Gorky Drama School trained over a thousand students who were subsequently organized into sixty troupes which gave performances in every corner of the countryside and on the front lines and took in new members from the rural districts of the Soviet Area. The peasants ardently wanted culture and they welcomed these troupes, volunteering to carry their props and belongings and offering food and lodging. The troupers, composed of playwrights, directors, actors and actresses, shared the life of the peasants. A close unity and friendship was built between them.

The Workers' and Peasants' Democratic Government also devoted great attention to the collection and propagating of folk songs. When the club members from the Yunchi District sang some very pleasant songs at a commemoration meeting it turned out that they were the most popular songs of the people of Kiangsi — the Song of Bamboo Strip, the Song of Chopping Firewood and Ten Curses to the Counter-Revolution. Chu Chiu-pai pointed out on the spot the importance of such work. He said: "The words of a popular song are of great educational value to the people. If you have nobody who can compose a song, then write out the words and sing them to the tune of a folk song which is familiar to the audience, pleasant to hear and easy to sing. Very quickly it will be sung by more and more people and the result will be even better than that of some of the new songs."

(3) The Historical Significance of the Art and Literary Movement in the Soviet Area

The art and literary movement in the Soviet Area had special historical significance because it was the first time in modern Chinese history that art and literature found access to the masses.

First, art and literature began to be taken up by the soldiers and peasants as part of their daily life. This was the most important development that had taken place in revolutionary literature since the days of the May 4 Movement. Under the difficult conditions of those days, theoretical study to any appreciable extent was out of the question. The theory that literature should serve the workers, peasants and soldiers was never clearly put forward; nevertheless, this was what was actually being done.

Secondly, as this movement was directly led by Mao Tse-tung and as it enjoyed a free and democratic environment under the Workers' and Peasants' Democratic Government, the work of popularizing art and literature, correctly guided and extensively practised, gained rich experience. This valuable experience, tested in practice over a long period of time, created concrete examples of literature serving the workers, peasants and soldiers and helped it to turn in this direction. It also prepared a basis for the further development of socialist realism in the subsequent period of the anti-Japanese war.

Thirdly, after 1927, when the country was cut into two by the enemy — the Soviet Area and the Kuomintang-controlled area — the movement for revolutionary literature was also cut into two. Isolated by the Chiang Kai-shek's forces, the revolutionary literature in the Kuomintang-controlled areas as represented by the League of Left-Wing Writers could not even make contact with the literary movement in the Soviet areas. But as the trend of struggle was basically the same, they co-ordinated very well in spite of the difficulties.

Section 5. The Struggles of the Camp of Revolutionary Literature Led by Lu Hsun Against the Reactionary Literary Trends

(1) The Struggle Against the Comprador-Bourgeois Crescent Clique

The Crescent clique had as its predecessor the Modern Review clique, whose principal members Hu Shih, Hsu Chih-mo and Chen Hsi-ying, were now joined by Liang Shih-chiu, Yeh Kung-chao, Shen Tsung-wen and others to form the Crescent Society. Before the Northern Expeditionary War, they opposed communism and relied on the favours of imperialism and the northern warlords. After the Northern Expedition, they turned their allegiance to a new master — Chiang Kai-shek and his reactionary regime — and came out against revolutionary literature.

In the very first issue of their monthly *Crescent* in 1928, they made clear their hostile attitude towards revolutionary literature. In the introductory remarks in this issue entitled "The Attitude of the Crescent," they stated their opposition to thirteen kinds of writers, among whom were "the utilitarians," "attackers," "extremists," "pedlars," "sloganeers," "*ism*-ists" and the "hot-headed." Their target was revolutionary literature.

They also put forth two principles of literature: that wholesomeness should not be impaired and dignity should not be demeaned. By wholesomeness, they meant that writers should refrain from attacking the dark side of society and from criticizing political corruption. By dignity, they meant that the carriage of a bourgeois gentleman should be upheld and nothing should be written about proletarian life. They alleged that there were too many schools of thought among literary circles at that time and that chaos reigned because there was too much freedom. They said: "Now that we have complete freedom of thought, the result is anarchic confusion." This was actually a proposal to their masters for thought control.

Liang Shih-chiu followed up with an article "Literature and Revolution" published in the *Crescent.* In opening his attack on revolutionary literature, he said: ' The term revolutionary literature can never stand. . . . A great literature is based on inherent and all-pervading human nature. . . . The majority has no literature; literature is not for the majority. . . . Literature is the creation of a few geniuses. . . ." Literature is independent, because "it implies no fixed class conception, much less a bias in the interests of a certain class."

To counter these literary theories of the reactionary comprador-bourgeoisie, Peng Kang and Feng Nai-chao of the Creation Society wrote articles, of which the main points were the following:

a. That there was in fact no freedom of thought at all. "Complete freedom" was but an advertising slogan for the reactionary regime;

b. The so-called "wholesomeness" and "dignity" were merely signboards used by the comprador-bourgeoisie to consolidate its reactionary rule;

c. That literature is not the creation of a few geniuses but is the product of the working masses through the medium of collective labour;

d. That there has never been such a thing as "inherent and all-pervading human nature." Human nature changes with the society; it has a class character. Human nature is man's social character and class character which literature reflects; and

e. That literature belongs to the masses; it serves the masses and the revolution. Those who refute this are spokesmen for the bourgeoisie.

As 1928 was a year when revolutionary literature was on the ascent, the attacks of the Crescent clique fell short of their mark. This handful of men, however, stubbornly hung on to their comprador-bourgeois standpoint and continued to assail revolutionary literature openly or covertly. Of course, they had nothing new to add to their reactionary theories which Lu Hsun again and again sharply refuted. In 1929 he pointed out:

> The critics of the Crescent Society disapprove of those who complain of the present order, but they have one complaint themselves—that such discontented individ-

uals exist. This must be a case of "paying a man in his own coin."[1]

Again in 1930 he wrote:

> Literature without human characters cannot show men's "nature" either. But once you use human characters, especially in a class society, you cannot get round their inherent class character. . . . If you say we must describe human nature because we are men, then workers must produce proletarian literature because they are workers.[2]

After repeated exposures, the Crescent clique gradually disappeared from the scene after 1930.

(2) The Struggle Against the Fascist "Nationalist Literature"

In June 1930, three months after the establishment of the League of Left-Wing Writers, a clique of Kuomintang-fostered writers, Wang Ping-ling, Huang Chen-hsia, Chu Ying-peng and others, issued a "Declaration on a Movement for Chinese National Art and Literature" and published *Vanguard Monthly, Literature Monthly* and other journals. They declared: "The self-styled left-wingers with their so-called proletarian art and literary movement have again kicked up a big fuss; they are chaining art to class." This was a clear statement of their aim of opposing the League of Left-Wing Writers.

The comprador-bourgeoisie and fascists frequently used "nationalism" as a signboard to hoodwink the people.

---

[1] Lu Hsun, *op. cit.*, p. 53.

[2] *Ibid.*, p. 76.

Under this signboard they exploited and oppressed the people to consolidate the rule of their own class. In fact, their so-called nationalism was only for a minority — their own class — and was against the interests of the people. The Kuomintang reactionaries who ruled the semi-colonial China being lackeys of imperialism, the "nationalism" they clamoured about was even more shameless than the "nationalism" sponsored by the bourgeoisie because it was precisely for selling out the nation. That was the true character of the "nationalist literary movement."

Lu Hsun made a scathing analysis of this base and insidious campaign. He pointed out that those who sponsored it were the lap-dogs of "foreign gentlemen," nothing but a heap of floating corpses. He said:

> Fearing that they would share the fate of their rulers, these lap-dogs and floating corpses inevitably collected themselves under the banner of "nationalist literature" put up by "loyal citizens" among a people victimized by imperialism; they joined their masters in a last-ditch struggle.[1]

Though a motley crew, these lap-dogs, "like their masters, oppress the proletariat by every means in an effort to prolong their last days."[2] More specifically Lu Hsun analysed some of the writings of these lap-dogs, pointing out their anti-Soviet and anti-Communist aims and their readiness to welcome Japanese imperialism. "They are," said Lu Hsun, "useful to imperialism and should be called the 'advanced detachments of their masters'; consequently

---

[1] Lu Hsun, *Collected Works,* Chinese ed., Vol. IV, pp. 245-46.

[2] *Ibid.*

the literature of the lap-dogs will continue to exist as long as vagabond politics."[1]

After this exposure by Lu Hsun, the slogan of "nationalist literature" could no longer deceive anyone. *Literature Monthly* had practically no readers though it continued to be published during the period of the anti-Japanese war.

(3) The Struggle Against the Petty-Bourgeois Reactionary "Theory of Freedom of Art and Literature"

The "theory of freedom of art and literature" appeared in 1932. There were two types of persons: the self-styled "free men" represented by Hu Chiu-yuan and the self-styled "third category" represented by Su Wen. The two men held similar views on literature — both were apologists for bourgeois reactionary literature from the standpoint of the reactionary petty bourgeoisie. But Hu Chiu-yuan donned himself in Plekhanov's cloak with which he was able to delude some young people at that time. He was a specific example of the type of person indicated in the 1931 resolution of the League of Left-Wing Writers calling on people to be on their guard against "reactionary and insidious characters camouflaged under various cloaks — 'left' or grey."

These men wrote many articles, mostly in *Modern Times,* putting forward their reactionary theories on art and literature. They claimed that art and literature could be free by detaching themselves from politics and class, did not have to serve any class and did not have

---

[1] *Ibid.*

to become a weapon of class struggle. They, therefore, were against allowing politics to interfere with art and literature. They said that writers of the "third category" had laid down their pens because the League of Left-Wing Writers had "interfered" with them by criticism. They were also against the popularization of literature as advocated by the League of Left-Wing Writers, and the use of popular forms like picture-books and opera scripts. They claimed that the members of the League of Left-Wing Writers were only "left" but did not "write." Finally they said that they might not succeed in becoming the "third category," but the third kind of literature was tenable.

Lu Hsun, Chu Chiu-pai, Chou Yang[1] and others sharply criticized such theories of art and literature, pointing out their reactionary character.

In an essay "On the 'Third Category,'" Lu Hsun wrote:

> The truth is that the "third category" have not "laid down their pens" because left-wing criticism is too harsh. The real reason is that there can be no "third category," and if no such men exist they cannot have pens — let alone lay them down.
>
> No writer living in a class society can transcend class, no one living in a time of wars can leave the battlefield and stand alone, and no one living today can write for the future — this is sheer fantasy. There are no such men in real life.[2]

---

[1] Chou Yang, born in 1908 in Yiyang, Hunan Province, is at present one of the Deputy Directors of the Propaganda Department of the Central Committee of the Chinese Communist Party and one of the vice-chairmen of the Union of Chinese Writers.

[2] Lu Hsun, *Selected Works*, English ed., Vol. III, pp. 162-63.

In answer to the attacks of Su Wen on picture-books and opera scripts, Lu Hsun said:

> And I believe that opera scripts may produce a Tolstoy or Flaubert. No one has a word against Michelangelo's paintings today, but were they not actually religious propaganda, and a picture-book of the *Old Testament*? They were done, too, for the artist's contemporaries.[1]

Chu Chiu-pai, in an article "On the Freedom of Art and Literature and the Lack of Freedom for Writers," said:

> In a class society there is no real and genuine freedom. When the proletariat openly demands art and literature as a means of struggle, whoever clamours "Don't violate art and literature!" unconsciously becomes a mouthpiece of the hypocritical bourgeois who hold that "art is above all."

He concluded by pointing out sharply: "The 'third category' only shied away from becoming openly the bootlickers of the bourgeoisie."

Editor's note:

The struggle between two roads on the art and literature front has been protracted and complicated. Finding it unpopular to openly oppose communism and the people, some of the Chinese bourgeois elements changed their tactics. They sneaked into the ranks of left-wing art and literature and put up Marxist signboards to sell their bourgeois wares. Hu Chiu-yuan was one of them but he was quickly exposed. He and Su Wen shifted from a position of shying away "from becoming openly the bootlickers of the bourgeoisie" to that of openly becoming bootlickers. Feng Hsueh-feng was another, though he remained hidden for a longer

---

[1] *Ibid.*, p. 164.

period. In the later stage of that literary debate, Feng wrote an article under the pen-name of Ho Tan-jen "On the Tendencies and Theories of the 'Third Kind of Literature,'" in which he blatantly declared that the writers of the "third category" opposed the landlord class and its literature and should be treated as "assistants" and "friends" in a common struggle. While defending the "third category," he swung his guns against what he called the serious errors of Chu Chiu-pai and Chou Yang in their appraisal of Su Wen — errors which he said must be corrected. He also propagated his erroneous view that "art is politics." The bourgeois ideas of art and literature of Feng Hsueh-feng, the self-styled Marxist, were not thoroughly exposed and criticized until the rectification campaign in 1957.

(4) The Struggle Against the "Analects" School of Literature and Other Reactionary Tendencies in Literature

In 1932 Lin Yu-tang, who had deserted the literary revolutionary camp of the May 4 Movement and joined the Kuomintang reactionary camp to become a semi-official jester, published *Analects* and in the following year *Human World,* advocating short humorous articles for leisurely reading. He said: "The short essays of today embrace all kinds of topics — as big as the universe and as small as a fly." As a matter of fact, only flies were discussed; humour meant telling jokes and leisure meant the leisurely villa life of the landlord. The purpose was none other than to distract people's attention from the dark reactionary rule of the Kuomintang in order that it might be consolidated. Such was the essence of the jester's literature.

These views came under severe criticism from Lu Hsun who pointed out that Lin Yu-tang's purpose in advocating humour was "to make people laugh away the cruelty of a butcher,"[1] and that his short articles were written to "emphasize the characteristics in common with old literature — ease, good style and finesse. It was to be a small 'show window' enjoyed by men of 'culture and refinement' and admired by young people, who might then discard rudeness for elegance."[2]

There were also other reactionary tendencies in art and literature. Shih Chih-tsun advised young people to study ancient literature and philosophy. Chou Tso-jen and Lin Yu-tang advocated reading the short essays of the Ming dynasty writers. Lu Hsun exposed and criticized the true character of such reactionary tendencies in art and literature. These exposures and criticisms exerted a great influence among the masses of people.

---

1 Lu Hsun, *Collected Works*, Chinese ed., Vol. IV, p. 435.

2 *Ibid.*, p. 442.

CHAPTER THREE

THE LEFT-WING LITERARY MOVEMENT (*Continued*)—THE ANTI-JAPANESE NATIONAL UNITED FRONT OF WRITERS AND ARTISTS AND THE DEVELOPMENT OF AND STRUGGLES AROUND THE THEORIES ON RESISTANCE LITERATURE

Section 1. The Formation of the Anti-Japanese United Front of Writers and Artists

After September 18, 1931, as Japanese imperialism carried its aggression deeper into China and the Kuomintang under Chiang Kai-shek hung on to its traitorous policy, the nation moved towards an increasingly grave crisis. On August 1, 1935, the Chinese Communist Party issued "An Appeal to All Countrymen for Resistance to Japan and Salvation of the Nation." On November 28 it followed this up with its Ten-Point Programme, calling for the formation of an anti-Japanese national united front, cessation of the civil war and unity in the struggle against Japan. On December 9 the students in Peking responded to the call of the Communist Party, which had organized and led them, by holding an anti-

Japanese national-salvation demonstration. This movement, known as the December 9 Movement, precipitated a nation-wide patriotic upsurge.

The deepening national crisis and rising tide of resistance to Japan resulted in new changes in the class relations within the country. As Mao Tse-tung pointed out:

> . . . The relationship among the various classes in China has changed, with an increase in the strength of the camp of the national revolution and a decrease in the strength of the camp of the national counter-revolution.[1]

He drew his conclusion by saying:

> The task of the Party is to form a united national revolutionary front by integrating the activities of the Red Army with all the activities of the workers, peasants, students, the petty bourgeoisie and the national bourgeoisie of the whole country.[2]

At the time of the December 9 Movement the cultural circles throughout the country echoed the demands of the students' movement and called for unity to ward off invasion, resist Japan and save the nation from extinction. On December 28, the National Salvation Association of the Cultural Circles in Shanghai was formed. In May 1936 the Federation of National Salvation Associations was established, its programme being in agreement with the August 1 declaration of the Chinese Communist Party — cessation of civil war and co-operation of all

---

[1] Mao Tse-tung, *op. cit.*, Vol. I, p. 160.

[2] *Ibid.*, p. 163.

political parties and groups to resist the aggression of the Japanese invaders. Publications on the resistance to Japan mushroomed, rising to over 1,000 in all.

In the spirit of the Party's August 1 declaration the writers and artists voiced a common demand that all writers and artists, irrespective of schools of thought — old or new — social status, and political affiliations (barring the collaborators) should unite under the general aim of resisting Japan and saving the country, use their pens as a weapon of resistance and form a united front of writers and artists.

In the interests of this united front and the unity of all writers, the League of the Left-Wing Writers declared itself dissolved in the spring of 1936. From then on, the left-wing writers devoted themselves to the task of uniting all authors and to literature furthering the resistance against Japan.

For left-wing literature, this new literary movement did not mean a step backward, but a big step forward, for it kept abreast of the actual situation. As for other kinds of literature, this movement met the common desire of the art and literary circles throughout the country in the new situation.

In October 1936 the "Declaration of the Writers and Artists for Unity Against Aggression and for Freedom of Speech" was issued. It was pointed out in the declaration that the Kuomintang government was incapable of uniting the country to resist aggression and should be called upon to make no more compromises. It urged all writers throughout the country, of old and new schools alike, to unite to save the country from Japanese aggression. Conformity in literature, it stated, should not be insisted upon, but there should be unity in the work of resisting Japan, so that action might be more effective; and the anti-Japanese forces should not be called upon to take up a uniform standpoint in their struggle against Japan, but united action should be brought about immediately. It was to be hoped, therefore, that while individuals and different groups may freely develop and write, patriotic literature and literature of national liberation would arise everywhere to heighten the morale of the people. Finally, it called upon writers and artists to fight for freedom of speech as an urgent matter.

The signatories to the declaration represented all spheres of art and literary life. The field was unprecedentedly wide. The declaration laid the foundation for the anti-Japanese national united front of writers and artists and prepared for the formation in 1938 of the All-China Resist-the-Enemy Federation of Writers and Artists.

This declaration was issued in early October 1936. On October 19, Lu Hsun, the standard-bearer of China's new culture and founder and leader of modern Chinese literature, died in Shanghai. His death was an irreparable loss to modern revolutionary literature in China as well as to the Chinese revolution. While the world mourned his passing, the progressive writers and artists in China and the broad masses of Chinese youth pledged themselves to learn from Lu Hsun and to carry on in his spirit. The great writer was dead. But his militant spirit and his immortal works remained always as a guide for the revolutionary literary movement in China.

Section 2. The Outbreak of the War of Resistance and Literature in the Service of the Resistance Movement

(1) Chinese Artists and Writers After the Outbreak of the War

On July 7, 1937, the Japanese imperialist aggressive army launched an attack on the Chinese forces at Lukouchiao (Marco Polo Bridge) on the southern outskirts of Peking. On August 13 Japanese forces attacked Shanghai. Under pressure of public opinion and on account of its conflict of interests with imperialism, the Kuomintang government had to put up a resistance.

Before the war broke out, the progressive writers, oppressed by the Kuomintang rule, could not openly come into contact with the masses. With the start of an all-out war, they could move about freely — to the front, to the small cities and towns and to the countryside — to take part in wartime work.

The writers and artists took an active part in the resistance, broadening their activities and coming into contact with the masses; and the masses, stimulated by the war and following its progress closely, felt an urgent need for more cultural life. The question of the popularization of literature therefore began to arouse general interest. Moreover, the war had taken the writers to the far corners of the country. The need for a central organization to facilitate mutual contact, to effect close unity and strive for political democracy and victory became more obvious.

(2) The Formation of the All-China Resist-the-Enemy Federation of Writers and Artists and Its Work

After a period of preparation, the All-China Resist-the-Enemy Federation of Writers and Artists was formed in Hankow on March 27, 1938, to lead the nation-wide movement for the art and literature of the resistance movement.

The formation of this federation marked the formal completion of the united front of the writers and artists. It was the culmination of the efforts that had begun in 1936. At the same time it co-ordinated its activities with that of the political united front. However, in the political united front, the Chinese Communist Party and other patriotic democratic people firmly stood for resistance, whereas the Kuomintang reactionaries took a wait-and-see attitude and were ready to compromise and surrender at any time. So in the writers and artists' federation, the progressive, patriotic writers under the leadership of the Communist Party persistently upheld the movement for a literature of the resistance while the minority of Kuomintang reactionary writers obstructed or sabotaged it. Fortunately the federation was from its very beginning led by the Communist Party. The progressive and patriotic writers and artists devoted their common efforts to the art and literature of the resistance movement. The role played by the Kuomintang writers was negligible.

Of the principal work the federation did after its formation were three things: Firstly, it called upon the writers to join the army or to go to the countryside. This was for the purpose of carrying out intensive propaganda for resistance and helping the writers to settle the many problems that had arisen in popularizing art and literature. This question had again come to the fore with the start of the war and the answers to the problems could only be found by having the writers go among the masses. Secondly, it called for and helped in the formation of local branches of the federation. And thirdly, it took part and persisted in the struggle against the Kuomintang fascist rule and in many other struggles for democracy.

The federation was renamed the All-China Federation of Literary and Art Circles in 1945 after the Japanese surrender. And at the National Congress of Writers and Artists convened in Peking in July 1949, after the victory of the Chinese revolution, it amalgamated with a number of literary organizations in the liberated areas to form the All-China Federation of Writers.

(3) Resistance Literature Under the Kuomintang Reactionary Rule

The Lukouchiao Incident on July 7, 1937 had compelled the Kuomintang reactionary government to resist Japan. Nevertheless, it did so with reluctance. After the loss of Wuhan in October 1938 it ceased to fight a war of resistance and adopted the role of onlooker. It attempted to compromise with the Japanese aggressors through the medium of other imperialist countries and even to negotiate a surrender. At the same time it increased its activities against the Communists and the people as a whole as a preparatory step for actual surrender. Consequently, whatever little active and progressive atmosphere there had been at the beginning of the War of Resistance now quickly evaporated. In its place was instituted a reign of fascist terror.

When the Kuomintang launched its first anti-Communist campaign many drama troupes and anti-Japanese propaganda teams in the Kuomintang-controlled areas were dissolved or compelled to stop their activities. Writers and artists were prohibited from going to the armed forces, factories or countryside. Freedom of speech, assembly or association was revoked. Books, periodicals and newspapers were increasingly censored, confiscated or banned.

After the Southern Anhwei Incident of January 1941[1] in which Kuomintang troops treacherously attacked the Communist-led New Fourth Army, the reactionary government intensified its repression of the progressive literary resistance movement. In 1941-42 new progressive art and literary publications almost completely disappeared from the Kuomintang-controlled areas while old ones were either banned or forced to suspend issue. Progressive writers and artists were likely to be arrested or murdered at any time and a large number of young authors were thrown into jails or concentration camps.

Under this sanguinary repression, despite the pessimism among a few of the writers and artists, the majority retained their confidence in ultimate victory in

---

[1] During the War of Resistance to Japanese Aggression Chiang Kai-shek, to weaken and destroy the Chinese Communist Party, ordered the Communist-led New Fourth Army, which was fighting the Japanese invaders in southern Anhwei, to cross to the north of the Yangtse River while laying an ambush for it on the way. In consequence, the New Fourth Army suffered heavy losses. Thereupon, he immediately ordered the New Fourth Army to dissolve and attacked its other units.

the War of Resistance. The tremendous strength of the armed forces and the masses of people in the liberated areas and in the enemy's rear led by the Communist Party was a constant and basic source of inspiration to the writers and artists in the Kuomintang-controlled areas. The art and literary movement continued to maintain its traditional, revolutionary militant spirit and consolidated the broad united front. The struggle against reaction was carried on in various ways — commemoration of anniversaries of writers' works, relief to fellow-writers, group discussions called by the branches of the federation, and art and literary forums. All these helped to enliven art and literary activities. The reactionary theory that "literature should have nothing to do with the War of Resistance" and the works of the collaborators and special agents were severely criticized and reactionary journals were boycotted. In the big enemy-occupied cities like Shanghai, the writing of resistance literature never ceased while progressive writers and artists working underground bravely held their positions and continued the struggle against the Japanese and the collaborators in all sorts of ways.

(4) Rapid Growth of Resistance Literature in the Shensi-Kansu-Ningsia Border Region and the Anti-Japanese Bases in the Enemy's Rear

In direct contrast with the Kuomintang-controlled areas, resistance literature in the Communist-led Shensi-Kansu-Ningsia Border Region and the extensive anti-Japanese bases in the enemy's rear was upheld and supported by the broad masses and the democratic government and enjoyed a rapid growth.

In 1939 the Cultural Association of the border region convened its first congress which issued a statement stressing the need to make joint efforts with the cultural circles in other parts of the country to strive for the success in the War of Resistance and in national construction. The congress opposed all ideas of pessimism, despair, disunity, retrogression, compromise and surrender, and endeavoured to broaden and consolidate the anti-Japanese national united front. It stated that the cultural movement should effectively serve politics and that the movement itself must continuously develop and progress. Art must be for the masses and must reflect reality. Education for the War of Resistance and universal education should be carried further. In the Kuomintang-controlled areas, the statement continued, efforts should be made to gain democracy and freedom and to oppose all kinds of political and cultural backsliding and suppression or restrictions on progressive ideas, speech and publication. The congress expressed its readiness to give more help to those engaged in cultural activities in their living conditions and work so that they might expend their energy to better purpose. It stated that it would help to do away with the state of homeless and wandering life of the cultural workers in the Kuomintang-controlled areas.

This was the general direction taken by the art and literature in the resistance movement in the border areas and it advanced on the basis of the excellent traditions of the art and literary movement in the old "Soviet areas." First of all, the writers and artists were encouraged to organize themselves and helped to go among the masses. Song and dance troupes, dramatic groups and work-teams were set up and sent to the front and the rear of the enemy. Participation in war efforts and going among the masses tempered the writers, enriched their experience and increased their political knowledge as well as their knowledge of art and literature.

Secondly, in the army and in the countryside, art and literature which followed and developed the fine traditions of the Red Army, were more enlivened. They thrived and rose to a higher level as large numbers of writers, artists and other intellectuals joined the army or went to the countryside. In the villages, art and literary forms familiar and acceptable to the countryfolk were freely adopted with some adaptations and improvements. Folk artists were consulted and invited to join in the work of studying and reviving folk arts and they were treated like teachers. Provisions were made for the training of new artists from among the workers, peasants and soldiers.

Finally, the border region attached special importance to the education of young writers and artists. The Lu Hsun Academy of Arts was set up to take charge of this work. The method of teaching was to combine theory with practice. The students were encouraged to study the conditions prevailing in art and literature in various places in the border region and in the army, and the experience and specific problems connected therewith. They were also encouraged to take part in practical work. Under this educational policy the academy graduated many art and literary workers who played a great role in the art and literary movement in the border region.

Notwithstanding the difficult material conditions, the border region published a number of art and literary periodicals, such as *Forward, Northwest Literature, Popular Literature, Literary Front*, and *Literary Blitz*. There were also countless mimeographed publications and wall newspapers.

Section 3. Discussions on the Question of Resistance Literature in the Kuomintang-Controlled Areas

(1) Certain Questions About Literature Serving the Resistance

For a short period after the outbreak of the War of Resistance there was a view current in the literary circles, particularly among the young writers, that literature had no practical purpose. But very quickly it was realized that the national liberation war was all-embracing and protracted. Consequently it demanded of everybody that they should be steadfast in their own post and persist in the struggle until victory. And art and literature were precisely the best weapons for propaganda and education. Thus, the role of literature in the war was affirmed and its importance was recognized.

Nevertheless, there were some who while agreeing that literature was important wanted to restrict the role of resistance literature to describing battles. Of course, some could write well on this subject. But others who had little or no experience of the battles could only write from imagination. In consequence there was a tendency towards formulism. This shortcoming was virtually remedied by discussion and criticism as the War of Resistance progressed. In the meantime, another issue arose on the question of exposure and satire.

If literature was not to be restricted to describing battles, if it should concern itself with the realities of every aspect of national life, then the bright and the dark side of the realities during the War of Resistance should both be dealt with. Under the Kuomintang's policy of compromise and surrender and under its fascist rule, there were more dark sides than bright. Should the dark sides not be described? Most of the writers were of the opinion that they should be exposed and satirized, and the critics were asked to call upon the writers to do this work.

(2) Discussions on the Question of the Popularization of Literature

The outbreak of the War of Resistance provided favourable conditions as never before for the popularization of literature, and the subject was raised with greater emphasis.

The discussions centred on three questions.

The first concerned the current task of popularizing literature. There were two different views. One was that the task should centre on making propaganda for the resistance movement, completely ruling out the need to raise literature to a higher level. This was the prevalent view in the early period of the war. Another was that the task involved two questions, both of them urgent — revolutionary political propaganda for resistance and the rapid elevation of literature. Between these two questions there were some contradictions, but popularization of literature could and would solve these contradictions. Obviously the first view was wrong since it reduced popularization to vernacularization or even vulgarization. The second view was a step ahead of the first. But it stressed the contradictions between literature and politics and put them on equal footing. In fact, literature cannot be separated from struggle. It is in itself a reflection of class struggle. It serves politics.

The second question concerned popularization and elevation. During the discussions on this question, different views were expressed. Some believed that popular literature should concentrate on spreading propaganda among the masses about the War of Resistance and that there was no need for elevation. They were satisfied with poorly-written or vulgar propaganda literature. Others claimed that the only purpose of popularization was for propaganda; it was not literature. These two views seemed to be incompatible. Actually they sprang from the same idea: that popularization and elevation were two separate things. There were others who did not hold either of these views, saying that popularization and elevation should go together. But as to the key questions of popularization for whom and elevation on what basis and the relation between popularization and elevation, there was no elucidation. The original question therefore remained unsolved.

The third question concerned form. The consensus of opinion was that new content should be injected into the old forms and that blind imitation should be discouraged. In other words, the old should be weeded through to let the new emerge. The reactionary poisons and feudal superstitions contained in the old forms should be differentiated from their progressive and popular aspects.

In short, the discussions were conducted on the prewar theoretical basis of popular art and literature, particularly of the period during which the League of Left-Wing Writers existed; but the discussions were on a bigger scale and were more specific than before. Nevertheless, those questions which had stood over from the days of the League of Left-Wing Writers remained unsettled. Particularly, that of the ideological remoulding of the writers and artists was still not given proper attention. Not until the publication of *Talks at the Yenan Forum on Art and Literature* by Mao Tse-tung were these questions fully and thoroughly settled.

(3) Discussions in National Forms

In October 1938, dealing with the question of study in his article "The Role of the Chinese Communist Party in the National War," Mao Tse-tung said:

> Our nation has a history of several thousand years, a history which has its own characteristics and is full of treasures. But in these matters we are mere schoolboys. The China of today has developed from the China in history; as we are believers in the Marxist approach to history, we must not cut off our whole historical past. We must make a summing-up from Confucius down to Sun Yat-sen and inherit this precious legacy. This will help much in directing the great movement of today. Communists are internationalist-Marxists, but Marxism must be integrated with the specific characteristics of our country and given a national form before it can be put into practice. . . . To separate the content of internationalism from national forms is the practice of those who understand nothing

of internationalism; we on the other hand must link up the two closely.[1]

After its publication this article became a subject of study in Yenan. Chen Po-ta, Chou Yang, and Ai Sze-chi wrote their impressions and discussed the question of how to adapt the old and create the new national forms. Views were expressed in the spirit of Mao Tse-tung's article, and there was no deviation. In the Kuomintang-controlled areas, however, a clash of views occurred during the discussions on this question in 1940.

Editor's note:

The counter-revolutionary Hu Feng was at that time moving among the ranks of the left-wing writers and artists. He published a booklet entitled *On the Question of National Forms* attempting to sum up the debate. He attacked all those who had taken part in the debate at Chungking and Yenan. Under the pretext of defending the new art and literature of the May 4 Movement, he completely repudiated national tradition, folk art and literature and the fact that the new art and literature must overcome their shortcoming of losing contact with the masses and establish a Chinese style and Chinese flavour which the common folk love to see and hear. His "theories" were admired by Feng Hsueh-feng and the like but were rejected by most of the progressive writers.

As time went on, Hu Feng became steadily more blatant in spreading his reactionary theories on art and literature. Finally he completely exposed his counter-revolutionary character.

(4) The Struggle Against the Reactionary Tendencies in Literature

As we have said earlier, when the War of Resistance began, a certain tendency towards formulism began to

[1] Mao Tse-tung, *op. cit.*, Vol. II, pp. 259-60.

show itself among writers who had little or no experience in the realities of the war. This was quickly overcome. While the discussions were in progress, however, Liang Shih-chiu, a comprador-bourgeois writer, demanded that "literature should have nothing to do with the War of Resistance."

Liang Shih-chiu's absurd theory met with prompt and sharp criticism. It was pointed out that everything had to do with the resistance in this period of the war. It was only natural that as soon as one began to write one could not forget the war. Moreover, Liang's allegation that "the stereotyped literature of the resistance movement was of no use to anybody," was combated as an arbitrary and slanderous statement. It was pointed out that in fact the reader actually benefited; even sketchy articles about the resistance widened his knowledge and strengthened his determination to resist. It was true that some of the literature lacked substance and depth, but precisely because of the need to remedy this shortcoming, the writers should have more to do with the War of Resistance in every way.

Liang Shih-chiu's absurd theories coincided with the first anti-Communist campaign launched by the Chiang Kai-shek reactionary clique, thus showing that he had political designs.

From that time on as Chiang Kai-shek strengthened his fascist rule, there appeared some reactionary literature spreading propaganda for fascism. About 1939, Chen Chuan, a flunkey of Chiang Kai-shek, gathered a group of backward, reactionary writers together in Kunming to publish a periodical called *Chan Kuo Tse* (Anecdotes of the Warring States) openly advocating fascism.

Chen Chuan himself wrote a play entitled *Wild Rose* exalting fascist agents.

Such reactionary tendencies in literature were promptly exposed and severely refuted by many writers and artists. At the same time they were rejected by the readers, who had become more politically conscious during the War of Resistance. These reactionary views and writings proved to be merely the clamour of a last-ditch struggle.

CHAPTER FOUR

CHINESE LITERATURE IN THE SERVICE OF THE WORKERS, PEASANTS AND SOLDIERS—THE PUBLICATION OF MAO TSE-TUNG'S *TALKS AT THE YENAN FORUM ON ART AND LITERATURE*

Section 1. The Publication of the *Talks at the Yenan Forum on Art and Literature*

After the fall of Wuhan in 1938, Chiang Kai-shek was ready to surrender to the Japanese imperialists at any moment. At the same time he whipped up his activities against the Communists and the people. From 1939 to 1941 he waged two anti-Communist campaigns, both of which collapsed in the face of the heroic counter-attacks by the army and people in the anti-Japanese bases, according to Mao Tse-tung's policy of self-defence.

Taking advantage of the lull in the situation from 1941 to 1943, when there were comparatively few changes either at home or abroad, the Chinese Communist Party organized a Marxist-Leninist study campaign throughout the Party in 1942. In this campaign, the Party led all its cadres and rank-and-file members to recognize and overcome the petty-bourgeois ideas and style of work operating under the cloak of Marxism-Leninism, which were prevalent in the Party at that time, thereby raising the members' political and theoretical level and heightening their sense of discipline. Mao Tse-tung's *Reform Our Study, Rectify the Party's Style in Work, Oppose the Party "Eight-Legged Essay"* were issued at the beginning of the movement and his *Talks at the Yenan Forum on Art and Literature* was also published at that time. These documents played a very important role in the study campaign.

After the May 4 Movement, big advances had been made in the literary movement. Being a component part of the new democratic revolution, the literary movement had always been influenced by communist ideas and guided by the Chinese Communist Party. It took the form of a united front, based upon the broad masses of the people. It had conducted a resolute anti-imperialist, anti-feudal struggle. The main trend of this movement was always realism, heading in the direction of socialist realism. This basic trend not only characterized the literary movement and theories but also penetrated the literary works. As a whole, the literary movement had made a great contribution to the Chinese revolution. But there was a long outstanding problem still awaiting solution. From the time of the May 4 Movement, although the writers and artists had set themselves the aim of taking the life of the broad masses of the people as their theme and of writing to serve the people, the problem of the "popularization of literature" had remained as the key problem in art and literature since the revolutionary literary movement of 1927, one on which many discussions had been held. But the problem was never completely solved. Many revolutionary writers and artists who, though admitting in theory that literature should serve the broad masses of the people, had at best a doctrinaire understanding, rather than a deep ideological grasp of the matter. Therefore the central task of literature — to serve the people — was neither clearly explained in theory nor effectively put into practice in literary works. As a result, a big contradiction arose, in that the actual practice of the writers was inconsistent with the aim of serving the people, as advocated by the movement.

This contradiction was caused by the fact that China was a country with a huge petty-bourgeois population, where petty-bourgeois writers and artists constituted an important force on the literary front as a whole. Following the May 4 Movement, the biggest bulk of the literary works portrayed the petty bourgeoisie and found their readers among them. The progressive petty-bourgeois writers, in spite of their declarations in favour of serving the masses, were still actually writing for the petty bourgeoisie. If and when they attempted to depict working people, the result was merely a petty-bourgeois intellectual in the garb of a worker or peasant. This actually represented the contradiction between proletarian and petty-bourgeois ideologies. It was a cardinal contradiction.

The problem found full expression in the literary circles of Yenan. Some of the writers and artists suffering from the oppression of the imperialists and Kuomintang reactionaries, had supported the working class and were willing to fight against the enemy under the banner of the working class. But when they came over to the area where the working class and the masses of the people had taken power into their hands, they became dissatisfied with the working class and the real situation there and even were at variance with them. There were others who had claimed that their work was to serve the masses of workers and peasants but when the objective conditions were ripe for them to do so they built up a wall with their own hands to separate themselves from the masses.

In his *Talks at the Yenan Forum on Art and Literature,* Mao Tse-tung hit right upon this main ideological problem and, armed with proletarian ideas, launched a vigorous struggle against non-proletarian ideas. The *Talks* systematically and thoroughly solved the above-mentioned contradiction between the proletarian and petty-bourgeois ideologies and the resulting inconsistency between the work of the writers and the stated purpose of the literary movement in advocating literature for the service of the people, as well as many other related problems. It summed up the history of literature since the May 4 Movement, pointed out a new direction for literature and ushered in a new era in the literary movement in China.

Section 2. *Talks at the Yenan Forum on Art and Literature* — Its Contents and Historic Significance

(1) The Question of "For Whom Our Literature Is Intended" and the Question of Ideological Remoulding of the Petty-Bourgeois Artists and Writers

In solving the problems in art and literature, Mao Tse-tung firmly grasped the key link, as he did with all other problems concerning Chinese revolution. In his *Talks* he first of all raises the fundamental problem of principle, "For whom are our art and literature intended?" He goes on to pose the question sharply to the artists and writers in the new literary movement, most of whom were of petty-bourgeois origin: Are our artistic and literary works intended in the first place for the workers, peasants and soldiers, or for the petty bourgeoisie? To this he gives the clear and definite answer: In the first place, for the workers, peasants and soldiers.

He warns that it is no easy matter for petty-bourgeois artists and writers to serve the workers, peasants and soldiers wholeheartedly and put them in the foremost place. The petty-bourgeois intellectuals had long been used to working individually or in very small groups and they had often been deeply influenced by the individualist bourgeois art and literature. All this had fostered their specific individualist habits and ways of thinking. Thus, in analysing and dealing with problems, they could not possibly take the proletarian stand. They could only take the petty-bourgeois stand. But if they were to serve the workers, peasants and soldiers they would have to take the proletarian stand instead of that of the petty bourgeoisie.

Mao Tse-tung proceeds to give a profound analysis and criticism of the petty-bourgeois ideas among the artists and writers:

> It is impossible today for writers who persist in their individualist petty-bourgeois stand to serve faithfully the masses of revolutionary workers, peasants and soldiers, because they are interested mainly in the small number of intellectuals of the petty bourgeoisie.

Here is precisely the reason why some of our comrades are unable to solve correctly the problem of for whom our art and literature are intended. I am not referring to their theory. In theory or in words, none in our ranks would consider the masses of workers, peasants and soldiers less important than the petty-bourgeois intellectuals. I am speaking of their deeds and actions. In deed and action, do they regard the petty-bourgeois intellectuals as more important than the workers, peasants and soldiers? I think they do. Many comrades are concerned with studying the petty-bourgeois intellectuals, analysing their psychology, giving emphatic expression to their life and excusing or defending their shortcomings, rather than with leading these people, together with themselves, to get closer to the masses of workers, peasants and soldiers, to participate in their actual struggles or to give expression to their life and educate them. Many comrades, because they are petty bourgeois in origin and intellectuals themselves, seek friends only in the ranks of the intellectuals and concentrate their attention on studying and describing them. This would be quite proper if they made such a study and description from a proletarian standpoint. But they do not do so, or do not fully do so. They take the stand of the petty bourgeoisie and produce their works as a kind of self-expression of the petty bourgeoisie, as can be seen in quite a number of our artistic and literary works. Quite often they express heart-felt sympathy for the intellectuals of petty-bourgeois origin, they sympathize with or even praise their shortcomings. As to the masses of workers, peasants and soldiers, they seldom come into contact with them, do not understand or study them, do not have bosom friends among them and are not adept at describing them and, when they do describe them, the result is merely petty-bourgeois intellectuals in the clothing of working people. In certain respects they also love the workers, peasants and soldiers and the cadres springing from them; but there are times when they do not love them, and there are some respects in which they do not love them — they do not appreciate their emotions, their manners, their budding art and literature (such as wall newspapers, murals, folk songs, folk tales, etc.). To be sure, sometimes they like these things too, but this is because of their novelty for the sake of embellishing their own works, or even for the backward qualities embodied in them. At other times they openly despise these things and prefer what belongs to the petty-bourgeois intellectuals or even the bourgeoisie. These comrades still stand on the side of the petty-bourgeois intellectuals, or, to put it more elegantly, their innermost soul is still a kingdom of the petty-bourgeois intelligentsia. Thus they have not yet solved or unequivocally solved the problem, "For whom are art and literature intended?"[1]

Therefore, he points out, to thoroughly solve this problem, the petty-bourgeois artists and writers would have to undergo ideological remoulding, and fuse their ideas and feelings with those of the workers, peasants and soldiers. To bring this about, they "must be determined to undergo a long and even painful process of remoulding."[2] Mao Tse-tung says:

---

[1] Mao Tse-tung, *op. cit.,* Vol. IV, pp. 72-3.

[2] *Ibid.,* p. 67.

> If our artists and writers from the intelligentsia want their works to be welcomed by the masses, they must transform and remould their thoughts and feelings. Without such transformation and remoulding they can do nothing well and will be ill-adapted to any kind of work.[1]

Ideological remoulding means to overcome all backward ideas and replace them with the advanced ideas of the working class. It comprises the complete transformation of a person's world outlook, a change of standpoint, and a change of ideas, feelings, psychology, habits and interests. Those who are to be remoulded must be prepared to undergo a considerable period of acute, painstaking inward struggle. As Mao Tse-tung points out:

> To solve this problem thoroughly, a long time is required, say, eight or ten years. But no matter how long it takes, we must solve it, and solve it unequivocally and thoroughly. Our artists and writers must accomplish this task and shift their stand — gradually shift it over to the side of the masses of workers, peasants and soldiers, to the side of the proletariat, in the course of going into their midst and into the heart of the actual struggle and in the course of studying Marxism and society. Only thus can we have art and literature that are truly for the workers, peasants and soldiers, and that are truly proletarian.[2]

---

[1] *Ibid.*, p. 68.

[2] *Ibid.*, p. 73.

(2) On the Question of How Literature Should Serve the Workers, Peasants and Soldiers

The ideological remoulding of the artists and writers is inseparable from their practical life and art and literary creations, and the individual artist's or writer's ideology, life and creations must be unified on the basis of his own labour and experience. The key point, however, for successful ideological remoulding, for real combination of art or literary works with the life of the masses of workers, peasants and soldiers and the class struggle of the masses, is to take an active part in the actual struggle of the masses. On this point Mao Tse-tung gives a penetrating explanation, emphasizing the life of the people as the only source of art and literature. He says:

> What after all is the source of any kind of art and literature? An artistic or literary work is ideologically the product of the human brain reflecting the life of a given society. Revolutionary art and literature are the products of the brains of revolutionary artists and writers reflecting the life of the people. In the life of the people itself lies a mine of raw material for art and literature, namely, things in their natural state, things crude, but also most lively, rich and fundamental; in this sense, they throw all art and literature into the shade and provide for them a unique and inexhaustible source. This is the only source, for there can be no other source.[1]

But the people's life itself is not the equivalent of art and literature. Mao Tse-tung proceeds to denote the

---

[1] *Ibid.*, p. 76.

important role played by art and literature in portraying the life of the people.

> Though man's social life constitutes the only source for art and literature, and is incomparably more vivid and richer than art and literature as such, the people are not satisfied with the former alone and demand the latter. Why? Because, although both are beautiful, life as reflected in artistic and literary works can and ought to be on a higher level and of a greater power and better focussed, more typical, nearer the ideal, and therefore more universal than actual everyday life. Revolutionary art and literature should create all kinds of characters on the basis of actual life and help the masses to push history forward.[1]

In short, since the life of the people is the only source of art and literature, and art and literature are intended to depict this rich life in sharper focus, making it more typical and nearer the ideal, the artists and writers must plunge themselves into this life.

(3) Popularization and Elevation in Art and Literature

In dealing with the question of popularization and elevation in art and literature, Mao Tse-tung begins by drawing the proper criterion for this question.

> Since our art and literature are basically intended for the workers, peasants and soldiers, popularization means extending art and literature among these people while elevation means raising their level of artistic

[1] *Ibid.*, p. 77.

and literary appreciation. What should we popularize among them? . . . We must popularize what is needed and can be readily accepted by the workers, peasants and soldiers themselves. Consequently the duty of learning from the workers, peasants and soldiers precedes the task of educating them. This is even more true of elevation. There must be a basis to elevate from. . . . It can only be raised from the basis of the masses of the workers, peasants and soldiers. This means not that we raise the workers, peasants and soldiers to the level of the feudal class, the bourgeoisie or the petty-bourgeois intelligentsia, but that we raise them up along their own line of advance, along the line of advance of the proletariat. Here again the task of learning from the workers, peasants and soldiers comes in. Only by starting from the workers, peasants and soldiers can we have a correct understanding of elevation and popularization and find the proper relation between the two.[1]

Mao Tse-tung stresses the task of popularization as the more urgent of the two. He says:

The problem facing the workers, peasants and soldiers today is this: Engaged in a ruthless and sanguinary struggle against the enemy, they remain illiterate and uncultured as a result of the prolonged rule of the feudal and bourgeois classes and consequently they badly need a widespread campaign of enlightenment, and they eagerly wish to have culture, knowledge, art and literature which meet their immediate need and are readily acceptable to them so

[1] *Ibid.*, p. 75.

as to heighten their passion for struggle and their confidence in victory, to strengthen their solidarity, and thus to enable them to fight the enemy with one heart and one mind. In meeting their primary need, we are not to "add flowers to a piece of brocade" but "offer fuel to a person in snowy weather." Under the present conditions, therefore, popularization is the more pressing task. It is wrong to despise and neglect this task.

But popularization and elevation cannot be sharply separated. Not only is it possible to popularize even now a number of works to a higher level, but the cultural level of the broad masses is also steadily rising. . . . The people need popularization, but along with it they need elevation too, elevation month by month and year by year. Popularization is popularization for the people, and elevation is elevation of the people. Such elevation does not take place in mid-air, nor behind closed doors, but on the basis of popularization. It is at once determined by popularization and gives direction to it. . . . This being the case, the work of popularization in our sense not only constitutes no obstacle to elevation but affords a basis for our work of elevation on a limited scale at present, as well as preparing the necessary conditions for our far more extensive work of elevation in the future.[1]

Mao Tse-tung goes on to emphasize the need for the experts in art and literature to build up a proper relationship with the popularizers and to maintain close contact with each other. He urges the artists and writers

---

[1] *Ibid.*, pp. 78-9.

to pay attention to crude forms of art and literature created by the workers, peasants and soldiers: the wall newspapers, the small drama troupes in the army and villages, and songs of the masses. He says:

> The experts should help and guide the popularizers as well as learn from them, and through them draw nourishment from the masses to develop and enrich themselves and to prevent their specialities from becoming empty, lifeless castles in the air detached from the masses and from reality.[1]

(4) The Criteria in Art and Literary Criticism

Turning to art and literary criticism as "one of the principal methods of struggle in the artistic and literary sphere," he emphasizes the need to develop it. Art and literary criticism presents a complex problem, whose main aspect is the criteria in criticism; when this point is solved all other problems, no matter how complex, can be solved without difficulty.

On this key question, Mao Tse-tung puts forward the following views:

> There are two criteria in art and literary criticism: political and artistic. According to the political criterion, all works are good that facilitate unity and resistance to Japan, that encourage the masses to be of one heart and one mind and that oppose retrogression and promote progress; on the other hand, all works are bad that undermine unity and resistance to Japan, that sow dissension and discord among the masses and

---

[1] *Ibid.*, p. 80.

that oppose progress and drag the people back. And how can we tell the good from the bad here — by the motive (subjective intention) or by the effect (social practice)? Idealists stress motive and ignore effect, while mechanical materialists stress effect and ignore motive; in contradistinction from either, we dialectical materialists insist on the unity of motive and effect. The motive of serving the masses is inseparable from the effect of winning their approval, and we must unite the two. The motive of serving the individual or a small clique is not good, nor is the motive of serving the masses good if it does not lead to a result that is welcomed by the masses and confers benefit on them. In examining the subjective intention of an artist, i.e whether his motive is correct and good, we do not look at his declaration but at the effect his activities (mainly his works) produce on society and the masses. Social practice and its effect are the criteria for examining the subjective intention or the motive. We reject sectarianism in our art and literary criticism and, under the general principle of unity and resistance to Japan, we must tolerate all artistic and literary works expressing every kind of political attitude. But at the same time we must firmly uphold our principles in our criticism, and adhere to our standpoint and severely criticize and repudiate all artistic and literary works containing views against the nation, the sciences, the people and communism, because such works, in motive as well as in effect, are detrimental to unity and the resistance to Japan. According to the artistic criterion, all works are good or comparatively good that are relatively high in artistic quality; and bad or comparatively bad that are relatively low in artistic quality. Of course, this distinction also depends on social effect. As there is hardly an artist who does not consider his own work excellent, our criticism ought to permit the free competition of all varieties of artistic works; but it is entirely necessary for us to pass correct judgements on them according to the criteria of the science of art, so that we can gradually raise the art of a lower level to a higher level, and to change the art which does not meet the requirements of the struggle of the broad masses into art that does meet them.[1]

Mao Tse-tung also makes a thorough and unequivocal analysis about the relation between the two criteria. He says:

There is thus the political criterion as well as the artistic criterion. How are the two related? Politics is not the equivalent of art, nor is a general world outlook equivalent to the method of artistic creation and criticism. We believe there is neither an abstract and absolutely unchangeable political criterion, nor an abstract and absolutely unchangeable artistic criterion, for every class in a class society has its own political and artistic criteria. But all classes in all class societies place the political criterion first and the artistic criterion second. The bourgeoisie always rejects proletarian artistic and literary works, no matter how great their artistic achievement. As for the proletariat, they must treat the art and literature of the past according to their attitude towards the people and whether they are progressive in the light of history. Some things which are basically reactionary from the

---

[1] *Ibid.*, pp. 84-5.

political point of view may yet be artistically good. But the more artistic such a work may be, the greater harm will it do to the people, and the more reason for us to reject it. The contradiction between reactionary political content and artistic form is a common characteristic of the art and literature of all exploiting classes in their decline. What we demand is unity of politics and art, of content and form, and of the revolutionary political content and the highest possible degree of perfection in artistic form. Works of art, however politically progressive, are powerless if they lack artistic quality. Therefore we are equally opposed to works with wrong political approaches and to the tendency towards so-called "poster and slogan style" which is correct only in political approach but lacks artistic power. We must carry on a two-front struggle in art and literature.[1]

(5) The Party's Artistic and Literary Activity, the United Front in Art and Literature and the Problem of Study

Speaking on the Party's work in art and literature, Mao Tse-tung remarks:

In the world today all culture, all art and literature belong to definite classes and follow definite political lines. . . . Proletarian art and literature are part of the entire cause of the proletarian revolution, in the words of Lenin, "cogs and screws in the whole machine." Therefore the Party's artistic and literary ac-

[1] *Ibid.*, pp. 85-6.

> tivity occupies a definite and assigned position in the Party's total revolutionary work and is subordinated to the prescribed revolutionary task of the Party in a given revolutionary period. Any opposition to this assignment will certainly lead to dualism or pluralism. . . . We are not in favour of erroneously over-emphasizing the importance of art and literature, but neither are we in favour of underestimating it. Art and literature are subordinate to politics, but they in turn also exert a great influence on politics. Revolutionary art and literature are part of the entire cause of the revolution, they are its cogs and screws; though in comparison with certain other parts they may be less important and less urgent and occupy only a secondary position, yet they are, as cogs and screws, indispensable to the whole machine, and form an indispensable part of the entire cause of the revolution. If we had no art and literature even in the broadest and most general sense, then the revolutionary movement could not be carried on to victory. It would be wrong not to realize this.[1]

Here Mao Tse-tung emphasizes:

> . . . In saying that art and literature are subordinate to politics, we mean here class politics and mass politics, not the politics of a few so-called statesmen. Politics, whether revolutionary or counter-revolutionary, represents the struggle of one class against another, not the activity of a few individuals. Revolutionary struggles on the ideological and artistic fronts must be subordinate to the political struggle because

---

[1] *Ibid.*, p. 82.

only through politics can the needs of the class and the masses be expressed in concentrated form.[1]

As to the question of the united front in art and literature, Mao Tse-tung points out that, like the united front in politics, it must carry out, under the leadership of the proletariat and the Chinese Communist Party, the policy of uniting with non-Party artists and writers and at the same time struggling against their wrong ideas.

Of the petty-bourgeois artists and writers in China, Mao Tse-tung states that they constitute an important force in the united front of art and literature, and goes on to say:

> Although there are many shortcomings in their ideology and in their works, they are comparatively inclined towards the revolution and comparatively close to the working people. Therefore it is especially important to help them to overcome their shortcomings and win them over to the front of serving the working people.[2]

The best way to help them, as he has often pointed out, is to help them remould their ideology.

Regarding the question of study, Mao Tse-tung points out in the *Talks* that all artists and writers must study Marxism and Leninism and must study it in a modest way. He says:

> We study Marxism in order to apply the dialectical materialist and historical materialist viewpoint in our observation of the world, society and art and litera-

---

[1] *Ibid.*

[2] *Ibid.*, pp. 83-4.

ture, and not in order to write philosophical discourses in our works of art and literature.[1]

And again:

Artists and writers should study society; i.e. study the various classes in society, their mutual relations and respective conditions and their physiognomy and psychology. Only when these things are clearly grasped will our art and literature be rich in content and correct in orientation.[2]

Speaking of the need for the artists and writers to study the fine literary legacy of China and that of the foreign countries, he says:

We should take over the rich legacy and succeed to the fine tradition of Chinese and foreign art and literature of the past, but we must do this with our eyes upon the broad masses of the people. We do not refuse to make use of the artistic and literary forms of the past, but in our hands these old forms, remoulded and filled with new content, also become things which are revolutionary and serve the people.[3]

He says again:

We must take over all the fine artistic and literary legacy, critically assimilate from it what is beneficial to us and hold it up as an example when we try to work over the artistic and literary raw material derived from the people's life of our own time and

---

[1] *Ibid.*, p. 90.

[2] *Ibid.*, p. 68.

[3] *Ibid.*, p. 71.

place. It makes an enormous difference whether or not one has such examples to look up to, a difference which explains why some works are refined and others crude, some polished and others coarse, some superior and others inferior, some smoothly done and others laboriously executed. Therefore we must not refuse to take over the legacy from the ancients and the foreigners and learn from such examples, whether feudal or bourgeois. But succession to a legacy and learning from examples should never take the place of the creation of our own work, for nothing can take its place. In art and literature, the uncritical appropriation and imitation of the ancients and foreigners represent the most sterile and harmful artistic and literary doctrinairism.[1]

(6) The Struggle Against Wrong Ideas in Art and Literature

Earlier in this chapter I mentioned the wrong views existing in the art and literary circles in Yenan at that time. Although these ideas came up in a concentrated form in Yenan, they existed generally in other parts of the country. In his *Talks* Mao Tse-tung severely criticizes some of the most widespread of these ideas and from the standpoint of proletarian ideology, launches a vigorous struggle against these non-proletarian ideas.

First of all, he denounces the absurd "theory of human nature." He says:

. . . There is only human nature in the concrete, no human nature in the abstract. In a class society

---

[1] *Ibid.*, pp. 76-7.

> there is only human nature that bears the stamp of a class, but no human nature transcending classes. We uphold the human nature of the proletariat and of the great masses of the people, while the landlord and bourgeois classes uphold the human nature of their own classes as if — though they do not say so outright — it were the only kind of human nature. The human nature boosted by certain petty-bourgeois intellectuals is also divorced from or opposed to that of the great masses of the people; what they call human nature is in substance nothing but bourgeois individualism, and consequently in their eyes proletarian human nature is contrary to their human nature. This is the "theory of human nature" advocated by some people in Yenan as the so-called basis of their theory of art and literature, which is utterly mistaken.[1]

In proceeding to refute the confused view that "the fundamental point of departure for art and literature is love, the love of mankind," he says:

> Love is a concept, a product of objective practice. Fundamentally, we do not start from a concept but from objective practice. Our artists and writers who come from the intelligentsia love the proletariat because social life has made them feel that they share the same fate with the proletariat. . . . As to the so-called "love of mankind," there has been no such all-embracing love since humanity was divided into classes. . . . Genuine love of mankind will be born only when class distinctions have been eliminated

[1] *Ibid.*, p. 86.

> throughout the world. The classes have caused the division of society into many opposites and as soon as they are eliminated there will be love of all mankind, but not now. We cannot love our enemies, we cannot love social evils, and our aim is to exterminate them.[1]

Two further views come in for reproval: One, that "art and literature have always described the bright as well as the dark side of things impartially, on a fifty-fifty basis," and two, that "the task of art and literature has always been to expose." Speaking on these wrong views, he says:

> Art and literature have not always done so. . . . Only truly revolutionary artists and writers can correctly solve the problem whether to praise or to expose. All dark forces which endanger the masses of the people must be exposed while all revolutionary struggles of the masses must be praised — this is the basic task of all revolutionary artists and writers. . . . For the revolutionary artists and writers the objects to be exposed can never be the masses of the people, but only the aggressors, exploiters and oppressors and their evil aftermath brought to the people. The people have their shortcomings too, but these are to be overcome by means of criticism and self-criticism within the ranks of the people themselves, and to carry on such criticism and self-criticism is also one of the most important tasks of art and literature. However, we should not call that "exposing the peo-

---

[1] *Ibid.*, pp. 86-7.

ple." As for the people, our problem is basically one of how to educate them and raise their level.[1]

There were still others who said at that time: "This is still a period of the essay, and the style should still be that of Lu Hsun." In discarding this view, Mao Tse-tung says:

> Living under the rule of the dark forces, deprived of freedom of speech, Lu Hsun had to fight by means of burning satire and freezing irony cast in essay form, and in this he was entirely correct. . . . In dealing with the people themselves and not the enemies of the people, Lu Hsun even in his "essay period" did not mock or attack the revolutionary masses and the revolutionary parties, and his style was also entirely different from that employed in his essays on the enemy. We have already said that we must criticize the shortcomings of the people, but be sure that we criticize from the standpoint of the people and out of a wholehearted eagerness to defend and educate them. If we treat our comrades like enemies, then we are taking the standpoint of the enemy.[2]

Still others said: "I am not given to praise and eulogy; works which extol the bright side of things are not necessarily great, nor are works which depict the dark side necessarily poor."[3]

Mao Tse-tung argues:

> If you are a bourgeois artist or writer, you will extol not the proletariat but the bourgeoisie, and if you are

---

[1] *Ibid.*, pp. 87-8.

[2] *Ibid.*, p. 88.

[3] *Ibid.*, p. 89.

> a proletarian artist or writer, you will extol not the bourgeoisie but the proletariat and the working people: you must do one or the other.[1]

Another opinion was: "The standpoint is correct, but the expression is faulty and produces a bad effect."[2] There were also some who said: "To call on us to study Marxism may again lead us to take the repetition of dialectical materialist formulas for literary creation, and this will stifle our creative impulse."[3] Mao Tse-tung refutes both of these ideas, pointing out the error of considering only the intention and ignoring the effect. The problem of effect, he says, is one of standpoint therefore one who has good intentions must sum up his experience, and correct the errors, so that the effect is better next time.

> We study Marxism in order to apply the dialectical materialist and historical materialist viewpoint in our observation of the world, society and art and literature, and not in order to write philosophical discourses in our works of art and literature. . . . Empty, cut-and-dried dogmas and formulas will certainly destroy our creative impulse; moreover, they first of all destroy Marxism. Dogmatic "Marxism" is not Marxist but anti-Marxist.[4]

In short, all these are non-proletarian ideas. Some are bourgeois and some are petty-bourgeois. All are antagonistic to proletarian ideas. The non-proletariat have set their minds on propagating their ideas by means

---

[1] *Ibid.*
[2] *Ibid.*
[3] *Ibid.*
[4] *Ibid.*, p. 90.

of art and literature. They wish to remould the Party and reform the world according to how the petty-bourgeois intelligentsia would like them to be. These ideas must be resolutely and ruthlessly routed out. The only method for this purpose is the method of ideological remoulding created by Mao Tse-tung, the method of the rectification campaign.

Editor's note:

Among those who showed anti-proletarian views in art and literature in Yenan at that time were Wang Shih-wei, Hsiao Chun, Lo Feng, Ting Ling and Ai Ching. Ting Ling was then the editor of the art and literary supplement of the Party organ *Jiefang Ribao* (Liberation Daily) published in Yenan. Articles written by Wang Shih-wei, Hsiao Chun, Lo Feng, Ai Ching and others who have since been exposed as reactionaries, were published in this supplement. Ting Ling herself also wrote a series of articles slandering the working class. They echoed with the views of Hu Feng and Feng Hsueh-feng in the Kuomintang-controlled area, and engaged in anti-Party disruptive activities with the aim of damping down the spirit of the revolutionary base. At that time the revolutionary artists and writers unleashed a resolute struggle against them. They vowed they would correct their errors and the Party tried its best to save them by giving them the chance to reform themselves.

When Ting Ling was in the countryside for ideological remoulding, she wrote the book *The Sun Shines over the Sangkan River*. The liberation of China and the publication of this book brought her fame and position but she forgot the criticism and education the Party had given her and taking the advantage of the post the Party and people had entrusted to her, she actively gathered a clique around herself. She, together with Chen Chihsia and Feng Hsueh-feng as editors of *Wenyi Bao* (Literary Gazette), endeavoured to make the journal their independent domain in opposition to the Party's directives on art and literature. Their anti-Party activities were completely exposed and criticized in 1955 and again in 1957.

(7) The Historic Significance of the "Talks at the Yenan Forum on Art and Literature"

Mao Tse-tung's *Talks at the Yenan Forum on Art and Literature* is of truly great historic significance, which cannot be overestimated.

This great significance lies not only in its direct contribution to literature but, like many of his important works, in its application of Marxism-Leninism in solving the specific problems of the Chinese revolution. In the course of discussing art and literary problems, it expounds many revolutionary theories, thereby enriching and promoting the development of Marxism-Leninism. All revolutionaries can learn from it the most profound and concrete revolutionary theories of dialectical and historical materialism. It is a part of the treasure-house of the world's Marxist-Leninist works.

Secondly, in respect of art and literature, it is a militant programme for the revolutionary art and literary movement of the Chinese people. It points out the correct direction for the development of China's revolutionary art and literature — to serve the workers, peasants and soldiers; it denotes that all revolutionary and progressive artists and writers must acquire a communist world outlook on life and art and must resolutely conduct ideological remoulding. It also emphasizes the need for them to master the correct way of thinking and writing, and to do their best to make art and literature one with the broad masses of workers and peasants and their class struggles. It guarantees the future course of art and literary work. The appearance of this work was an unprecedented event in the history of modern

Chinese literature, one that has brought immense happiness to all the artists and writers throughout China.

Thirdly, by affirming the aim of literature as one of serving the workers, peasants and soldiers, the *Talks* ushered in a new era in modern Chinese literature in line with the development of revolutionary literature since the May 4 Movement. The change it brought in literature was even greater and more profound than that brought about by the May 4 Movement. Not only has it swept away all the imperialist and feudal reactionary art and literature, it has also initiated sharp criticism against the various petty-bourgeois ideas and tendencies existing in art and literature, marking the distinction between proletarian and all non-proletarian ideas and safeguarding the purity and strictness of proletarian ideology. By declaring that art and literature must serve the workers, peasants and soldiers, it has fundamentally solved the problem of uniting art and literature with the broad masses of the people, a problem which had not been solved since the May 4 Movement. These theories of Mao Tse-tung on art and literature have armed all Party and non-Party revolutionary artists and writers and taken them along the road of identifying themselves with the masses of workers, peasants and soldiers. Illuminated by Mao Tse-tung's theories, socialist realism in Chinese literature has achieved greater development and success since the publication of the *Talks*.

CHAPTER FIVE

LU HSUN, STANDARD-BEARER OF THE CHINESE PEOPLE'S NEW CULTURE AND COMMUNIST THINKER

Section 1. His Life and Ideological Development

Lu Hsun, whose real name was Chou Shu-jen, was born on September 25, 1881, in Shaohsing, Chekiang Province. His grandfather held an official position in Peking at the time of Lu Hsun's birth. His father was a scholar with no official position. When Lu Hsun was thirteen his grandfather was involved in a case of bribery and sent to prison. His father fell seriously ill about this time and died three years later. His mother, whose family name was Lu, was a capable peasant woman. It was from her that Lu Hsun took his *nom de plume*. Her broad vision and perseverance had a tremendous influence on her son.

From his boyhood Lu Hsun was strikingly intelligent. When he was six, he began to receive a traditional style of education at a private school where he remained until he was seventeen. During these years he read a great number of the Chinese classics and had the courage to challenge the established traditional ethics of the feudal, patriarchal society. He took full advantage of his opportunities to come in contact with rural life, making friends with the simple and straightforward peasant boys and learning to know the labouring people. He took a special interest in folk art and literature — New Year pictures, stories, legends, and village opera.

All this prepared the background for his later literary and revolutionary career. Of greater influence on his ideas were, of course, the momentous social changes taking place during his formative years. It was the age when imperialism was intensifying its aggressive activities in China. The corrupt and decadent Ching (Manchu) dynasty kowtowed to the foreign powers while suppressing the people's patriotic struggles. Lu Hsun was deeply disturbed at the humiliations being brought upon his country. About that time his family fell into poverty, causing him to suffer the many snobbish slights which opened his eyes to the oppressive nature of the feudal, patriarchal society, and taught him to hate and despise this society.

At eighteen Lu Hsun left his home-town for Nanking where he entered the Naval Academy. In the following year he changed to the School of Railways and Mines. During his four years' stay in Nanking Lu Hsun came into contact with the new ideas advocated by the "Reform Movement of 1898" which aimed at setting up a constitutional monarchy. The movement, however, influenced him very little since he rapidly formed the conclusion that the reformists' ideas fell far short of what was needed. It was rather the translations of some literary and scientific works, particularly Huxley's *Evolution and Ethics*, which had a tremendous influence upon him at this time. Darwin's theory of evolution remained for a long period as his guide in his mental development. It was during his school days in Nanking when his anti-imperialist and anti-Manchu national revolutionary consciousness was steadily growing, that he acquired his ardent feelings of patriotism.

In 1901 he graduated from the School of Railways and Mines, and the following year was awarded a government scholarship to study in Japan.

As a thoroughgoing patriot, Lu Hsun pledged his life to the work of reviving his country. He took part in patriotic activities and joined the anti-Manchu revolutionary party Kuang Fu Hui (Restoration League) in 1908.

While in Japan he studied medicine. Later he saw a film about the Russo-Japanese War which stirred him to his depths. It showed the execution by the Japanese of a Chinese who had acted as a spy for tsarist Russia, while a crowd of Chinese looked on apathetically. Deeply hurt, Lu Hsun began to change his mind about his profession. He felt that it was more important to cure the apathy of his people than to cure their physical ills, and that the best treatment for the spirit of the people was literature. So he abandoned medicine for literature.

Lu Hsun spent eight years in Japan during which he read a large number of books on European science, philosophy and literature in search of a road of national revolution. Darwin's progressive theory of evolution helped him to become a revolutionary democrat and patriot.

In 1909, two years before the 1911 Revolution which led to the overthrow of the Manchu regime, Lu Hsun returned to China. He taught in the Chekiang Normal School and Shaohsing Middle School and later became the principal of the Shaohsing Normal School. After 1911 he was appointed a member of the Ministry of

Education under Minister Tsai Yuan-pei. He remained in this position until 1926.

From the time he returned from Japan until 1918, Lu Hsun kept in touch with the complicated practical politics and social realities of China. Disturbed by the corruption in political life, this fervent patriot groped in the dark, perplexed and struggling between hope and despair. Quietly he continued his search for a way forward for the Chinese revolution. And with the revolution in view, he observed, studied and analysed the Chinese people, society, history and culture. In 1918 he broke his silence. This was the beginning of his revolutionary struggles.

In the first period of his revolutionary struggles, from 1918 to 1927, Lu Hsun fought all the old forces in a spirit of uncompromising opposition to imperialism and feudalism. At the same time, he underwent a process of self-remoulding from the theory of evolution to the theory of class struggle.

In April 1918 Lu Hsun published his first short story, "A Madman's Diary," in the *New Youth* magazine. This all-out, penetrating attack on China's old feudal ethics was the first work of modern Chinese fiction. About the same time, he wrote the first of his terse, trenchant and militant essays criticizing social conditions, in which he opened fire on all feudalists, traitors, slanderers of revolution and other enemies of the people, with deadly effect.

During this period Lu Hsun came in touch with many young people. From 1920 he taught in Peking University and the National Teachers' College, edited newspaper supplements, gave guidance to young people in setting up literary organizations and wholeheartedly helped them revise their manuscripts. In 1925 he enthusiastically supported the students of the Peking Women's Normal College in opposing Chang Shih-chao, then Minister of Education. On March 18, 1926, the warlord government under Tuan Chi-jui killed over forty patriotic students of Peking. Lu Hsun came out boldly to protest against the massacre. He became an authority among the thinkers of the time and gained great prestige among the young people.

Persecuted by the reactionary warlords regime, Lu Hsun left Peking in August 1926. He went to Amoy University to teach. In January 1927 he went to Canton to become the dean and concurrently the head of the department of literature in Sun Yat-sen University. In April of the same year Chiang Kai-shek betrayed the revolution, massacring the Communists and revolutionary students. Frustrated in his attempt to save the students, Lu Hsun resigned in protest. In October he left Canton for Shanghai.

Between 1918 and 1927 Lu Hsun published two collections of short stories, five volumes of essays, one volume of prose poems and one volume of prose, and translated a number of foreign works, including Soviet works on theories of art and literature.

In this period, Lu Hsun was still a revolutionary democrat. He had not yet clearly and definitely accepted Marxism-Leninism, retaining the influence of the theory of evolution and individualism. But he was coming into closer contact with Marxist-Leninists and attacking ever more fiercely imperialism, feudalism and the right-wing of the bourgeoisie. He had particular hatred and disgust for the feudal ruling class — the warlords and their lackeys — whom he sharply satirized. All this testified to the thorough and uncompromising character of his anti-imperialist and anti-feudal stand.

Indeed, Lu Hsun's process of advancing "from the theory of evolution to that of class struggle, from individualism seeking emancipation to the militant collectivism determined to transform the world"[1] was completed only after 1928. Nevertheless, his efforts and struggles along this direction began from and continued throughout this period.

From October 1927, when he came to Shanghai, up to 1936, the time of his death, he remained in the city, no longer teaching but devoting himself to the revolutionary literary movement under the leadership of the Chinese Communist Party. It was during these later years of his life that he waged his courageous and resolute battles in the cause of communism.

In 1928 Lu Hsun founded the magazine *Torrent*. He pursued the study of Marxist-Leninist social sciences and translated Marxist-Leninist theories of art and literature. He came into closer contact with the Chinese Communist Party and took part in the mass movements and political struggles initiated by the Communists.

In 1928 he joined the Revolutionary Mutual-aid Society.[2] In 1930 he was one of the founders of the China

---

[1] Chu Chiu-pai, *op. cit.*, p. 57.

[2] "Revolutionary Mutual-aid Society" or "Mutual-aid Society" was the popular name for the "China Aid Society" which was established in 1923 after the "February 7" strike to raise funds to aid the families of revolutionary workers in trouble.

Freedom League.[1] In the same year he sponsored the formation of the China League of Left-Wing Writers and became its most influential figure. In 1933 he joined the China League for Civil Rights[2] and in May of the same year he went personally to the German Consulate in Shanghai and handed in a protest against the brutalities of the Nazis. In the following September he helped the convocation of the International Anti-imperialist and Anti-fascist Conference[3] and was one of its honorary presidents.

During the last ten years of his life, Lu Hsun wrote nine volumes of essays, more profound and covering a wider field than those of his earlier period. He also completed a volume of short stories on historical subjects and many more translations, the most important of which

---

[1] This was a revolutionary mass organization established in February 1930 in Shanghai, and supported and led by the Communist Party. It strove for freedom of speech, press, assembly and association and opposed the Kuomintang's reactionary rule. Lu Hsun was one of its founders.

[2] A people's organization formed under the sponsorship of Soong Ching Ling, Tsai Yuan-pei and others, on January 17, 1933 in Shanghai, with a branch in Peking, to oppose the Kuomintang dark rule and strive for the protection of civil rights.

[3] This was the Far-Eastern Conference convened in Shanghai in September 1933 by the World Anti-Imperialist Committee. As Shanghai was then dominated by the reactionaries, the conference was held in secrecy with the help of the underground Chinese Communist Party. The participants included Lord Marley of Britain, Paul Vaillart-Coutourier, a French writer and the then editor-in-chief of *L'Humanité* and Soong Ching Ling of China. Lu Hsun was elected the Honorary Chairman of the Presidium of the Conference. During the preparations for the conference Lu Hsun rendered his support and donated money to it.

were those on the theories of art and literature by Plekhanov and Lunacharsky, *The Nineteen* by Fadeyev, *October* by Yakovlev, *Russian Fairy Tales* by Gorky and *Dead Souls* by Gogol. He gave guidance to and took part in the editorial work for many journals. He introduced and guided the new revolutionary woodcut art in China. He read and revised the manuscripts of young writers and corresponded with them. He seldom took a rest even during illness.

This was the decade of the sanguinary reactionary rule of the Kuomintang in its desperate attempts "to encircle and annihilate" the revolution. In the face of the constant danger of arrest and assassination, Lu Hsun never once retreated. On the contrary, he succeeded in breaking through and smashing the Kuomintang's ten-year campaign of "encircling and annihilating" the revolutionary cultural movement. As Mao Tse-tung said:

> . . . It was in the very midst of such campaigns of "encirclement and annihilation" that Lu Hsun, the communist, grew to be the giant of China's cultural revolution.[1]

On October 19, 1936, this giant of China's cultural revolution, suffering from overwork and tuberculosis, died in Shanghai.

Lu Hsun's undaunted struggle against reaction and his contributions to the cause of communist culture over the last ten years of his life are of permanent value to China. This was mainly because in this period he became a great communist and a true internationalist. Resolutely and unreservedly he supported and followed the

---

[1] Mao Tse-tung, *op. cit.*, Vol. III, pp. 149-50.

leadership of the Chinese Communist Party. When the Red Army safely reached northern Shensi after its Long March, he sent a telegram to Mao Tse-tung and Chu Teh offering his congratulations on the success. In his letters in reply to the Chinese Trotskyites, he considered it an honour to mention Mao Tse-tung and other Communists as his comrades. At all times he was concerned with the Party, and at all times the Party helped him, influenced him, gave him great strength, enabled him to develop his genius to the utmost, and encouraged him to wage his struggles fearlessly.

In *On New Democracy,* Mao Tse-tung gave this high appraisal of Lu Hsun:

> Since the May 4 Movement . . . a brand-new cultural force of fresh strength has appeared in China. . . . For the last twenty years, in whatever direction this new cultural force has turned its spearhead, a great revolution has taken place in both thought-content and form (such as the style of written language). Its influence is so great and its power so tremendous that it is practically invincible wherever it goes. The vast scope of its mobilization is unparalleled in any other period in Chinese history. And Lu Hsun was the greatest and the most militant standard-bearer of this new cultural force. He was the supreme commander in China's cultural revolution; he was not only a great man of letters, but also a great thinker and a great revolutionary. Lu Hsun had the most unyielding backbone and was totally free from any trace of obsequiousness and sycophancy; such strength of character is the greatest treasure among the colonial and semi-colonial peoples. Lu Hsun, representing the great majority of

> the people, was an unprecedented national hero on the cultural front, the most correct, the bravest, the firmest, the most loyal and the most zealous hero who stormed and broke up the enemy's front. The line he took is precisely the line of the new culture of the Chinese nation.[1]

These words of Mao Tse-tung are in effect a summary of the militant life of Lu Hsun.

Section 2. Lu Hsun's Works of Fiction—from Thorough, Critical Realism to Socialist Realism

Between 1918 and 1925 Lu Hsun wrote over a score of works of fiction which were later compiled into *Call to Arms* and *Wandering*. These few earlier works, which were highly successful, marked Lu Hsun as a pioneer in Chinese realistic literature and a figure of world stature in twentieth century realism. They helped to lay a firm foundation for such literature in China.

Basically these short stories belong to the critical, realistic method of writing. But in their critical thoroughness and revolutionary character they go far beyond the confines of the general run of critical realism. This was due to Lu Hsun's out-and-out anti-imperialist and anti-feudal ideas at that time. His writings of the later period, from 1927 onwards, when he had become a communist, belong to the category of socialist realism.

Lu Hsun's realism in his earlier period can be attributed to his absorption of the fine realistic traditions of an-

---

[1] *Ibid.*, pp. 143-44.

cient Chinese literature as well as to his contacts with critical realism in world literature. The result was a unique style of realism, characterized by a keenly critical and revolutionary quality. In this it differed from both the realism in Chinese classical literature and the critical realism in world literature.

About "A Madman's Diary,"[1] Lu Hsun said that this was intended to expose the abuses of the patriarchal family system and ethics but that it contained a much deeper degree of indignation than Gogol had expressed on his similar theme. His penetrating criticism and revolutionary quality were mainly the product of the period in which Lu Hsun was writing — the early days of China's new-democratic revolution. Not only did he personally take part in this struggle and become a part of it but he was also a staunch vanguard of the revolution, through which his genius found full expression.

Lu Hsun abandoned his study of medicine for literature chiefly because of his deep love for his country. He wanted to cure the spirit of the Chinese people and he felt that creative writing was the best means to this end. This ardent revolutionary patriotism was expressed in his fiction.

First, it showed itself in his affection for the working people. In more than half of Lu Hsun's stories, working people play the principal role and the author shows his deep attachment to them. In "My Old Home" he describes his friendship for the peasant Jun-tu in his boyhood. In "Village Opera" he expresses his feeling for the simple, straightforward peasants with whom he had

---

[1] Lu Hsun's "A Madman's Diary" was modelled on Gogol's "Madman's Diary."

become friends in his younger days and for the rural life he once lived. In "Kung I-chi" and "The Divorce" he sympathizes with the plain, good-hearted peasants who were persecuted and misunderstood by the feudal society. In "The New Year's Sacrifice" and "Tomorrow" he manifests his indignation at the old ethical codes which crushed the peasant women.

Again, it showed itself in his hatred and abhorrence for the feudal system and its detrimental effects on the country and the working people. In "Preface to My Selected Works," Lu Hsun writes:

> . . . I could not help slipping in certain exposures of the root of all evil in the old society, mixed up with warnings and the hope that some cure might be found.[1]

In "How I Came to Write Stories," he says:

> So my themes were usually the unfortunates in this abnormal society. My aim was to expose the disease and draw attention to it so that it might be cured.[2]

In his first story "A Madman's Diary," he attacks the dark feudal society through the mouth of a madman, mercilessly, sharply and thoroughly:

> I tried to look this up, but my history has no chronology, and scrawled all over each page are the words: "Virtue and Morality." Since I could not sleep anyway, I read hard half the night, until I began to see words between the lines, the whole book being filled with the two words — "Eat people."[3]

---

[1] Lu Hsun, *op. cit.*, p. 173.

[2] *Ibid.*, p. 230.

[3] *Ibid.*, Vol. I, pp. 11-12.

Such a scathing exposure of the true nature of deception and hypocrisy of the history of class society found no contemporary equal. In the same work Lu Hsun, in exposing the essential character of the reactionary ruling class, describes it as possessing "The fierceness of a lion, the timidity of a rabbit, the craftiness of a fox,"[1] and indignantly calls for the overthrow of "This cannibalistic society" in order to "save the children!"

In "Soap" Lu Hsun exposes the hypocrisy of the "virtue and morality" of the small feudal-minded urban intellectuals. In "Master Kao" he portrays the loathsome character of the old intellectuals who pretend to have changed after the Revolution of 1911. In "In the Wine Shop," "A Happy Family," "The Misanthrope" and "Regret for the Past," he describes the various types of intellectuals who have been beaten by the old forces: pessimists who muddle through life, dreamers who finally capitulate, wounded fighters and women who are victimized for their modern ideas. His merciless exposures and thoroughgoing criticism arose from his deep love for his country and the working people, to whom such corrosive influences were extremely detrimental.

Thirdly, his spirit of revolutionary patriotism showed itself in his insight into the antagonism between social classes and his ability to reflect them. In this he exposed both the conflicts between classes and the internal contradictions in the social order that the exploiting class tried to maintain. Although Lu Hsun was not yet a Marxist and could not yet have analysed the essence of such contradictions between social classes, he had come under the influence of the Russian October Revolution

[1] *Ibid.,* p. 14.

and could therefore keenly feel and write about such contradictions. In "A Madman's Diary" he writes:

> Those people — some of them have been pilloried by the magistrate, some slapped in the face by the local gentry, some have had their wives taken away by bailiffs, some have had their parents driven to suicide by creditors; yet they never looked as frightened and fierce then as they did yesterday.[1]

Here he is actually revealing a conception of class struggle. Lu Hsun knew what to love and what to hate. He held dear what he loved because it had a bright future. While rejecting the old, he affirmed the new in which he placed his hope. He expressed his sentiment in the following words:

> And I, for my part, did not want to infect with the loneliness I had found so bitter those young people who were still dreaming pleasant dreams, just as I had done when young.[2]

In these respects, Lu Hsun's works differ from the general run of classical, critical realism. They are imbedded with the rudiments and elements of socialist realism.

The True Story of Ah Q, Lu Hsun's most outstanding work, completed in December 1921, is a landmark in the history of modern Chinese literature. Taking the 1911 Revolution as his background, he points out the ills of Chinese society, or, in his own words, "exposes the frailty of the people" — through the experiences of

---

[1] Lu Hsun, *op. cit.*, p. 10.

[2] *Ibid.*, p. 6.

a vagabond farm labourer, Ah Q, in whose characterization he vividly typifies the spirit of Ah Q-ism — "ways to win moral victories."

In content, *The True Story of Ah Q* is clearly far more than a simple story about the peasants in general, for it reflects the lessons of the failure of the 1911 Revolution as well as describing rural life, the peasants and the question of peasant revolution.

Ah Q-ism had its historical basis, inseparable from the characteristics of modern Chinese society. It was a product of a historical period in which China had become subject to imperialist penetration, a product of a semi-feudal and semi-colonial society. The semi-feudal and semi-colonial characteristics of China at that time dominated the life of the Chinese people. On the one hand, imperialist aggression, oppression and exploitation bred and stimulated the growth of their national revolutionary consciousness, and, on the other, imperialism, together with feudal culture, implanted in them slavish ideas. Therefore, as long as China's semi-feudal and semi-colonial society existed, Ah Q-ism had a basis to rest on. Once this society crumbled Ah Q-ism vanished with it.

Nevertheless, the Ah Q-ism which existed within Ah Q's own class was very different from that which existed within the ruling class. Lu Hsun hated the latter, and hoped it would quickly vanish together with the ruling class. He hated the former because it created defeatism among people of Ah Q's class — farm labourers. This was a class that he felt should never give way to defeatism; it should carry on struggles, even defeated, until it won. To ensure victory it should know clearly its own weaknesses, mercilessly criticize them and fight against them. Lu Hsun's ardent love for the Chinese working people, particularly the peasants, made him hate and detest any poisonous element which caused defeatism among them and led to their defeat. He hoped they would throw off the poison.

In 1934-35 Lu Hsun wrote five historical stories: "Against Aggression," "Pacifying the Flood," "Gathering Thornferns," "Beyond the Frontier" and "Resurrection." All except the first were written in 1935. These works, together with his earlier works "Mending Heaven" (1922), "The Flight to the Moon" and "Forging the Sword" (1926), were compiled into *Old Tales Retold*. These works, in the form of historical stories, attacked and exposed the dark rule of the Kuomintang reactionary government and its despicable hirelings, the "scholars" and "celebrities." They also satirized some intellectuals and praised the new ideal personalities. In fact, they are too realistic and militant to be treated as purely historical stories. Compared with his three earlier stories, the themes of the five stories written in 1934-35 were more constructive and more daring. "Against Aggression" and "Pacifying the Flood," in particular, were already socialist realist literature of the calibre of Lu Hsun's later essays.

CHAPTER SIX

LU HSUN, STANDARD-BEARER OF THE CHINESE PEOPLE'S NEW CULTURE AND COMMUNIST THINKER

(Continued)

Section 1. Lu Hsun's Essays—Socialist in Content and National in Form

Lu Hsun's works of fiction are a landmark in the history of modern Chinese literature. Nevertheless, his essays have contributed far more than his works of fiction to modern Chinese literature and the Chinese revolution.

When we say Lu Hsun's essays have socialist content, we are referring mainly to those of the later part of his life, although the earlier ones are not entirely devoid of socialist elements.

Lu Hsun in his earlier years was a revolutionary democrat. His essays in this period, like his short stories and novels, are works of critical realism, but more militant and political in nature. Lu Hsun always stood for reform, and against conservatism and decayed traditions, and put great emphasis on the spirit of revolt against the old social order. Because his viewpoint was based on the theory of progressive, militant evolution, his earlier essays contain the elements of materialism. For that matter, Lu Hsun had always been a clear-headed, militant realist right from the beginning of his literary career, and this also had bearing on his essays. In his approach to any matter, he invariably proceeded from reality, from the interests of the people and from the standpoint of progress and development. This standpoint of progressive evolution and these elements of materialism and militant realism, combine to form the factors of socialist realism in his earlier essays and the basis of the proletarian and communist outlook of his later years.

In his later years, Lu Hsun became a Marxist and fought an unflinching battle in the cause of communism right up till his death. His main weapon of this period was the essay. It is only natural that these essays should be works of socialist realism. Lu Hsun's ideological development from a revolutionary democrat to a Marxist is fully and clearly shown in his later essays. He openly declared that he had placed himself alongside the proletariat and would always fight for the proletarian cause of liberation. He also put forward the view that proletarian literature "should be an intrinsic part of the proletarian struggle for liberation."[1] In a courageous and vigorous fight against political reaction and its literature, he won a great victory. He openly proclaimed his support for the Chinese Communist Party. He considered it an honour to mention Mao Tse-tung and other members of the Communist Party as his comrades. In following the lead of the Party, he loyally and uncondi-

[1] Lu Hsun, *op. cit.*, Vol. III, p. 96.

tionally carried out its policy, never once slackening his efforts in the struggle for the revolutionary cause. His wholehearted support for the Soviet Union is shown in his declaration that he wanted "to fight the devils who attack the Soviet Union," and that he considered "this is our road to life too."[1] He also waged a struggle against all the incorrect ideological tendencies which showed themselves within the ranks of the revolutionary writers. By applying Marxism-Leninism in the conditions of Chinese cultural revolution, he scored a great victory on the cultural front in China.

Just as Lu Hsun's essays are socialist in content, they are thoroughly national in form.

"Miscellaneous essays" or "miscellaneous thoughts" is how Lu Hsun himself described his self-created style of essay. The characteristics of this style, its influence and the reasons for its creation are best explained by Chu Chiu-pai:

> Lu Hsun's essays are actually publicist articles, polemical *feuilletons*. Anyone bearing in mind the situation during the last two decades can understand the reason for the rise of such writing. Tempestuous social struggles make it impossible for a writer to mould his thoughts and feelings at leisure, or to express them in concrete images and types in his work. Moreover, savage despotism and oppression make it impossible for him to express his views in the usual forms. So Lu Hsun's native wit helped him to find an artistic form to express his political stand, his penetrating observations on society and his warm sympathy for the people's struggle. Not only so, the emergence of

---

[1] *Ibid.*, p. 155.

> this form mirrors the history of the battle of ideas in China since the May 4 Movement. Because of Lu Hsun, the miscellaneous essay will become a literary genre. It will not, of course, take the place of other forms; but what distinguishes it is the directness and speed with which it reflects daily happenings in society.[1]

Lu Hsun's *feuilletons* always merged with the revolutionary reality in China, relentlessly criticizing all the backward and reactionary phenomena which appeared in Chinese society. Each article is a highly militant political essay. But Lu Hsun did more than adopt the ordinary form of political essay. He created an artistic genre which combines poetry with political polemics. His essays are sharp and penetrating, compact and terse. They are as trenchant as a dagger and as mellow as well-matured wine. Profound in thought, they serve as a powerful weapon in the battle of ideas. The artistic form which Lu Hsun created has no precedent in Chinese literature. Yet, because of Lu Hsun's penetrating insight into Chinese society, history and culture, the form is typically Chinese, genuinely national. Commenting on Lu Hsun's essays Comrade Mao Tse-tung says:

> Living under the rule of the dark forces, deprived of freedom of speech, Lu Hsun had to fight by means of burning satire and freezing irony cast in essay form, and in this he was entirely correct. We too must hold up to sharp ridicule the fascists, the Chinese reactionaries and everything endangering the people; but

---

[1] Chu Chiu-pai, *op. cit.*, p. 41.

in our border region of Shensi-Kansu-Ningsia and the anti-Japanese base areas in the enemy's rear, where revolutionary artists and writers are given full freedom and democracy and only counter-revolutionaries are deprived of them, essays must not be written simply in the same style as Lu Hsun's. Here we can shout at the top of our voice, and need not resort to obscure and veiled expressions which would tax the understanding of the broad masses of the people. In dealing with the people themselves and not the enemies of the people, Lu Hsun even in his "essay period" did not mock or attack the revolutionary masses and the revolutionary parties, and his style was also entirely different from that employed in his essays on the enemy. We have already said that we must criticize the shortcomings of the people, but be sure that we criticize from the standpoint of the people and out of a wholehearted eagerness to defend and educate them. If we treat our comrades like enemies, then we are taking the standpoint of the enemy. Are we then to give up satire altogether? No. Satire is always necessary. But there are all kinds of satire; the kind for our enemies, the kind for our allies and the kind for our own ranks — each of them assumes a different attitude. We are not opposed to satire as a whole, but we must not abuse it.[1]

This correct directive of Comrade Mao Tse-tung should be regarded as a guiding principle for the study of Lu Hsun's essays.

---

[1] Mao Tse-tung, *op. cit.*, Vol. IV, pp. 88-9.

Section 2. Lu Hsun's Earlier Essays

(1) Spirit of Militant Realism

In his earlier period Lu Hsun wrote five collections of essays entitled *The Grave, Hot Air, Bad Luck, More Bad Luck, And That's That.* Nearly every essay in these collections mirrors the struggles of the time, each more militant, more penetrating and with a stronger imprint of dialectical materialism than the one before. These five collections may rightly be considered as a record of the conflicts in political thought in China from 1918 to 1927.

There is a basic characteristic in the earlier essays of Lu Hsun, namely, the militant spirit of realism which showed itself even in the essays he wrote on the eve of the May 4 Movement in 1919.

In 1918, Lu Hsun wrote a series called "Random Thoughts" for the magazine *New Youth.* Lu Hsun wrote in his "Preface to *Hot Air*":

> Some of the articles were directed against the practice of planchette, sitting in meditation and boxing, some against those who advocated the preservation of "national characteristics," some against the boastfulness of the old bureaucrats in telling of their experiences, and some against the cartoons carried by the Shanghai *Times.* I remember that *New Youth* was then attacked from all sides and that I only dealt with a handful of the attackers. It is unnecessary for me to talk about the big events which have already appeared in the magazine.[1]

---

[1] Lu Hsun, *Collected Works,* Chinese ed., Vol. I, pp. 367-70.

These words were, of course, the modest expression of an author, but it is not difficult to see that each of the "Random Thoughts" was aimed at the dark reality of that time. From the very outset, Lu Hsun's essays bear the imprint of militant realism.

Lu Hsun's militant realism finds expression in his penetrating insight into reality and makes itself felt primarily in his attacks on the prevalent feudalism of his time. He pointed out more than once in his essays that feudal "national characteristics" endangered the very existence of our nation. "Certainly self-preservation comes first," he wrote. "All we ask is whether a thing has the power to preserve us, not whether it is characteristic or not."[1]

His penetrating insight is also reflected in his understanding of the events that took place in his day. After the 1911 Revolution Lu Hsun came to realize that the revolution was incomplete and had failed. Later, in *Bad Luck* he had this to say about the revolution:

> It seems to me the Republic of China has for a long time not existed. I felt I was a slave before the revolution. Shortly after the revolution I was deceived and became a slave again. It seems to me many citizens of the Republic are really its enemies . . . and the blood of many martyrs were trodden under foot, though unintentionally. It seems everything has to be started all over again.[2]

Lu Hsun's profound understanding of reality gave him an objective in his fight, namely, to change the existing

---

[1] Lu Hsun, *Selected Works*, English ed., Vol. II, p. 29.

[2] Lu Hsun, *Collected Works*, Chinese ed., Vol. III, pp. 12-3.

conditions. And his fight against the present was for the purpose of achieving a bright future. Lu Hsun had full confidence in the future and believed the darkness of his time could not last for ever.

But by then he had already realized that no one could sit back and wait passively for the "bright future" to come of itself. He was no believer in the helplessness of man in the face of social circumstances. Rather, he held that man could, on his initiative, promote social progress and advance himself in the wake of social progress. Therefore, he called upon the people to launch a struggle against the dark society of the time. "What is a road?" he wrote. "It is trodden from where there is no road; it is blazed from where there are only thorns."[1] And again:

> Anyone who is capable of doing something should do it; anyone who is capable of speaking up should make himself heard. Produce as much light as the heat you possess. Don't wait for the big torch, even the firefly can produce a spot of light in the darkness.[2]

And further: "If there are still men in the world who really want to live on, they must first dare to speak, laugh, cry, rage at, revile, fight, and defeat this accursed age in this accursed place!"[3]

As Lu Hsun's spearhead was directed against the dark reality and towards a bright future, he was able to fight

---

[1] *Ibid.*, Vol. I, p. 434.

[2] *Ibid.*, p. 400.

[3] Lu Hsun, *Selected Works*, English ed., Vol. II, p. 120.

with no thought of personal considerations. He wrote in *Hot Air*:

> If there was no torch in the future, I'll be the only light. Should there be a torch or the sun come out, we would naturally be glad to extinguish ourselves. Not only we will bear no grudge, but will admire without envy the torch or the sun, for it will shine upon mankind, including myself.[1]

Later, Chu Chiu-pai commented on the selfless spirit of Lu Hsun:

> The leaders of a new cultural movement invariably want to be the new guides of the young. Lu Hsun alone sincerely desired to be "a foot soldier scouting before the main forces of the revolution." These words are true of him: "Burdened as a man may be with the weight of tradition, he can yet prop open the gate of darkness with his shoulder to let the children through to the bright, wide-open spaces." . . . Lu Hsun considered himself simply as "a stone or plank in a bridge, not as any goal or model for the future," and predicted that his writing "should be lost as time goes by." ("Postscript to *The Grave*") But precisely for this reason, the bridge he built reached to the other bank and his work has become the first milestone in China's new literature. Precisely because of this, he has truly become "the leader of young rebels."[2]

---

[1] Lu Hsun, *Collected Works*, Chinese ed., Vol. I, p. 400.

[2] Chu Chiu-pai, *op. cit.*, pp. 49-51.

(2) "Stubborn Struggle" Tactics

Because of Lu Hsun's penetrating study and analysis of Chinese history and society, he had a profound understanding of the enemy of the Chinese revolution. This enemy, he also regarded as his own. He knew that the enemy was strong, obstinate, and well experienced in ruling. The revolutionary struggle in China, therefore, must be a long and hard one which required resolution and bravery on the one hand, and tact and flexibility on the other. No rashness could bring any results for the revolutionary struggle. Based on his long-term observation and his own experience, he worked out tactics in accordance with the Chinese scene which proved fatal to the enemy — to carry on the struggle in a stubborn way. He said that what China needed was "not sacrifices which cause a temporary stir, but persistent and stubborn struggles."[1]

By "stubborn struggle" he meant thoroughgoing, persistent, unswerving struggle with no considerations of "benevolence" or "morality" in dealing with the enemy. In *The Grave* Lu Hsun clarified this point further by using the metaphor of beating a dog that has fallen into the water. He said: "I think all dogs that bite men should be beaten, whether they are on the land or in the water."[2] This is because, he said, "it is hard for a dog to change its nature."[3] And he issued the following warning to the revolutionaries of the time:

---

[1] Lu Hsun, *op. cit.*, p. 274.

[2] Lu Hsun, *Selected Works*, English ed., Vol. II, p. 209.

[3] *Ibid.*, p. 211.

> If there is no fight to the finish between darkness and light, and simple souls go on making the mistake of confusing forgiveness with giving free rein to evil, and continue pardoning wicked men, then the present state of chaos will last for ever.[1]

Lu Hsun also pointed out that in order to carry on the struggle steadfastly and to the finish, the revolutionaries must pool their strength. They must not, he said, fight violent battles without finesse, for that can only harm them and bring no damage to the enemy. The key points of Lu Hsun's tactics lie in his emphasis on firmness, perseverance, heightened vigilance and the concentration of strength. These correct tactics fully show Lu Hsun's ideas to have been based not on wishful thinking, but on reality and in full accord with the truth of revolutionary struggle. They also show that Lu Hsun and the blind, impetuous petty-bourgeois revolutionaries had nothing in common.

(3) A Great Leap in His Ideological Development

Lu Hsun's ideas went through continuous change until 1928, from those of an evolutionist to those of a Marxist, from those of a revolutionary petty bourgeois to those of a proletarian, from those of a revolutionary democrat to those of a communist.

In 1918, Lu Hsun was still essentially an evolutionist. In 1927 when he was in Canton, his ideas began gradually to change. In the "Preface to *Three Leisures*" which he wrote in 1932 he gave the reason for this change:

---

[1] *Ibid.*, p. 216.

> I always believed in evolution, and was sure that the future would be better than the past, that the young would be better than the old. Indeed, I had such respect for young people that if they stabbed me ten times I would only strike back once. Later, however, I realized my mistake. I was not taken in by any materialist argument or revolutionary writing, but in Canton I saw young people divided into two great camps some of them acting as informers, or helping the authorities to make arrests! So my earlier way of thinking went by the board, and I started looking sceptically at the young instead of respecting them all indiscriminately.[1]

Lu Hsun's ideas of evolution were thus thrown overboard. From his personal experience and profound observation he came to realize that regardless of age a man in a class society belongs to a given class and serves the interests of that class. At this point he made a further study of Marxism-Leninism and, after arming himself with revolutionary theories and tempering himself in practice, he eventually advanced from the standpoint of an evolutionist to that of a proletarian fighter.

Section 3. Essays of the Later Period

(1) Fight for the Cause of Liberation of the Proletariat

From 1928 onwards Lu Hsun accepted Marxism-Leninism and became a communist thinker. Between

---

[1] *Ibid.*, Vol. III, pp. 146-47.

1928 and 1936, when Lu Hsun died in Shanghai, he wrote a large number of essays which are compiled into nine collections: *Three Leisures, Two Hearts, Mixed Dialects, False Liberty, Semi-Frivolous Talk, Decorative Literature, The Essays of Chieh-chieh-ting, The Essays of Chieh-chieh-ting (II), The Last Essays of Chieh-chieh-ting.* Other essays are also found in *Miscellaneous Collections (I)* and *Miscellaneous Collections (II).*

In these works Lu Hsun declared his proletarian stand and expressed his firm belief in communism. In "Preface to *Two Hearts*" he made a sincere analysis of himself and his changed ideas:

> . . . And my way of talking constantly of myself, of how I keep "knocking my head against a wall" and of what a snail I am, as if all the miseries in the world were concentrated in my person and I was a scapegoat for everyone else, is a bad failing of middle-class intellectuals. It is true, though, that while I started by simply hating my own class which I knew so well, and felt no regret over its destruction, later on the facts taught me that the future belongs solely to the rising proletariat.[1]

From the proletarian standpoint Lu Hsun launched, first of all, a relentless battle against the Chiang Kai-shek gang with his essays. He attacked boldly and persistently the "encirclement" campaigns launched by Chiang Kai-shek against the revolutionary bases. In "Irresponsible Tanks" he strongly protested against Chiang Kai-shek using tanks to attack the revolutionary bases. In "Above and Below," the bombardment of the

---

[1] *Ibid.*, pp. 151-52.

revolutionary bases by Chiang's planes was severely denounced. In "Let the Barbarians Fight the Barbarians" and "On Writing and the Choice of a Subject" Lu Hsun pointed out that the attack on the revolutionary bases was carried out by Chiang in league with imperialism. The imperialists, he said, often resorted to the method of "Letting Chinese fight Chinese" by "selling aeroplanes to one group of Chinese so that they can bomb others." He assailed vehemently the non-resistance policy of Chiang Kai-shek, pointing out that Chiang Kai-shek first claimed that "The suppression of internal troubles makes it impossible to resist foreign aggression," then switched to "It would be better to invite the foreign forces to suppress internal troubles," and finally reached the conclusion that "As foreign forces have become a part of our domestic forces, resistance to foreign aggression is out of the question."[1]

Lu Hsun also waged a heroic struggle against Chiang's merciless slaughtering of cultural workers. In February 1931, when Jou Shih, Hu Yeh-pin, Pai Mang, Li Wei-sen and Feng Keng — all members of the League of Left-Wing Writers, together with 18 other revolutionaries were murdered by the Kuomintang government, and when Lu Hsun himself was in great danger, he, instead of beating a retreat, stood out in the open and lodged a strong protest against the Kuomintang atrocities. He pointed out that the Kuomintang reactionaries were "creatures of darkness about to perish." He said:

> Since the rulers knew their flunkey-writers were no match for the revolutionary literature of the proletariat . . . they have sunk to the lowest tactics of

---

[1] Lu Hsun, *Collected Works*, Chinese ed., Vol. V, pp. 87-8.

> all — arresting and imprisoning left-wing writers and putting them to death in secret.[1]

He went on to stress that the butchery practised by the Chiang Kai-shek gang would by no means stop the advance of revolutionary literature. He wrote:

> Our proletarian literature will continue to grow, however, because it belongs to the great ranks of the revolutionary toilers; and as long as the people exist and gain in strength, so long will this revolutionary literature grow.[2]

As an exposure of the reactionary character of the Kuomintang government, he also wrote an article entitled "The Present Condition of Art in Darkest China"[3] for the progressive American magazine *New Masses*. In 1933, he published his famous article entitled "In Memory of the Forgotten" in which he expressed deep condolence over the deaths of his comrades and the firm conviction that "a time will come when others will remember them and speak of them. . . ."[4]

The firm conviction of Lu Hsun in the victory of the revolution dealt a crushing blow to the reactionary rulers then in power and greatly boosted the morale of the writers within the camp of revolutionary literature. Until his death in 1936 Lu Hsun never once ceased to attack the Kuomintang's "encirclement" campaign against the revolutionary writers. In "Written After

---

[1] Lu Hsun, *Selected Works*, Vol. III, p. 107.

[2] *Ibid.*, p. 108.

[3] *Ibid.*, pp. 109-13.

[4] *Ibid.*, p. 213.

Midnight" which was published shortly before his death, Lu Hsun pointed out that the degree of misery in the areas ruled by the Kuomintang was greater than what is described in "Inferno" of Dante's *Divine Comedy*. "It is," he said, "a hell where misery has become so common that nobody seems to see it."[1]

Lu Hsun mercilessly exposed the reactionary measures practised by the Chiang Kai-shek clique, although under the circumstances his essays on this topic had to be written in a rather obscure way. But few of them are difficult to understand. In one, he vividly describes the civil strifes between the warlords:

> So in spite of all these fierce battles year in and year out, the chiefs are quite all right. Their misunderstandings are suddenly cleared up, and they drink happily together, uniting to resist the foe and swearing to serve the country till suddenly. . . . It goes without saying — suddenly of course they start fighting each other again.[2]

After the "Mukden Incident" which broke out on September 18, 1931, Lu Hsun had written a number of essays attacking the traitorous policy of non-resistance adopted by the Kuomintang government. Under his mighty pen all the reactionaries from Chiang Kai-shek, Wang Ching-wei, Tai Chi-tao, Wu Chih-hui down to Hu Shih were fully exposed in their true colours.

In particular, Lu Hsun concentrated his fire on rumours and slanders spread by the reactionaries against

---

[1] Lu Hsun, *Collected Works,* Chinese ed., Vol. VI, p. 410.

[2] Lu Hsun, *Selected Works,* English ed., Vol. III, p. 189.

the Chinese Communist Party, warning the people of the country not to be duped by such venomous lies.

Lu Hsun's support for the Chinese Communist Party reflects itself fully in the heroic struggles he waged for the cause of liberation of the proletariat. He wrote on the eve of the War of Resistance to Japanese Aggression: "I consider it an honour to regard those as my comrades who, standing firmly on the ground, are fighting and shedding their blood for the existence of the Chinese nation."[1] The fighters referred here are the Communist Party headed by Mao Tse-tung and the Workers' and Peasants' Red Army.

(2) His Spirit of Internationalism

Lu Hsun is not only a great patriot, but also a great internationalist. In him patriotism and internationalism are well integrated. In his later years Lu Hsun became fully aware that the Soviet Union is the motherland of the proletarian dictatorship and is the model of world proletarian liberation and national liberation. He realized that only by following the Soviet Union's example could China find a way out. His unreserved support for the Soviet Union led him to expose continually the rumours and slanders against her concocted by the imperialists and Chinese reactionaries. He said, ". . . a brand-new, truly unprecedented social system has emerged from hell — hundreds of millions of common folk have taken their destiny into their own hands."[2] And again,

---

[1] Lu Hsun, *Collected Works*, Chinese ed., Vol. VI, p. 474.

[2] Lu Hsun, *Selected Works*, English ed., Vol. III, p. 143.

". . . Their plans are all quite rational, and they are simply living like human beings — there is nothing strange or peculiar about them."[1] Explaining why the imperialists wanted to invade the Soviet Union, he said:

> For workers and peasants to live like human beings is very much against the interests of capitalists and landlords; hence their greatest wish is to wipe out the country which serves as a model for toilers everywhere. The more normal the Soviet Union, the more they tremble.[2]

And again, "The better the Soviet Union does, the more impatient they are to attack it, for the sooner they will face destruction."[3] He also said:

> We have been duped too long by the imperialists and their lackeys. Ever since the October Revolution they have been telling us how poor the Soviet Union is growing, what savages and vandals they are. Yet what are the facts? The world has been made to sit up by their export of petroleum and wheat. The leaders of the Industrial Party (A counter-revolutionary clique unmasked in 1930. Most of its members were engineers or technicians who carried on sabotage — *Ed.*) — their immediate enemies — have been sentenced to merely ten years' imprisonment. No libraries or museums have been blown up in Leningrad or Moscow. The works of such writers as Serafimovich, Fadeyev, Gladkov, Seifulina and Sholokhov are

[1] *Ibid.*, p. 142.

[2] *Ibid.*

[3] *Ibid.*, p. 153.

> admired from Western Europe to Eastern Asia. And though I know very little about their art, according to K. Umansky's *Neue Kunst in Russland*, there were twenty exhibitions in Moscow in 1919, and two in Leningrad. From this we can judge the healthy situation today.[1]

As a result of the lies and slanders spread by the imperialists and the Kuomintang reactionaries to defame the Soviet Union, the Chinese people knew little about the real conditions in that country. Lu Hsun's truthful presentation of the Soviet Union and his analysis of the motives of the imperialists to slander her served as a beacon for the Chinese people at that time.

On the basis of such an analysis, Lu Hsun further pointed out to the people of the whole country that they must oppose the imperialist attack upon the Soviet Union, that they must protect the Soviet Union as they would their own country and that imperialism was the common enemy of the Soviet Union and China. "The civilized countries are sucking China's blood, seizing China's territory, and killing Chinese people," he said. "If such great cheats defame the Soviet Union and want to attack it, that is to the credit of the Soviet Union."[2] He went on:

> The imperialists' interests and ours — I am not speaking of their flunkeys — are diametrically opposed. Since our sores are their treasures, their enemies must naturally be our friends. They are tottering to ruin, unable to prop themselves up, but

---

[1] *Ibid.*

[2] *Ibid.*, p. 143.

hoping to stave off their final fate by hating the Soviet Union for its advance. When slander, curses and hatred prove ineffective, as a last resort they must prepare to fight — they cannot sleep till the enemy is destroyed. But what of us? Are we going to be duped again?

. . . .

The imperialists' flunkeys want to fight. Let them go with their bosses and fight — our interests are diametrically opposed. We oppose any attack on the Soviet Union. In fact we want to fight the devils who attack it, no matter what honeyed words they use, nor how just they pose as being.

This is our road to life too![1]

For a man like Lu Hsun who was strongly attached to his motherland and its labouring people, who treasured science and truth, who was thoroughly opposed to feudalism and imperialism and devoted himself to the cause of the liberation of the proletariat, it is perfectly natural and logical that he loved and supported wholeheartedly the Chinese Communist Party and the Soviet Union, a model country which stands for the liberation of the proletariat and national liberation throughout the world.

(3) His Contributions to Art and Literary Theories

The later essays of Lu Hsun were an invaluable contribution to the ideological content of revolutionary Chinese literature. He was constantly educating the

[1] *Ibid.*, pp. 154-55.

writers and young people at that time in the Marxist ideological outlook and wholeheartedly helping them in the writing of revolutionary works. Under his enthusiastic guidance, many writers, both established and young, produced works beneficial to the revolution.

Again and again he emphasized the danger of petty-bourgeois ideas to revolutionary literature and pointed out how important it was for a revolutionary writer to take part in actual struggles and to go deeper into real life. Apart from this guidance on principles, he also dealt with a number of practical questions.

In the first place he put forward valuable suggestions concerning the question of popularization and elevation in art and literature. Lu Hsun thought highly of popular works. He said:

> There is a need for a great number of writers who, considering the interests of the masses, try their best to produce works simple and easy to understand, so that everybody can read and enjoy and much of the old rubbish can be done away with.[1]

Meanwhile Lu Hsun pointed out that it was not right at the start to set too high a standard for works written for the masses, for that would completely stifle their growth and "seal their coffin." He himself wrote some popular satires in ballad form like "Song of Good Things." Lu Hsun held the view that the masses were not as foolish as some of the intellectuals might have supposed. He said:

> They need knowledge and new things. They want to learn and are able to do so. Of course, they will

[1] Lu Hsun, *Collected Works,* Chinese ed., Vol. VII, p. 579.

> understand nothing if your talk is full of new phrases and terms. But if you teach them the essential things step by step they will be able to catch them. Their ability to understand may well surpass those of the more prejudiced intellectuals.[1]

Here Lu Hsun pointed out that popularization and elevation could not be sharply separated, but the former may gradually bring about the latter.

Secondly, Lu Hsun during this period repeatedly passed on his valuable experience in writing to the young writers — experience which was and still is an excellent guide for those engaged in creative writing. Talking on his experience, he mentioned that creative writing must first serve humanity and be able to better it. In "A Reply to the Magazine *The Dipper*" Lu Hsun summarizes his experience under eight points:

a) Take an interest in everything and see as much as you can. Don't write as soon as you have seen a little.
b) Don't force yourself to write when not in the mood.
c) Don't choose definite models for your characters, but create them out of all that you have seen.
d) Read your story through at least twice after finishing it, and ruthlessly cut all words, phrases and sections that are not essential. It is better to compress the material for a story into a sketch than to stretch the material for a sketch into a story.
e) Read foreign stories, especially those of Eastern and Northern Europe, as well as Japanese works.

---

[1] *Ibid.*, Vol. VI, pp. 83-4.

f) Never make up adjectives or phrases that no one else can understand.
g) Never believe any talk about "rules of writing."
h) Never trust Chinese "literary critics," but read the works of reliable foreign critics.[1]

Thirdly, he offered some penetrating comments on literary criticism. Lu Hsun criticized above all the unprincipled, vulgar and sectarian reviews then prevailing in the field of art and literature. Since such reviews could only smother the progressive art and literature and were not in the least constructive, Lu Hsun was of the opinion that Chinese "literary critics" should never be trusted. But this does not mean that Lu Hsun was against criticism. On the contrary, he always stood for correct criticism. He said:

> There are three things which we hope the critics can do: First, point out what is bad; second, recommend what is good; third, recommend what is tolerable when there is nothing good. . . . If even that is lacking, then point out those parts of a bad translation which may be beneficial to the reader.[2]

Although what Lu Hsun says here is about criticism on translation his practical principles of criticism can nevertheless be applied to creative writing. In this period Lu Hsun wrote many pieces of literary criticism which played an important role in raising the quality of creative writing.

Last but not least was the question of the heritage of ancient Chinese literature. Lu Hsun always respected

---

[1] Lu Hsun, *Selected Works*, English ed., Vol. III, pp. 138-39.

[2] Lu Hsun, *Collected Works*, Chinese ed., Vol. V, p. 236.

this heritage, but such respect should not be confused with blind worship. It was a respect for Chinese history, for its dialectical development. He held the view that modern culture is derived from the old.

> As the new class and its culture do not come suddenly from heaven, but are developed largely from the struggle against the old rulers and their culture, that is, from the conflict between the old and the new, therefore, the new culture has inherited and selected all that is worthy in the old culture.[1]

In this, Lu Hsun gives a dialectical explanation of the relation between the old and the new culture. What he meant by "all that is worthy" was the best part of the old culture, the part that is popular and revolutionary, which should be kept. As for the rest, the feudal and backward, that should be thrown away.

---

[1] *Ibid.*, Vol. VII, p. 586.

CHAPTER SEVEN

KUO MO-JO AND OTHER WRITERS BEFORE AND AFTER THE MAY 4 MOVEMENT

Section 1. Kuo Mo-jo's Literary Works

(1) The Spirit of Patriotism: Escape from Bondage and Fight Against Darkness

Kuo Mo-jo came from a landlord family in Loshan, Szechuan Province. Believing that it was necessary to make China wealthy and strong, an idea which was current in the latter part of the last century, he was patriotic in outlook even in the days of his youth. In 1914 he went to Japan to study medicine. As an amateur writer, he was one of the founders of the Creation Society, along with his friend Cheng Fang-wu. Beginning from 1924 he was influenced by Marxism. He did much to promote revolutionary literature and took part in the First Revolutionary Civil War. When the war ended in failure, he fled back to Japan[1] and took up the study of ancient Chi-

[1] In October 1927, after the defeat of the First Revolutionary Civil War, Kuo Mo-jo came to Shanghai and left for Japan on February 24, 1928.

nese history in which he became a scholar of some renown. When the War of Resistance to Japanese Aggression broke out in 1937 he returned to China and joined the people's struggle against the invaders. Meanwhile he continued his historical studies and wrote historical plays. In 1949 he was elected Chairman of the All-China Federation of Writers and Artists.

Kuo Mo-jo's literary works are deeply imbued with the spirit of romanticism. But owing to the fact that he lived in a semi-feudal and semi-colonial society they are also deeply coloured by patriotic feelings against feudalism and imperialism. This spirit was a product of the actual social conditions of the time which were the main source of inspiration of Kuo Mo-jo's works. This is why his works, although imbued with the spirit of romanticism, are yet fundamentally realistic. This is clearly shown even in his earlier works and still more so in his works of 1924 and after, when he had become a pronounced adherent of Marxism and socialist realism. During the War of Resistance when his works became even more realistic, they still retained their spirit of romanticism.

The philosophy of Kuo Mo-jo during the earlier period of his life may be best described in his own words: "In the past I have always stood for individuality and freedom."[1] The phrase "individuality and freedom" belonged of course to bourgeois terminology, and represented ideals which were incapable of realization at that time when China was still a semi-feudal and semi-colonial country. As soon as he came into contact with the reality of society, these ideas evaporated, leaving in his mind, however, a certain lingering attachment. Meanwhile he

---

[1] Kuo Mo-jo, "Preface to My Collection of Critical Essays."

developed a strong sense of revolt against the society which had shattered his ideals. This attachment and spirit of revolt can both be seen in his earlier works.

Most of his earlier poems are included in the collection *The Goddesses.*[1] These poems fully reflect his mental state at the time. Their style is characterized by great freedom and modulation. They have an irrepressible force about them, like a torrent rushing down from the top of a mountain. They are written in powerful and sonorous language which, like a heavy rainstorm, fills the reader with a sense of awe. At the same time this style has a tendency towards monotony. It is too abstract and lacks depth.

These characteristics are also seen in his earlier dramatic compositions. In his *Three Rebellious Women,* for instance, in which he takes three famous women — Wang Chao-chun, Cho Wen-chun, and Nieh Ying — from Chinese history as his theme, he mercilessly attacks the moral code of the old society under the guise of opposing the corrupt feudal system. His rebellious spirit is also clearly seen in such works as *The Death of Chu Yuan, Pyrus Flower,* and *The Two Princes of Kuchu.*

But Kuo Mo-jo's ideas did not end where they started — they underwent a constant process of development. Moreover, the progress of the revolutionary situation in the country — marked by the outbreak of the great "February 7" strike of the Peking-Hankow railwaymen in 1923 — and the tribulations in his own life compelled him to look reality in the face and turn his steps towards the path of revolution. Thus his rebellious spirit as shown

---

[1] *Selected Poems from "The Goddesses"* was translated and published in English by the Foreign Languages Press, Peking, in 1958.

in *The Goddesses,* which craved the destruction and overthrow of almost everything, underwent a change in about the year 1923. He now had a clearer target to fight for; he also grasped to a certain extent the idea of class struggle. The change in his thinking showed itself in his collection of poems entitled *Front Rank.* The following is an example:

> The road is not paved with cement;
> It is paved with the blood, sweat, and life of the
> working people.
> Under the wheels of the rich men's cars
> Roll lives and lives streaming blood.
> Listen, brothers! I believe that one day
> A volcano is going to erupt
> In the middle of Bubbling Well Road.
>
> — "Morning in Shanghai"

This passionate tone is also found in "Forward March" and other poems in the collection.

Kuo Mo-jo's earlier works, especially his poems, represented the ideas and emotions of the revolutionary petty bourgeoisie, especially the young intellectuals of the period between the May 4 Movement and the May 30 Incident. Frustrated with the darkness of the time, they sought after revolution, looked in vain for the right path, and became violently rebellious in spirit. This accounts for the fact that Kuo Mo-jo's works were widely read by young people and wielded a great influence over them.

(2) Revolutionary Poems and Songs

But it was about 1924 that Kuo Mo-jo's thinking underwent a decisive change. This was what he said in his preface to his *Selected Works*:

> In the overlapping period between spring and summer in 1924 I spent two months in studying Marxism by reading Dr. Kawakami Hajime's *Social Structure and Social Revolution.* This book, of which I made a translation, was a great help to me. It led to a radical change in my thinking, a change which was to stay. As a result I became a Marxist.

Again he said in 1925 in his preface to *A Collection of Critical Essays*:

> In the last one or two years I sometimes came into contact with the people of the pitiful lower strata of society. From these contacts I came to see that in an era when most people have lost their freedom and individuality in spite of themselves it is presumptuous for a small number of people to assert their right to the same. . . . Individuality should be developed and freedom of living enjoyed by all people alike. But before the time comes when everyone can develop his individuality and live in freedom the small number of people who are ahead of their time should sacrifice their own individuality and freedom to fight for those of the masses so as to enable the masses to regain their individuality and freedom.

Soon after writing these lines Kuo Mo-jo took part in the First Revolutionary Civil War. With the war ending in failure he went to Shanghai to work for the promotion of revolutionary literature. In the following years he wrote many revolutionary poems and songs which were later collected in the volume entitled *Restoration.*

Restoration shows a further advance in Kuo Mo-jo's ideas. In the poem "My Thoughts Alight on Chen Sheh and Wu Kuang"[1] he sang the praises of the workers and peasants, and pointed to the imperialists and their lackeys — the feudal warlords, compradors, bureaucrats and landlords — as the greatest enemy of the revolution.

Why is the life of the peasants so wretched?
Because, friends, many Shih-huang-ti's[2] now rule over China.
Furthermore there is oppression by the foreign imperialists,
Five million times as bad as that of the Huns.

Their gunboat policy hovers over our head.
Their economic aggression sucks dry our blood.
Their lackeys — warlords, compradors, landlords and bureaucrats —
Are the new Shih-huang-ti's of China.

But our peasants, over 320 million, fight though cornered.
I, for one, do not believe that we're at our wit's end.
I do not believe that we shall never be able to stand up,
That there will never be any Chen Sheh's or Wu Kuang's among us.

Remember we have five million industrial workers.
They can give us cannons, rifles, and military tactics.
Friends! Let the peasants revolt under the lead of the workers.
This is our way out; herein lies our strength to transform the world.

---

[1] Chen Sheh and Wu Kuang were leaders of a great peasant uprising which led to the collapse of the Chin dynasty (221-206 B.C.).

[2] Shih-huang-ti was the first emperor of the Chin dynasty.

Thus in these lines he expressed his wrath against the enemies of the revolution and his recognition of the workers and peasants as the pillars of the revolution. After the sanguinary lesson of the big bourgeoisie's betrayal of the revolution in 1927 he learned to distinguish friend from foe. In "A Dialogue Between the Yangtse and the Yellow Rivers" he wrote:

> Friendly relations should be sown with all the small nations of the world.
> An alliance should be formed with all the workers of the world.
> But those speaking for our nation must never be the warlords, old or new,
> They can never pass for the people of our land.

Chiang Kai-shek's massacre of Communists and patriots stirred Kuo Mo-jo to the depths of indignation. In the poem "Great Terror" he spoke out with all the heroism of a revolutionary, "We do not fear your terror," and "For every single one you kill a hundred more will rise."

During this period Kuo Mo-jo's poems were still imbued with the spirit of romanticism and were full of emotional outbursts. But the nature of these outbursts had changed — they were now mainly in praise of the proletarian revolution. Although they may appear monotonous and even lacking in depth they nevertheless played a positive historical role by reflecting the spirit of the time, when revolution was riding high, and the dauntless spirit of the revolutionary fighters.

This period of Kuo Mo-jo's literary life ended with his flight to Japan. There he devoted himself almost entirely to the study of the ancient history of China. His literary life was only resumed on the outbreak of the War of Resistance to Japanese Aggression.

Section 2. Novelists of the Late May 4 Period

(1) Yeh Shao-chun and His Works

Among the members of the Literary Research Society Yeh Shao-chun,[1] sometimes known as Yeh Sheng-tao, was one of those who have made the greatest contribution. It was the belief of the members of the society that literature should reflect social tendencies, reveal and discuss the various problems of life. This was precisely Yeh Shao-chun's aim in writing.

Yeh Shao-chun wrote many short stories before 1926, which appeared in the collections *Misunderstanding, Conflagration, Below the Horizon* and *In the City.* After 1926 he wrote the novel *Schoolmaster Ni Huan-chih*[2] and some shorter pieces. He also wrote a number of stories for children and some essays.

With regard to Yeh Shao-chun's earlier works Mao Tun had this to say:

> Yeh Shao-chun looks at life with a cold indifference; he writes about the nondescript and trifles of life in an objective and realistic way. In some of his earlier works as in the stories "A Friend," "Bitter Herb," and "Misunderstanding" there is a tendency towards the problem novel. As his technique matured his works also became more objective and realist. As typical

---

[1] Yeh Shao-chun was born in 1894 in Soochow, Kiangsu Province. He is now one of the vice-chairmen of the Union of Chinese Writers.

[2] Translated and published in English by the Foreign Languages Press, Peking, in 1958.

> examples we may mention the short story collections *Below the Horizon* and *In the City,* written between 1923 and the first half of 1926. If someone should ask me which writer of the "first decade"[1] reflected the gloomy life of the petty urban intellectual, my answer would be Yeh Shao-chun.

This is a true assessment. For many years Yeh Shao-chun was a teacher and an editor in a publishing house. He had frequent contact with the intellectuals of the lower middle class and knew well the gloomy life they led. This accounts for his successful delineation of this type of character, especially those drifting through life in small cities.

But Yeh Shao-chun was far from accepting life as it was. He was particularly dissatisfied with the backward state of education. Unfortunately he did not know under what economic system could education be expected to improve. Nor did he understand anything of the real relations between men, that is, class relations. Consequently he was not able to judge people from this point of view. His attitude as a bystander, however, prevented him from breaking away from the bounds of reality. Nevertheless, he saw the beauty of nature and the love that arose from heart-to-heart understanding as the essential things of life, by which dullness could be transformed into light and happiness. Beauty and love became for him the ideals of life. Needless to say these ideals were unable to withstand the harsh impact of reality. Failing to see bright prospects, Yeh Shao-chun sometimes showed a tendency towards melancholy and pessimism.

---

[1] The "first decade" means the period from 1917 to 1926.

After the May 30 Movement his ideas underwent a change. He began to make a deeper analysis of reality. This was reflected in the long novel *Schoolmaster Ni Huan-chih.*

The appearance of *Schoolmaster Ni Huan-chih* was a notable event in the literary circles at that time, for two reasons. First, it was the first novel whose scene was set within its own decade. Second, it was the first novel to describe the ideological change of a petty-bourgeois intellectual who, swung by the tide of the time, goes over from educational work to the mass movement, from libertarianism to collectivism.

Ni Huan-chih, the hero of the novel, was a typical petty-bourgeois intellectual. Although the events of his day gave him a new understanding of life, he was weak and vacillating, as were all petty-bourgeois intellectuals, and unable to go completely with the tide. Nor could he be ahead of his time. He had no clear idea of the progress of the revolution being led by the Chinese Communist Party, and he did not know how to push it forward. At the critical moment of revolution he became nervous and felt as if a final catastrophe was impending. After the collapse of the revolution when the reactionaries were massacring the revolutionaries he returned to his old haunt — the bar. He never saw the real strength of the revolution, that is, the masses of workers and peasants, nor its protracted, tortuous and complicated course. So he found himself in a quandary when events took a sudden turn. On his deathbed he saw in a delirium the workers being crushed to powder under a pile of stones. He pinned his hope on his wife and son. To the last moment of his life he never recognized the masses as the main strength of the revolution.

The hero of *Schoolmaster Ni Huan-chih* was typical of one section of the petty bourgeoisie. There was another more courageous section who joined the camp of the proletariat. When the revolution suffered a setback they followed the main forces into the countryside, persevering in their revolutionary work. There were many of these people. But unfortunately they do not appear in *Schoolmaster Ni Huan-chih*. What does this mean? This means that the author did not have a sufficient understanding of the revolution in China as led by the proletariat. He only saw the setback of the revolution, which was temporary, and did not see the strength of the workers and peasants, which was invincible.

Yeh Shao-chun is not only a novelist but also an essayist. His earlier essays, like his novels, were written in a sombre and matter-of-fact manner. They show the spirit of calmness characteristic of the Chinese gentry. But with the progress of his ideas he was sometimes unable to maintain this spirit. In the essay "In the Rainstorm of May the Thirty-first," for instance, he broke through the wall of calmness and came out with a violent attack on the dark forces of imperialism and feudalism.

After 1930 Yeh Shao-chun became interested in teaching Chinese. Although he retained his original realistic style, few of his works appeared from then on.

(2) Yu Ta-fu's Novels

Yu Ta-fu's works consisted of eight full-length novels, two shorter ones — *Stray Sheep* and *She Is Only a Woman* and several volumes of essays and miscellanea.

The keynotes of these novels, melancholy and despondency, predominate even in his later works. His earlier works were on the one hand expressions of personal dissatisfaction and on the other a protest against the ugliness of reality, since his dissatisfaction was in essence a reaction against the ugliness of reality. In his works he bluntly demands creature comforts, lays bare all the grief and sorrow in his mind, and boldly describes his frustrated sexual desire. In so doing, he in fact exposed the hypocrisy of the old moral code, while at the same time revealing his own morbid state of mind.

After the May 4 Movement, when communist ideas became more and more popular, Yu Ta-fu also came under their influence. Thus in his earlier works, apart from airing personal sentiments, he wrote two short stories more or less coloured by socialist thought. They were "Intoxicating Spring Nights," with a woman worker as the main character, and "A Humble Sacrifice,"[1] on a ricksha puller, in which the author attempted to describe the life of the ordinary worker and to show the simplicity, honesty and nobility of the working class. Yu Ta-fu's great disgust with the capitalists' oppression of the workers is also apparent in these books. His hatred of the capitalists did not, however, go beyond this emotional reaction.

In the works he wrote after the First Revolutionary Civil War, Yu Ta-fu adhered to his former style of writing. There was one exception — the novel *Flight*, written in 1935, which describes the landlords' cruel exploitation of the peasants, their greed, their selfishness and their methods of infiltrating into the revolutionary camp. The

---

[1] These two stories were translated and published in English in *Chinese Literature*, No. 3, 1957.

novel shows an evident hatred for the landlords and may be considered a progressive work.

It seems that *Flight* was Yu Ta-fu's last novel. After the War of Resistance broke out he went to Singapore and Indonesia to engage in cultural work. He was killed in Sumatra in September 1945 by Japanese police after the Japanese surrender.

(3) Other Writers

Realism was the main tendency in the literary world both before and after the May 4 Movement. Under the direction and influence of Lu Hsun, the pioneer of realism in the history of modern Chinese literature, many realist writers appeared. Those who concentrated their attention on the life of the petty-bourgeois intellectuals and lower middle class included Wang Tung-chao, Lo Hua Sheng (the pen-name of Hsu Ti-shan), Miss Kan (the pen-name of Feng Yuan-chun), and Huang Lu-yin.

Wang Tung-chao wrote *An Evening of Spring Rain, One Leaf,* and *Dusk.* The ideas revealed in these works are somewhat similar to those of Yeh Shao-chun in the earlier period of his literary life while placing greater emphasis on abstract love and beauty. These ideas were to change after 1927, as revealed in the novel *Mountain Rain* in which he describes the phenomena and causes of the decline of village life in North China and the awakening of the peasants. While his description of the collapse of village life is very vivid, that of the peasants' awakening is not so successful.

Lo Hua Sheng wrote the *Weaving Spider.* Although coloured by ideas of romantic fatalism, it also contains elements of realism and democratic thought. In the latter period of his literary life his ideas of democracy were further developed. In the short story "Spring Peach" although social problems are not studied from the class point of view the noble character of the working people and their strong class solidarity is well described. During the War of Resistance his ideas made even greater headway, when he joined the anti-Japanese democratic movement led by the Chinese Communist Party in Hongkong. In 1941 he fell ill and died.

Miss Kan wrote *Cockleburs* in which she boldly describes the Chinese women's attempts to free themselves from the fetters of Confucian morality. Huang Lu-yin wrote *A Friend from the Seaside,* describing the various perplexities of the women in their search for emancipation. These novels may be said to be true portrayals of the women intellectuals after the May 4 Movement.

Those who wrote of rural life included Hsu Chieh, Wang Jen-shu and Wang Lu-yen. Hsu Chieh wrote *Sad Mist, Drifting* and *Crater of the Volcano.* Wang Jen-shu was the author of *Martyrdom, Jail, The Vagabondage of Ah Kuei, In Decline* and *Old House.* Among the works of Wang Lu-yen are *Pumelo, Gold, The Tragedy of Childhood, Under the Roof, The Heart of Hsiao Hsiao, Riverside* and *The Enraged Village.* These authors drew a realistic picture of the countryside, showing the characteristic stubbornness of the peasants as well as their ignorance and gullibility. They write with great sympathy of the peasants' blind struggle and their inevitable failure. But their common standpoint was that of traditional humanitarianism; they did not see the class relations and struggle in the countryside. This was why they could not see the victories the future would bring to the peasants.

Miss Ping Hsin (the pen-name of Hsieh Wan-ying) was another well-known writer of the period under discussion. Her short stories of the period 1919-23 were published as *A Collection of Short Stories by Ping Hsin.* Ping Hsin did deal with certain problems of life in her stories. But her method of solution was one of bourgeois idealism, that is, by a concept of love that stood above class. The short story, "I Alone Am Disconsolate," tells how a father forbids his sons to take part in a students' movement, threatening to stop their education if they disobey. Although the elder sister sympathizes with her younger brothers she does not want her brothers to disobey their parents; in other words her love for her family is stronger than her love for society.

Section 3. Realism in Poetry and Drama Before and After the May 4 Movement

(1) Movement of Vernacular Poetry

After the call for a revolution in literature was put forth in 1917 the first product of the new literature was poetry in the vernacular. In line with the revolutionary situation and the nature and aims of the literary revolution the vernacular poets took up from the very beginning the task of fighting against feudalism and imperialism, thus becoming a wing of the cultural revolutionary front. Their method of writing had to be realistic.

The vernacular poetry of the early period had two characteristics. First, it centred largely upon describing social phenomena and discussing social problems, the understanding of these phenomena and problems differing, of course, according to the writer's level of political understanding. Second, it was marked by a resistance to the feudal ethics and a search for truth with regard to the problems of life. Just as by far the greater number of novels written in the early period of the new literature dealt with the theme of love, so it was with the poetry. But in a period when the important thing was to oppose feudal ethics this had a certain positive significance.

These two characteristics determined the form and style of the new poetry in its early period. What the new poets aspired to was to free themselves from conventions. They did not want to write in a florid style or to seek for unusual effect. Most of their works are in free verse. As in folk songs and ballads, many of the words and expressions they use are colloquial or drawn from local dialects. One thing they took great pains to avoid and that was pedantry. Although all this shows a sound spirit of realism, the new poets were unable to analyse problems from the class point of view. As a result their description of events is often cursory and hence superficial.

(2) Drama Movement

Like other writers of the period the playwrights were also inspired by the anti-feudal, anti-imperialist spirit of realism. This was most clearly seen in their critical attitude towards the old dramas, which was similar to the critical attitude towards feudal literature among the writers. But as their understanding of the old dramas was incomplete, their opinion was rather one-sided. They even demanded the total abolition of the old dramas which are in reality a kind of folk art. Many of these contain popular elements which should be distinguished from the backward feudal elements and should of course be preserved. But as a matter of historical progress, their violent attack on the old dramas conformed with the spirit of the time and produced a salutary influence politically.

The spirit of these playwrights also showed itself in their ardent promotion of realism in dramatic writing. In 1918, for instance, the journal *New Youth* issued a special number (Vol. IV, No. 6) on Ibsen and translated many of Ibsen's plays. Ibsen, with his bold attack on the society of his time, and his exhortations to people to free themselves from traditional ethics, law, prejudices, and practices, won warm approval among the Chinese reading public and exerted a great influence on their ideas. Most of the dramas written in this period dealt with social problems though few of these received any solution at the hands of the writers. Nevertheless, the fundamental spirit of these dramas was realistic. In 1921 Shen Yen-ping, Cheng Chen-to, Chen Ta-pei, Ouyang Yu-chien, and nine other people formed the Popular Drama Society. This was what they said in their manifesto:

> At least we can say this much: the era when people go to the theatre for recreation only is gone. The theatre occupies an important place in modern society. Like the wheels of a cart it gives motion to society and impels it forward. Like an X-ray it searches out

> the basic troubles of society. It is also a just and unbiased mirror faithfully reflecting the moral and intellectual conditions of the people. . . . This kind of theatre does not exist in China at the present time. It is the kind of theatre that we, weak though we are, are trying to create.

As the aim of the promoters of this theatre was to uncover "the basic troubles of society" and impel society forward their spirit could not but be that of realism. They also founded a journal known as *Drama*. Although only ten numbers were published it was not without influence on the new drama movement.

At the beginning of this period most of the plays produced were directed against the feudal marriage system. Both *Lan-chih and Chung-ching* written by Hsiung Fo-hsi, and *The Virago* written by Ouyang Yu-chien, were intended as an attack on the patriarchal family system and a bid for freedom of marriage. The plays *A Night in a Cafe* and *The Night When the Tiger Was Captured* written by Tien Han were also of this nature. The positive import of this kind of play was that they raised the problem of free marriage which the petty-bourgeois intellectuals were anxious to solve. But they merely aired the problem and that was all. As to its solution, the writers had no ideas.

The problem of marriage, as presented in the dramas of the early period, mainly concerned the petty-bourgeois intellectuals. It proceeded mostly from the individual point of view and had therefore a rather limited scope of significance. Following the progress of the revolutionary movement, drama dealt with a much wider range of themes. Consequently greater and more important social problems were gradually brought to the fore. The *Yama Chao* written by Hung Shen, for instance, had as its theme the opposition to the civil war waged by the warlords. But owing to the limitations of the writer's knowledge of the nature of China's revolution his understanding of reality could not but be superficial. He condemned the warlords for their crimes and sympathized with the people for their sufferings. And there he stopped. Hu Yeh-pin's *The House of the Mason* deals with the sufferings of the oppressed. His *A Gentleman's Invitation* is a satire on the corruption of the ruling class. Neither of these plays do more than expose the evils of the old society; neither contain any clearly revolutionary ideas.

After the May 30 Movement, drama came out in an open attack on imperialist aggression. Tien Han's *Death of Ku Cheng-hung*, written at about this time, shows strong anti-imperialist feelings. The three plays — *Protest, Crisis* and *Sacrifice* — by Cheng Po-chi also have anti-imperialism as their theme. After the appearance of these works came the First Revolutionary War. As with other forms of literary writing, drama also became a part of revolutionary literature in general.

CHAPTER EIGHT

REVOLUTIONARY WRITERS, PROGRESSIVE WRITERS, AND LITERARY SCHOOLS OF THE DECLINING BOURGEOISIE

Section 1. Revolutionary Writers

In 1927 and 1928 the movement of revolutionary literature was fully unfolded. In the theoretical field it was concluded, in accordance with the principles of Marxism-Leninism, that literature has a class character, is a weapon of class struggle, and should serve the needs of politics and revolution, and that writers should try to acquire a proletarian outlook. This gave great impetus to the literary movement though it also gave rise to shortcomings. Among the shortcomings was the failure to lay sufficient emphasis on the importance of remoulding the ideology of the petty-bourgeois writers and to see that this is a long-term, difficult and delicate task.

Under the inspiration of this theory many literary works appeared which though deeply coloured by romanticism, were fundamentally revolutionary. In evaluating these works we should first of all point out their merits. These works formed in a sense a wing of China's revolutionary movement, and, as such, they performed their function well. They exerted a great influence on the young people and undoubtedly served to quicken the pace of the revolution. They paved the way and laid the foundations for the revolutionary literary movement and helped it with experience and lessons.

But owing to the fact that the authors of these works were mostly intellectuals of the petty bourgeoisie, whose ideas had not been remoulded, and hence their works contained many defects and unhealthy elements. Probably the most common defect of all is the tendency to individual heroism. The main character is invariably a hero, more or less a superman. He appears in society like a bolt from the blue. He makes speeches, holds meetings, does revolutionary work, and scores successes. It seems as if he alone can determine anything. Even the leadership of the Party was described by these authors in terms of individual heroism, in a way typical of their petty-bourgeois revolutionary outlook and their lack of contact with reality. Another defect of these works is their romanticism. The aim of revolutionary literature is to describe the revolutionary movement of the proletariat and the life of the working people. But the authors lacked understanding of the real nature of revolutionary work. They never took part in revolutionary work and never lived among the workers and peasants. They could therefore only rely on their subjective imagination instead of on objective reality. They thought that it was enough for a writer to apply the dialectical materialist method to writing. This accounts for the fact that most of their works were merely a matter of abstract formulism. Their emphasis on romantic love was a further defect. Outside of the main topic of revolution, many of these books deal with nothing but love. Some even reverse the relative position of the topics and make love the main topic interspersed with minor revolutionary episodes. In short, a mixture of revolution and love affairs became the literary vogue of those days.

To point out these defects of the revolutionary literature does not deny their historical importance. Revolutionary literature was a new thing in those days and as a new thing it could hardly be free from defects. And it was precisely from these defects that the writers learned better methods of writing. In other words, revolutionary literature grew from its struggle against mistakes and defects.

The better known revolutionary writers in this period included Hua Han (the pen-name of Yang Han-sheng), Shih Yi (the pen-name of Lou Chien-nan), Kung Ping-lu, Hung Ling-fei, Chiang Kuang-tzu, Yin Fu, Hu Yeh-pin and Tien Han. Hua Han wrote *The Tenth Sister's Melancholy, The Last Day* and *Spring*. Shih Yi wrote *Struggle, Illness and Dreams*, and *The Third Period*. Hung Ling-fei's works included *Flight, The Front, Change, Tomorrow* and *Sellers of Strength*. Kung Ping-lu wrote *Coal Miners* and other works. But among these writers Chiang Kuang-tzu, Hu Yeh-pin, Yin Fu and Tien Han wielded the greatest influence.

(1) The Poems and Novels of Chiang Kuang-tzu and Hu Yeh-pin

Chiang Kuang-tzu was one of the first writers to attempt revolutionary literature. He was a prolific writer and the influence of his works was great.

In 1925 he published a collection of his poems entitled *New Dream*. In 1926, after publishing a novel called *The Young Wanderer* he wrote a further collection of poems entitled *War Drum* and ten collections of short stories including *On the Yalu River*.

Chiang Kuang-tzu began to write poems as early as 1921. The collection *New Dream* included the poems he wrote in the period 1921-24 when he was staying in the Soviet Union. In these poems the writer praises the life of the Soviet people after the October Revolution and shows his patriotic revolutionary anti-imperialist and anti-feudal spirit, which is also seen in his novels.

Chiang Kuang-tzu's novels deal with a great variety of themes and his characters represent many types of people. Besides intellectuals there are strikers, shop assistants, revolutionaries, peasant leaders, and women who are moved by the spirit of rebellion. His novels also reflect the main contradictions and struggles of society. Important events — such as the students' movement to boycott Japanese goods, the strike of the workers of the Canton-Hankow Railway, the three uprisings staged by the Shanghai workers, the Nanchang Uprising, and the peasants' movement of Hunan — all appear directly or indirectly in his novels.

As his novels contain analyses of the main motive forces of revolution and descriptions of important revolutionary events they won warm approval among the younger people of those days. *The Moon Forces Its Way Through the Clouds*, for instance, ran into seven editions in the first year of its publication. These big circulations spread the influence of the revolution and won many new readers to revolutionary literature. His contribution to the revolution should therefore never be forgotten.

That does not mean to say that his works have no defects. As a matter of fact practically all the defects common to the revolutionary works of his time appear in his works too. But what should be remembered is that these defects can by no means blur the lustre of his achievements. In propagating the revolutionary ideas of the proletariat, in rousing the revolutionary ardour of the masses, and in taking a lead in writing revolutionary literature Chiang Kuang-tzu did excellent service.

Hu Yeh-pin was one of the writers murdered by the Kuomintang reactionaries in Shanghai, on February 7, 1931. He began his literary career in about the year 1924. Among his other works, he wrote the *Manuscript of Saintly Poems* and *Whither?* Love is the theme of most of his works. In fact they are full of the spirit of petty-bourgeois romanticism. But as the author was a shop apprentice in his youth and remained long in poverty his novels do show the sufferings of the poor. In 1928 he went from Peking to Shanghai. There he came under the influence of Marxism-Leninism. In the words of a literary critic, while he did not know the meaning of revolution, he cursed life and sang the praises of love. But as soon as he came into contact with revolutionary thought he unhesitatingly began to study diligently theories which were entirely new to him. In Shanghai, apart from doing revolutionary work, Hu Yeh-pin wrote two novels, *To Moscow* and *The Light Before Us*. His ideas and style of writing, as these two works show, had evidently changed.

To Moscow, written in 1929, is a story of revolution and love, full of the spirit of romanticism. The end of the story shows the writer's firm belief in the revolution: Su Shang, the heroine, succeeds in freeing herself from the clutches of Hsu Ta-chi, a counter-revolutionary, and leaves by train for Moscow.

The Light Before Us, completed in 1930, was Hu Yeh-pin's last work. Compared with *To Moscow* it shows a further advance in his ideas. Although this is also a story of revolution and love the story is woven around an ideological struggle — between the Marxism-Leninism of Liu Hsi-chien, the hero, and the anarchism of Pai Hua, the heroine. In the end Marxism-Leninism prevails over anarchism. Compared with other stories of revolution and love it is deeper in thought content.

(2) Yin Fu's Poems and Tien Han's Plays

Yin Fu was also known as Pai Mang. At twenty-two, he was among those murdered in Shanghai. His poems were collected under the titles *Children's Pagoda, Black Waves of the Volga* and *107*. *Mother,* a collection of short stories and miscellany, is another of his works.

The poems of this young poet show great revolutionary zeal and firm belief in the cause of the revolution. They were veritable flowers and gems of the revolutionary literature of his time. His poems are deeply moving. They hold a reader spellbound. There is hardly a sign in his works of the defects common to those of his contemporaries, such as sloganizing, generalizing, and formulism. Lu Hsun spoke highly of Yin Fu's work in his introduction to *Children's Pagoda*:

> This is a ray of light in the east, a sounding arrow in a dense forest, a bud or sprout at the end of winter, and the first step in a march. It is a banner of love for the forerunners and an epitaph of hatred for the vandals. None of the works marked by "mature thought and skilful writing," or showing "calm grace

> and awe-inspiring profundity," need be compared with these poems, for they belong to a totally different category.

In other words, Lu Hsun maintained that it was neither the works of the romanticists and old realists nor those of the revolutionary poets of his day, could compare with those of Yin Fu.

Tien Han[1] began play-writing early in life. He was a serious student of the art of play-writing and also the most prolific writer of his time.

His earlier works were imbued with the spirit of romanticism. His later works, of 1928 and after, were fundamentally sound in their class stand and revolutionary viewpoint though still more or less coloured by romanticism.

The plays he wrote after 1928 drew on much wider sources for their characters. Besides delineating intellectuals and petty citizenry he also drew workers and peasants. The *Dance of Fire*, for instance, compares the life of the workers with that of the capitalists. The *Flood* describes the life and struggle of the peasants in an inundated area. The *Drought* contains a most ghastly scene of cannibalism. Although the writer did not have close contact with the life of the working people and was unable to avoid the common defects of the revolutionary literature of this period, these plays were nevertheless a great contribution to the propagation of revolutionary ideas.

---

[1] Tien Han was born in 1898 in Changsha, Hunan Province. He is now the Chairman of the Union of Chinese Dramatists.

After the Mukden Incident of 1931 Tien Han wrote many plays on the theme of national salvation and resistance to Japanese aggression, like *Disorderly Bell, Sweeping Fire, Comrades-in-arms, Moonlight Serenade of 1932, Song of the Return of Spring, Night of the First Snowfall, Mother of Abyssinia* and *Evening Party.* The performance of these plays, which overflow with patriotic ardour and hatred of Japanese imperialism, did much to fan the resistance movement.

It is because most of Tien Han's plays proceed from the motive of objective demand that they faithfully reflect the disturbances and struggles of the time in the light of class relations. Written as they are in passionate and colourful language, they are good stage plays.

Tien Han is not only a prolific playwright but also a great promoter of the movement of revolutionary drama. He was the first leader of the South Country Club and has never since abandoned his position as a fighting dramatist. His influence has touched many playwrights as well as promoters of progressive drama. In the movement for revolutionary drama he has also exerted great influence.

During the War of Resistance to Japanese Aggression Tien Han produced less plays than he did in the previous period. Among the better known ones are *Autumn Dirge* and *Song of Beautiful Ladies.* It was during this period that he became interested in the revision of old plays. Among these he revised are included *New Story of Heroic Sons and Daughters* and *Fisherman's Song,* which have helped to push forward the movement for reforming traditional drama.

Section 2. Progressive Writers

After 1928 the revolutionary literary movement gained further ground. Translations of foreign works on the Marxist-Leninist theory of art and literature frequently appeared on the market and were eagerly snapped up, especially by young people. In 1930 the China League of Left-Wing Writers was formed. Under the leadership of the Chinese Communist Party and the personal direction of Lu Hsun the movement of proletarian revolutionary literature swept across the whole country. Under the influence of this movement many revolutionary writers appeared, a large number of literary works were produced, and the principle of socialist realism in writing found a wider circle of acceptance. But there were also a number of petty-bourgeois writers who had a dual outlook on life. While they were dissatisfied with the reactionary Kuomintang rule they had only a vague conception of the strength and future of China's revolution. As they had no firm working-class standpoint, they were unable to study society and life from a scientific point of view. They failed to understand the new-democratic revolutionary movement led by the Chinese Communist Party. Their attitude towards this movement was that of bystanders and their outlook on the political situation was confused and despondent. They were neither willing to consider themselves as one of the reactionary writers nor willing to join the revolutionary literary camp. This was reflected in their writings, which remained in the stage of the old type of realism.

From the point of view of objective historical conditions, works written according to the principle of the old type of realism were not without progressive significance. At least they increased the readers' dissatisfaction against the reactionary rule. Therefore, they played a useful part in fulfilling the main task of the revolution which was to oppose feudalism and imperialism.

These progressive writers were represented by Lao Sheh and Pa Chin in the field of novels, by Wen I-to in that of poetry, and by Hung Shen and Tsao Yu in that of drama.

(1). Novels by Lao Sheh and Pa Chin and Poems by Wen I-to

Lao Sheh[1] is the pen-name of the writer Shu Sheh-yu, who was born in Peking in 1899. In his own words, "I was from childhood used to a life of poverty. My philosophy of life was always one expressed by the common saying 'It's all a matter of fate!' "[2] Although he was speaking of his life before the May 4 Movement his experience shows itself in the content and style of his later writings. His life of poverty could not but have left the desire to resist the oppressors of the people, be they individuals or government. But because his outlook on life was one of fatalism he frequently expressed these feelings by a kind of humour characteristic of the lower middle class. This humorous touch weakens the will to resist. In his own words, "humour dilutes one's sense of justice." His earlier works, like *The Philosophy of*

---

[1] Lao Sheh is the Chairman of the Peking branch of the All-China Federation of Writers and Artists and a deputy to the National People's Congress.

[2] "Preface to the *Selected Works of Lao Sheh.*"

Old Chang and *Master Chao Says,* were all written in this humorous vein.

In 1924 Lao Sheh went to London to teach Chinese in the School of Oriental Studies, London University. As he did not return to China until 1930 he had no direct experience of the two big events, the May 30 Movement and the First Revolutionary Civil War. On his return, he taught in universities and so had little opportunity to gain first-hand experience of the revolution. His ideas therefore made little progress.

During this period he wrote many novels. His own origin shows itself in his range of characters which are not limited to intellectuals but include the labouring people and the oppressed too. But as he was too far removed from the scenes of revolution he had no direct knowledge of it. How he delineated his characters of the labouring masses may be best summed up in his own words:

> That was because I had tasted the bitterness of life in my youth and had been oppressed; I wanted to give vent to my grievances with borrowed themes. I had a strong sense of justice and injustice, but it was that of a petty bourgeois and it was precisely because of this that I did not dare to be a revolutionary. Nor did the characters of my novels dare to be revolutionaries. In the novels I merely expressed my sympathy with them but dared not point out a way for them. In their language, appearance, life, and so on, I painted a picture of gloom and darkness. There was no struggle and hence no hope or light.[1]

[1] Lao Sheh, "Chairman Mao Gave Me a New Lease of Literary Life," *Renmin Ribao* (People's Daily), Peking, May 21, 1952.

In his famous novel *The Ricksha Boy*, one of his best novels of pre-liberation days both in content and style, his main character was an honest, industrious ricksha boy who died under the oppressive and destructive forces of the old society, the darkness of which no light could penetrate. After reading this book, a worker asked Lao Sheh: "If the ricksha boy died like that what hope do we have?" He was unable to answer the question. Some of his better known short stories, like "Crescent Moon"[1] and "Going to Take Up an Official Appointment," suffer from a similar defect, they give no ray of hope to the oppressed.

But this defect of Lao Sheh's works does not rule out their merits. Lao Sheh is above all a good realist writer with keen analytic powers. He has in his writings mercilessly criticized all the evils and corruptions of the old society so far as they were within the scope of his knowledge. Being poor when he was young he had for a long period of time close contact with the working people. In later days he continued to maintain friendly relations with them and loved them with all his heart. So he not only knew their life but understood their psychology. This is why his characters of working people are so realistic, lively and touching. They are real people and not mere abstractions or cold concepts. Being Peking born, Lao Sheh uses the Peking dialect, especially the dialect of the common people, with great versatility. The Peking dialect of his novels is seldom found to such perfection in the novels of previous authors. Lao Sheh, as has been indicated before, was dissatisfied with the

---

[1] Translated and published in English in *Chinese Literature*, No. 4, 1957.

old society and was its stern critic. He was patriotic and loved the working people. During the War of Resistance to Japanese Aggression he was active in the movement of resistance literature and achieved great results in rallying the artists and writers to the cause of resistance and in opposing separatist activities. During the war he was able to gain a deeper understanding of the anti-Japanese democratic movement and the Chinese people's revolutionary movement as also of the fascist and traitorous activities of the Chiang Kai-shek clique. This was why he returned to China from the United States immediately after liberation.[1] He loved New China in the same way as he loved the motherland and the working people. He did everything to remould himself. Subsequently he wrote such popular plays as *Dragon Beard Ditch*[2] and *Fang Chen-chu.* He was honoured with the title of "People's Artist;" a title which he eminently deserves.

Pa Chin[3] is the pen-name of Li Fei-kan, who was born into a landlord family in Szechuan Province in 1904. About 1927, when the tide of revolution was sweeping over the whole country and many intellectuals of the younger generation were flocking to join the revolution, he was in faraway France and therefore unable to take part in this great revolutionary struggle. His life in France at that time was monotonous and lonely. This

---

[1] In 1946 Lao Sheh went to the United States to teach and came back to China in 1949.

[2] Translated and published in English by the Foreign Languages Press, Peking, in 1956.

[3] Pa Chin is one of the vice-chairmen of the Union of Chinese Writers.

was what he said in the preface he wrote for his *Selected Works*: "To console my young and lonely heart I began to write down the things I learned from life." This was how his first novel *Destruction* came to be written.

His early works show Pa Chin's strong petty-bourgeois sense of justice. His heart burns with the flames of youth. His indignation at the evils of the feudal social system is great and his spirit of rebellion strong. But owing to the fact that he had no knowledge of the revolutionary theory of Marxism-Leninism, had no experience in actual revolutionary struggle, and spent much of his life in solitude his enthusiasm and spirit of rebellion led him astray and landed him on the path of anarchism. His novel *Destruction* is full of anarchistic ideas.

Revolution and love form the main theme of *Destruction*. The central idea of the novel is that all those who build their happiness on others' sufferings will be destroyed but those who first stand up to oppose the oppressors will also be destroyed. This is tantamount to saying that both revolutionaries and non-revolutionaries will end in destruction, a very untenable theory. After the publication of *Destruction* Pa Chin wrote the following novels: *New Life, The Sun That Has Died, Dream at the Bottom of the Sea, The Antimony Mine, Snow* (also published under the title *Sprouts*), and *Autumn in Spring*. In content, style, and tone these novels are at bottom similar to *Destruction*. The theme of *The Antimony Mine* is the wretched life of a miner, and that of *Snow* the life of kiln workers. Although in theme they differ from *Destruction* they carry practically the same message.

Pa Chin's later works include the "Trilogy of Love": *Fog*, *Rain*, and *Lightning*. All of them express in one way or another his anarchistic ideas.

Pa Chin's three novels — *The Family*, *Spring*, and *Autumn* — known as the "Trilogy of Turbulent Currents," enjoyed more popularity than the others. The novel *The Family*, in particular, was widely read among the youth. It touched the right chord in rousing them to rebel against their feudal family life. The story is woven around a rapidly declining feudal family. The author mercilessly attacks the feudal family system and the dark old society with its "cannibalistic" moral code. He exposes the corrupt and shameful life of the feudal landlords and bureaucrats, shows his sympathy with the young men and women who were painfully caught in the cogwheels of the feudal society, and describes how they tried to oppose the system. Chueh-hui, the principal character in the novel, is a young man of strong character. He resolutely fights against the feudal system and finally flees from his family. The author makes a strong indictment against feudal society but unfortunately is unable to point out the right way for his hero after his flight. The author's ideas were bound up with anarchism and his idea of revolution was one which had neither leadership nor mass support.

During the War of Resistance Pa Chin wrote the novel *Fire*. It was a war novel, full of the spirit of patriotism. In this novel, the general trend of his ideas show little change. Because his motive for writing was his dissatisfaction with life he tried by every means to destroy, in his novels, the ugly life which he hated so much. This he has succeeded in doing and herein lies the merit of his works.

Pa Chin was a great enemy of "traditional ideas" and this character of his was in keeping with the revolutionary trend of that time. Although his works were tainted by romanticism they were fundamentally realistic. His spirit of romanticism, in fact, enabled him to hit all the harder. Another marked characteristic of his works is that they overflow with intense emotions. He passionately attacked the feudal system and the dark society; he passionately praised revolution — the revolution as he imagined it. This gave a magnetic power to his novels and made them very popular among the unsophisticated youth of the petty bourgeoisie who were dissatisfied with reality but could find no way out.

Wen I-to was originally a bourgeois poet and an aesthete, who later changed his outlook when he made more contact with the realities of life. Having overcome these contradictions in his mind he took bold steps forward and became a staunch partisan of democracy. During the earlier period of his literary activities he had close connections with members of the Crescent school. The line of the development his ideas took, however, differed from that of the latter.

The real turning point in the life of Wen I-to came during the War of Resistance to Japanese Aggression. Circumstances compelled him to leave his study and come into contact with the outside world. Honest, loyal and patriotic as he was, he began to scan reality anew. He saw with his own eyes the avarice, corruption and traitorous activities of the Kuomintang reactionaries. He also saw the tremendous strength of the working people under the leadership of the Chinese Communist Party which he was hitherto prevented from seeing. At last he had found the right path. With great courage he joined the revolutionary struggle of the people and marched forward with the country's army of revolutionaries. Unfortunately his life ended in a tragic death in July 1946 when he was assassinated in Kunming by secret police of the Chiang Kai-shek clique. Although during the later years of his life he had not written any poems in ink he did write an epic in blood.

(3) Plays by Hung Shen and Tsao Yu

Hung Shen was comparatively young when he became a playwright. The progress in his ideas in the early period of his literary career is best described in his own words taken from his preface to his *Selected Works*: "After I had read some books on the social sciences and joined the League of Left-Wing Writers. . . . I began to experience some change in my personal and political views." It was following this that he wrote in 1930-31 his "Trilogy of the Countryside": *Wu Kuei Bridge*, *Fragrant Rice* and *Blue Dragon Pond*.

During the War of Resistance Hung Shen wrote the plays *Flying General*, *Pao Teh Hsing*, *Money and Painting*, and *Look at the Sky When the Cock Crows*. In his own estimation, none of these works were as good as *Wu Kuei Bridge*. He was probably right.

Tsao Yu[1] is an outstanding realist playwright of contemporary China. Before the War of Resistance he wrote three plays: *Thunderstorm*[2] (1934), *Sunrise* (1936),

---

[1] Tsao Yu is the head of the Peking People's Art Theatre.

[2] Translated and published in English by the Foreign Languages Press, Peking, in 1958.

and *The Wilderness* (1937). All three enjoyed great popularity among the petty bourgeoisie and other city-dwellers.

Tsao Yu is the pen-name of Wan Chia-pao, who was born of a well-to-do feudal family in 1910. He studied for several years in Nankai Secondary School and Tsinghua University, both dominated by the capitalist way of thought. He was therefore familiar with China's feudal culture as well as with the literary theories of the Western bourgeoisie. This had a great influence on his ideas, and he paid little attention to the revolutionary theory and practice of his time. The December 9 Movement of 1935, which was led by the Chinese Communist Party, broke out in Peking where he was studying but he hardly noticed it. Of his own plays, he had this to say, "I was engrossed in thought about many ultimate problems," and, "I was not aware of any conscious effort of correcting, attacking, or satirizing anything." But he was after all living in a semi-feudal and semi-colonial country; he saw, and heard about, the evils of that society. He was a conscientious artist and the fire of youth burned in his heart. He had to take the things that he knew for the themes of his plays, and this was how he wrote *Thunderstorm*, a social play exposing the evils of the big feudal family. Thanks to his superb literary technique, the characters he delineates are realistic and lively. They moved the heart of millions and made them ardent admirers of his plays. But the audience was not moved to tears as might be expected; instead, they were moved to pondering about the fate of China as a semi-colonial country. Herein lies the real merit of *Thunderstorm*. This merit should not, however, be overestimated as the author has his limitations. It is true he exposed the evils of society but he did not point out how to wipe out these evils. Still worse, he fell into the quagmire of fatalism.

After *Thunderstorm* Tsao Yu wrote *Sunrise*. From taking the family as his tragic theme he now began to take society. From talking about the "mysterious unknown" in *Thunderstorm* he began to attempt to solve important social problems. This was a big step forward. But in the play *Sunrise* the author lays all the blame on "a terrible dark force," "an invisible force which controls the people in the scene," that is, a gang leader of Shanghai. Hope for a bright future is pinned on the tamping workers on the construction site at a big building. But these workers never appear in the play and nothing is said about the leadership and organization of these workers. Reviewing his own work this is what Tsao Yu says in his preface to his *Selected Works*:

> Thinking over the past I remember that when I was writing the play I did want to pose certain problems and provide their solutions. But I was from beginning to end dominated by strong emotion. I did not write in a thoroughgoing fashion and so failed to make known the real origins of the evils I described. The play *Sunrise*, for instance, is evidently a denunciation of the old semi-feudal, semi-colonial society. But in writing it I unwittingly allowed imperialism, the greatest of evils, to pass without a single blow. This made the play read like a grandiloquent indictment of the evils of urban society which thinking men liked to read in those days. Another thing, I laid great stress on the life of the henchmen of the reactionary

> ruling class — their licentiousness and cruelty. But I never wrote about serious revolutionaries, the positive force of society, about their life-and-death struggles waged against the enemy.

The author's self-criticism, though perhaps over-modest, was made with great sincerity. In all fairness it must be said that the author did bring up certain problems in *Sunrise*. Besides he described with great force the licentious and shameful life of the henchmen of the ruling class as well as the miserable life of the oppressed people. He dealt a serious blow to the dark old society. It was a play that had a positive effect on the society of those days.

After *Sunrise* came *The Wilderness.* In this play he turned his attention from the city to the countryside. *The Wilderness* is the story of a peasant's revenge on a despotic landlord. The theme is good, but unfortunately the author was unfamiliar with the life of the peasants, the chief class contradictions and class struggle in the countryside. Besides, his ideas were dominated by a belief in fatalism. As a result the play, which could have been treated in a most realistic way, became full of mysterious, abstract, and even strange conceptions. Mysticism, symbolism and psychological analysis combined to rouse a sense of terror and give the play its atmosphere of dismay. The play gives the impression of being detached from reality. It does not seem like a real story. *The Wilderness* must therefore be counted as a failure.

During the War of Resistance Tsao Yu wrote three multi-act plays: *Transformation, Peking Man*, and *The Family* (adapted from Pa Chin's novel of the same title).

Compared with *The Wilderness, Transformation* showed a big advance in the author's ideas. Caught up in the current spirit of enthusiasm, he set out to write about "the phenomenon of our people's riddance of the old and emergence of the new during the War of Resistance." His intention was good, but he did not know the cause of the phenomenon which he called the "old" or under what political and social conditions the phenomenon which he called "new" could be brought about. The light and happiness he describes in his play sprang purely from his imagination; they had no basis in objective reality.

Such false optimism was soon to meet with disillusion as the War of Resistance progressed. When this happened, he did not seem to have tried to find out the whys and hows. He dropped the theme of the War of Resistance and wrote other kinds of plays, like *Peking Man* and *The Family.*

Anti-feudalism was the theme of both the *Peking Man* and *The Family.* Although these two plays show little progress in the author's ideas they do show an advance in his technique of character delineation. Like the two plays *Thunderstorm* and *Sunrise*, *Peking Man* and *The Family* expose the evils of the old society without giving any advice as to how such evils can be wiped out. Nevertheless, they sounded the unmistakable dirge of the old society. Anyone seeing the play must be roused to instant indignation and revolt against the "cannibalistic" moral code of the feudal system.

As a critical, realistic writer Tsao Yu is probably one of the best playwrights in the history of modern Chinese literature. He has a good knowledge of the dregs and dark forces of society and hates them with all his heart.

He brings them on to the stage, thoroughly exposing their guilt and ruthlessly criticizing them. This is exactly what the people want a playwright to do, and Tsao Yu has done it and done it well. His characters are living people, with the power to move an audience, even to hold them spellbound. People who see Tsao Yu's plays feel that they represent their own ideas and express their own thoughts, and hate these dark forces he describes from the bottom of their hearts. That his plays have had a positive influence on the Chinese public cannot be gainsaid.

Section 3. Literary Schools of the Declining Bourgeoisie

After the May 4 Movement a rift began to appear in the literary circles of China. A number of bourgeois intellectuals in the camp of revolutionary writers showed a tendency towards compromise with the enemy, i.e., the reactionaries. They became known as the Modern Review group and Hu Shih was their bell-wether. After the First Revolutionary Civil War the bourgeoisie betrayed the cause of the revolution. The intellectuals under their patronage turned about face too and went over to the camp of counter-revolution. Many reactionary, decadent literary groups, such as the Crescent group appeared at this time.

These literary groups stood against the interests of the people in the sphere of politics and against realism in the sphere of literary writing. They were therefore an anachronism in the history of modern Chinese literature.

These anachronistic elements were not very numerous and did not last very long. They were active only during the period from 1928 to 1931, when the class struggle was most acute and the reactionary rule at its blackest. It was therefore comparatively easy for such persons to make a showing. Before this they had written but little and the influence of their works was negligible. After 1931 their works were overshadowed, if not entirely pushed out, by the great tide of revolutionary literature under the guidance of the Chinese Communist Party, and found little favour with the reading public. Still later they converged with the literature of the fascists and special agents; they fell so low that it is beyond the dignity of a literary critic to comment upon them.

(2) The Crescent and Other Groups

The members of the Crescent group, reactionary in both their political views and views on literature, were represented by Hsu Chih-mo and Shen Tsung-wen.

Hsu Chih-mo came from a bourgeois family. He received his college education in Britain and was full of the ideas of the British upper-class society. He was much influenced by the doctrines of aestheticism and impressionism (in literature) which were in vogue in the later period of the nineteenth century. His mental make-up was thus entirely a product of the British-American capitalist civilization. It was his hope that a parliamentary democracy of the British-American type would some day come into being in China. His earlier works, typified by *Chih-mo's Poems,* were full of the spirit of optimism and enthusiasm which characterized the outlook of the Western bourgeoisie in the early stage of their development.

One thing should be noted and that is the fact that the Crescent poets paid great attention to form in poetry. In this Wen I-to in the earlier period of his literary development agreed with Hsu Chih-mo and they jointly did much to promote the doctrine of formalism in poetry. They laid great emphasis on the correct number of words and lines in a poem, on the use of metres, and on the structure of the verses. In these respects they were successful. The composition, rhythm, and diction of their poems show great care and skill. In the opinion of Mao Tun their poems have a perfection of form but so scanty a content as to amount to almost nothing. Be that as it may their poems did have a certain amount of influence on the work of their contemporaries. Later their works deteriorated to slavish imitation of the forms of the poems written by bourgeois poets of the West. They wrote sonnets and other forms of Western poetry which were form for the sake of form with little or no content. Bourgeois poets resort to elaborate form to conceal their poverty of thought and lack of real feeling. This has often happened in the history of literature and is characteristic of the art of all declining classes.

Shen Tsung-wen, the other representative of the Crescent group, was a prolific writer. More than thirty collections of his short stories have been published. In his works he deals with a wide range of subjects. His characters include soldiers, peasants, landlords, gentlemen, minority nationals, and so forth. But though his range of characters is great their delineation is poor.

They do not seem like real people; they are like puppets, mere figments of the writer's imagination.

The works of Shen Tsung-wen show very clearly his political stand and outlook on life. He describes social life from the standpoint of the bourgeoisie and feudal landlords. He is too subjective to know what is really beautiful and what really ugly, what is really good and what really bad. He frequently distorts reality and truth. The characters of his works have no resemblance to real people — they have no class character. They are the products of his imagination — they are what he, with his bourgeois and landlord outlook, thought they should be.

In the realm of the declining bourgeois literature, there were at this time, in addition to the Crescent group, the Symbolists and the Modern school.

Symbolism in literature first appeared in France as the product of the declining period of capitalism. The Symbolists were believers in aestheticism and in the theory of art for art's sake. In China the Symbolists, however, held similar views to these of the members of the Crescent group.

The first Chinese writer to write symbolist poetry was Li Chin-fa, a returned student from France. In 1925 he published a volume of his works entitled *Light Rain*. Commenting on his works Chu Tzu-ching, a well-known literary critic, said: "His poems follow no definite rules. The meaning of the sentences, if taken separately, is clear enough. But taken as a whole his poems are hard nuts to crack." This is a correct description of Li Chin-fa's works.

The Crescent group disappeared in about 1931. Then came the Modern school. The works of the members of the Modern school were usually carried by the journal *Modern Times*. Their general tone of aestheticism was similar to that of the works of the members of the Crescent group and the Symbolists. A typical writer of the Modern school was Tai Wang-shu, whose poems are included in *Recollections* and other collections.

"I have tried to make a pair of shoes that would fit my own feet," Tai Wang-shu said in commenting on his own poetical works. It was in France that he found a pattern for his "shoes." "Neither to hide nor to reveal oneself" — this was the "pattern" of his "shoes" and the keynote of his symbolist poems. His works differed, however, in one respect from those of Li Chin-fa; for whereas Li Chin-fa's poems are abstruse in the extreme Tai Wang-shu's are more easily understood though they show a deep sense of melancholy.

CHAPTER NINE

MAO TUN AND THE REVOLUTIONARY WRITERS OF THE PERIOD OF THE LEAGUE OF LEFT-WING WRITERS

Section 1. Mao Tun and His Literary Works

(1) Earlier Novels and Short Stories

Mao Tun is the pen-name of Shen Yen-ping.[1] He began his literary career around the time of the May 4 Movement, as the editor of *The Short Story Monthly,* and literary critic. After the May 30 Movement he took part in actual revolutionary work. His first novel written after the failure of the First Revolutionary Civil War was a trilogy entitled *The Canker — Disillusion, Vacillation,* and *The Search.* With regard to these three works, Mao Tun had this to say:

> They represent three stages in the mental development of a young man under the impact of the great tide of revolution: (1) excitement and enthusiasm on the eve of revolution and their disappearance when

---

[1] Shen Yen-ping was born in Tunghsiang, Chekiang Province, in 1896. He is now Chairman of the Union of Chinese Writers and the Minister of Culture.

revolution actually comes; (2) vacillation at the time when revolution is in full swing; and (3) a consequent feeling of isolation, which gives rise to a desire for new adventures.

Speaking of the shortcomings of the above-mentioned three works Mao Tun made the following analysis:

> In *Disillusion* and *Vacillation* my observation and analysis of the revolutionary situation were incorrect in some respects. My outlook on the future of the revolution was pessimistic. In *The Search*, my analysis of the state of mind of the petty-bourgeois intellectuals of the period following the failure of the Great Revolution[1] was one-sided. I laid too much emphasis on their pessimism, scepticism and despondency, and did not criticize these faults sufficiently strongly. My state of mind during the time I was writing these three novels was one of pessimism and dejection. This was one of the main reasons why I was unable to draw any positive characters. . . . Didn't I come across any positive characters among my acquaintances of various walks of life during the period of 1925-27? Yes, I certainly did. It was my own pessimism and dejection that made me unaware of the existence and the trend of activity of these people. An author's own thoughts and feelings are often the decisive factors in his choice of themes and characters from real life. This is a rule the truth of which I did not see at first. Later when I understood it and repented of my error it was already over a year since the publication of *The Search*.[2]

---

1. That is, the First Revolutionary Civil War from 1924 to 1927.
2. The author's preface to *Selected Works of Mao Tun*.

But looking at them against their historical background these three novels, for all their defects, did reflect and expose the erroneous ideas of a section of the petty-bourgeois intellectuals of that period as well as their character, which was determined by their ideas, and made appropriate criticisms of them. In this respect these works are not without historical significance.

After the publication of the trilogy Mao Tun wrote the long novel *Rainbow*; the two shorter novels *Three Companions* and *The Road*; *Midnight*, a long novel and a masterpiece of revolutionary literature which created a furore when it was published in 1932; and many short stories.

Generally speaking Mao Tun's short stories were written from a revolutionary standpoint. They reflected real conditions and their materials were drawn from a wide range of facts. Among the scenes described are the miseries and struggles of the peasants of economically ruined villages; the life of the lower middle class and the merchants in the big and small cities under the economic control of the imperialists; pessimistic government clerks who lived from hand to mouth; young men and women muddling through life; and the dregs of society. As the author had rich experience, a profound observation of life and a conscientious attitude towards his profession the quality of these short stories was very high, in fact, better than those of most of his contemporaries. The short stories "Spring Silkworms," "Autumn Harvest," "Winter Ruin," and "The Shop of the Lin Family"[1] were all excellent whether judged by their content, style or technique.

---

[1] These four stories were included in the selection of Mao Tun's short stories published under the title *Spring Silkworms and Other Stories* by the Foreign Languages Press in 1956.

(2) "Midnight"

Mao Tun's *Midnight* is a masterpiece of revolutionary literature in modern China.

Midnight was completed in 1932, two years after the formation of the League of Left-Wing Writers of which he was a member. The publication of *Midnight* gave prestige to the league. This was a thing of great political significance at that time.

Mao Tun, when speaking of the motives which impelled him to write *Midnight,* has this to say:

> In the spring of 1930 Shanghai began to feel the repercussions of the world depression. . . . I decided that my novel should deal with three aspects of the current situation: (1) how Chinese industrialists, groaning under foreign economic aggression, were hindered on the one hand by the feudal forces and threatened on the other by the control of the money-market by comprador-capitalists, and how they tried to save themselves by employing even more brutal methods and intensifying their exploitation of the working class; (2) how, as a result, the working class was obliged to put up a fierce resistance; and (3) how the national capitalists, at enmity alike with the Communist Party and the people as a whole, were finally reduced to the only alternative of capitulating to the compradors (the tools of the imperialists), or becoming compradors themselves.
>
> A novel of such content, of course, would offer scope for dealing with quite a number of problems, but I decided to restrict myself to a refutation of the Trotskyist fallacy. I would use my facts to prove that

China, far from becoming a capitalist country, was being reduced to the status of a colony under the pressure of imperialism. There were a number of people among China's bourgeoisie, it is true, who had much in common with the old French bourgeoisie; nevertheless the China of 1930, unlike eighteenth-century France, was a semi-colony, which meant that the outlook for China's bourgeoisie was particularly bleak — it was, in fact, utterly hopeless. Such were the circumstances which gave rise to the attitude of vacillation in the national bourgeoisie. I intended also to refute some of the fanciful theories advanced by bourgeois scholars in those days. Typical of these theories was the following: China's bourgeoisie could save itself — by which they meant developing industry and setting up a bourgeois regime — by opposing the national, democratic revolutionary movement led by the Communist Party and at the same time opposing feudalism and comprador-capitalism. As it turned out, Chinese capitalists like Wu Sun-fu, who opposed both the working class and the national, democratic revolution led by the workers' party, were left with no alternative but to become compradors themselves.[1]

As the author has said in his postscript to *Midnight,* it was certainly "an attempt to describe Chinese society at large." Shanghai, China's economic centre at that time and a typical semi-colonial and semi-feudal city, is the background of his novel. The chief character is Wu Sun-fu, a national capitalist and the owner of a silk mill who is an able man with the ambition of building up

[1] Mao Tun, *Midnight,* Foreign Languages Press, Peking, 1957, pp. 6-7.

China's national industry. The story woven around this character is a complicated one fully reflecting the contradictions of the time. Among the things described are the economically ruined countryside and peasant uprisings, the decline of national industry under the pressure of imperialist economic aggression, the capitalist exploitation of the workers, the workers' protests and strikes, the all-powerful stock exchange, the life and quarrels of the families of the capitalists, and so forth. The characters include national capitalists, comprador-capitalists who are the brokers of the American imperialists, Communists leading the workers' movements, lackeys who organize "yellow" trade unions for the capitalists, die-hards of the feudal society, loafing intellectuals of the petty bourgeoisie, women of the bourgeoisie, and workers and peasants. In all, *Midnight,* with its skilful weaving of all these characters and scenes into one long, complicated story, was the first novel of its kind in the history of Chinese literature.

Through these many big, contradictory, and complex events and characters, the author succeeded in realizing his plan. He drives home one important truth and that is that the imperialists, to save themselves from collapse, strengthen their hold on semi-colonial countries, make them more and more colonial, and hold them back from taking the road to capitalism. For this reason the national industry of semi-colonial and semi-feudal China was not only unable to develop but had to accept imperialist control and suffer imperialist encroachment. To save themselves from ruin the national capitalists had to increase their exploitation of the workers on the one hand and compromise with the feudal forces, give way to the imperialists, and act as compradors on the other. This is why Wu Sun-fu, the able national capitalist in *Midnight,* eventually had to give in to Chao Po-tao, the broker of the American imperialists. The author not only forcibly refuted the Trotskyists' erroneous theory that China would develop along the path of capitalism but also blew high the dream of the intellectuals of the middle and upper strata who had forgotten that China's chief enemy was the imperialists and who vainly hoped that China would develop her national industry, take the path of capitalism as did the European and American countries, and become strong and wealthy. The author discusses the above-mentioned problems with great literary skill, and it is thanks to this skill that he is able to express his views so vividly and concretely, and convince his readers more effectively than many another author using other forms of writing. *Midnight* is precisely what the revolutionary struggle of those days required, that is, a book which would propagate revolutionary ideas, educate people, and push forward the revolutionary movement. This the author achieved, and herein lies the great historical significance of the novel.

The author also succeeded in showing the vacillating, comprador, and reactionary character of the national bourgeoisie, that the main strength of China's revolution was the workers and peasants led by the Communist Party, and that it was only the workers and peasants who could resolutely fulfil the task of fighting against imperialism and feudalism. He gave a clear picture of the future of China's revolution and, to a certain extent, encouraged revolutionary sentiments among his readers.

His third achievement lay in his delineation of certain typical characters like Wu Sun-fu, the national capitalist, Chao Po-tao, the comprador, and their associates. He drew a vivid picture of one of the aspects of Shanghai society. In this he has made a great contribution to modern Chinese literature.

But *Midnight* also has shortcomings which may be best summarized in the author's own words. This was what he said in his preface to the *Selected Works of Mao Tun,* published in 1952:

> This novel deals with three kinds of men: comprador-capitalists, reactionary industrial capitalists, and revolutionaries and workers. My knowledge of the first two was derived from first-hand experience while that of the latter was derived from indirect experience, being taken either from first-hand observers or other indirect sources. For this reason my description of the comprador financial capitalists and of the reactionary industrial capitalists is fairly lively and faithful while that of the revolutionaries and the workers is less satisfactory. The greatest shortcomings of the novel are, however, the following: (1) Although it was my aim to analyse and criticize the revolutionary work done in the city neither the analysis nor the criticism was sufficiently thorough. (2) The novel does not reflect the entire revolutionary situation of the time. It was my intention to give a comprehensive picture of the revolutionary situation of the time through a comparison of the conditions in the countryside, where the revolutionary forces were developing vigorously, and those in the cities, where the strength of the enemy was concentrated and hence greater, so as to promote optimism with regard to the future of the revolution. This was why in Chapter Four of the novel I described the taking of a town by the revolutionary forces in

the countryside. This was intended to be the beginning of a theme to be further developed. But the plan was too big and it was beyond my ability to carry it out at that time. It had to be abandoned when I reached the latter half of the novel. Meanwhile I was unable to persuade myself to strike out Chapter Four to which I had taken a fancy. It was retained but became rather isolated. The worst thing is not, however, that in failing to do what I had planned I warped the organic structure of the book as a whole but that I failed to give a complete picture of the revolutionary situation in the country as a whole. The writing of *Midnight* was a great lesson to me. As we were born and bred in the old society our powers of observation are enough to enable us to describe the men and things in that society. But to faithfully describe the workers and their struggles the first thing one must do is to live among them. Otherwise no matter how rich and good the materials one draws from indirect sources, one cannot write a realistic and vivid account of the actual people and events.

Section 2. Various Sides of Social Life Reflected in the Novel

With the formation of the League of Left-Wing Writers and under the patronage and direction of Lu Hsun revolutionary literature soon became the dominant force in the literary world and socialist realism in literary writing also gained further ground. Lu Hsun's essay, "Thoughts on the League of Left-Wing Writers," is in fact an introduction to the method of writing according to the principles of socialist realism. In this essay he emphasizes the importance of the task of bringing up "a host of new fighters."[1] He himself made great efforts towards the fulfilment of this task, spending almost half of his time in teaching young writers how to write, discussing the problems of writing with them, corresponding with them, and polishing their manuscripts. Under his patronage and direction a large number of new revolutionary writers appeared during the period from about 1930 to the outbreak of the War of Resistance to Japanese Aggression. Although their works were not entirely socialist-realist in character they showed an increasing tendency towards socialist realism and the number of readable works produced during this period was greater than that of any previous one.

The more outstanding revolutionary writers of this period, so far as the novelists are concerned, were Chang Tien-yi, Yeh Tzu, and Hsiao Hung.

(1) Novels by Chang Tien-yi

Chang Tien-yi's[2] first work, *The Three-and-a-Half-Day Dream,* was published in 1929. In 1930 he wrote *From Hollowness to Substantiality* and in 1931 *Twenty-one.* His works published after 1931 include the following: *Bees, Removal, Diary of Ghost Land, A Year, In the City, "Chingming" Festival, Wan Jen-yo, Counter-Attack, Pulse of Time, Three Brothers, Reunion,* and *Spring Breeze.* He also wrote books of juvenile literature, like

[1] Lu Hsun, *Selected Works,* Vol. III, p. 96.

[2] Chang Tien-yi, born in 1906 in Nanking, is the editor-in-chief of *People's Literature,* a monthly.

A Strange Place, The Bald King and *Stories of the Rain Forest.*

During the period 1929-31 when the stereotyped revolution-plus-love literature was out of fashion and subject to criticism and works of the old realist school could not meet the need of readers as being unable to show clearly the way to revolution, Chang Tien-yi came forward with his new short stories written from the revolutionary standpoint and in a realist way.

Chang Tien-yi's works cover a wide range of themes and an equally wide range of characters. They include petty-bourgeois intellectuals and their gloomy life; snobbish petty citizenry who cringe before their superiors, strut among their subordinates, and will go to all lengths to climb the social ladder; the landlords and bureaucrats, the contradictions between them, and their avarice and exploitation; peasants and soldiers and their noble characteristics.

Besides writing about the dregs and parasites of society Chang Tien-yi also peopled his books with characters he liked, as the children of the revolutionary workers in "After Moving"; the soldiers in *Twenty-one* who, awakened to truth, revolted against the civil war; the soldiers in *The Last Train* and *Road* who stood for resistance to Japanese aggression; the peasants in revolt in *Bees* and *Even the Bodhisattva Cannot Help*; the peasant refugees in *Hatred* who, from class solidarity, reconciled themselves to the soldiers; and Hei Erh and Ta Tsai in *Children,* who opposed the landlords' collection of levies. All these characters and events were dealt with by the method of class analysis.

Needless to say Chang Tien-yi's works are not without defects. Like many other writers his experience of the life of the workers and peasants was insufficient and his description of them is therefore rather abstract. Though a past-master in satirical writing his satires are sometimes not to the point. They are too flippant and even vulgar, thus greatly diminishing their effect. This is particularly evident in the author's earlier works such as *An Unlikely Chivalrous Man.* Another defect in his works is that some of his descriptions are carried to too great a length. There is yet a third defect. Owing to his fondness for humour, he nearly always shows his attitude towards a character as soon as that character appears. The merit of this method of treatment is clarity and straightforwardness. But the writer's lack of reserve robs the reader of the suspended interest. By the time of the War of Resistance, however, the author had already rid his writing of this defect. His two later works, *Mr. Hua Wei* and *New Life*, are clear and straightforward without imparting a sense of superficiality.

In his mastery of the language of the people Chang Tien-yi stood out prominently among his colleagues. He not only possessed a rich vocabulary of popular idiom, but had the ability to use it in such a way that it impresses the reader with enormous freshness. His skilful use of idiom enabled him to draw a vivid word picture of his characters that hold the attention of his readers to the end. This was one of the reasons why his works were so popular.

Chang Tien-yi was also a writer of juvenile literature. He was familiar with the psychology and language of children. He instilled a new and correct ideological content into the works he wrote for youngsters — a bold venture that was ahead of his time. This opened a new path for juvenile literature, in itself no mean achievement.

(2) Novels by Yeh Tzu and Hsiao Hung

Yeh Tzu was born in Yiyang County, Hunan. During the First Revolutionary Civil War he joined the great peasant uprising of Hunan which was led by the Communist Party. The peasant uprisings, in those days, came like a hurricane with such a tremendous force that the reactionaries — landlords, bureaucrats, warlords, and even the imperialists — were dumbfounded and trembled with fear. Many of them found they could no longer stay in their homes and had to flee for safety to the cities. But unfortunately the revolution failed shortly afterwards and the landlords, bureaucrats and warlords regained their power. They came down on the peasants with great cruelty — shooting, beheading, dismembering, burying alive, flogging, torturing and intensifying their exploitation of the peasants. The countryside was swept with an atmosphere of terror. On the surface, the peasant movement was suppressed but the desire for revenge smouldered in their hearts, awaiting the first opportunity to explode.

Yeh Tzu saw all these things with his own eyes. His whole family took part in the struggle. He saw the rapid rise of the peasant movement and its cruel suppression, and he knew the deep hatred concealed in the peasants' heart. All these things weighed on him like a boulder, forcing him to speak out.

It was in this mood of anger and grief that he felt impelled to write the stories collected under the titles of *Harvest*,[1] published in 1935, and *One Night in a Mountain Village* and *Star*, both published in 1936.

[1] "Harvest," one of the stories in this collection, was translated into English and published in *Chinese Literature*, No. 1, 1955.

With the exception of one or two, all these stories deal with the life and class struggle of the peasants. As he had actually lived in the countryside and taken part in the peasants' struggles the scenes he describes were all drawn from personal experience. Speaking of his own works Yeh Tzu said:

> They are nothing but bursts of fiery temper, a pile of facts written with blood and tears, all raw material. Sometimes I feel like jumping into the story myself and picking a fight with someone.

Lu Hsun, in his preface to *Harvest,* has this to say:

> The events described in these six stories seem surprising in time of peace but they are now common occurrences. And precisely because they are common so they are intimately related to us and are therefore very important. The author is still a young man, but he already has as much experience as submissive people could gain in a century's time in time of peace. In a life of constant change it is impossible to expect him to practise "art for art's sake."[1]

And again:

> In the face of the destructive measures (destructive measures taken by the Kuomintang reactionaries against revolutionary literature — *Ed.*) his works gained in maturity. They not only won the warm approval of many young people in China but also of readers of other countries as with "Outside the Electric Wire-Netting" when published in the magazine *New Land*

[1] Lu Hsun, *Collected Works,* Chinese ed., Vol. VI, p. 176.

> *of Literature* under the title of "Uncle Wang." The author fulfilled his immediate task in giving his answer to the oppressors: "Literature is militant!"[1]

In fact, every piece of Yeh Tzu's work may be said to have fulfilled its militant task.

In all the above-mentioned works the author described with great force the avarice, villainy, and malice of the landlords and reactionary military officers. In "Harvest" the peasant Yun Pu suffers from hunger and cold and has to sell his daughter to avoid starvation. In the autumn he gathers a record harvest but all the grain is taken by the landlord. In "Fire" the landlord orders his guards to shoot at the peasants. In "Outside the Electric Wire-Netting" the reactionary police squeeze Uncle Wang of his last dollar and burn his house to the ground. Then they machine-gun the peasants — men, women and children.

But the peasants in Yeh Tzu's novels and short stories were no weaklings. Some of them were well trained in the struggles of the peasant movement led by the Chinese Communist Party. They knew how to defend themselves with their own strength. With such characters the author weaves a moving story of class struggle. At the end of the story "Fire," the peasants storm into the landlord Ho Pa's house and beat him to death. They take over the weapons of the guards. When the reactionary troops come to deal with them they have already gone to the mountains to join the Workers' and Peasants' Red Army, leaving the troops only a stretch of deserted land.

---

[1] *Ibid.*, pp. 176-77.

It was the author's intention to write a book of some length. But he never did it. He did not even complete *Water Chestnut*, a short novel. His life ended in poverty and illness. In 1939 he died in Hunan, his native province.

Hsiao Hung (the pen-name of Chang Nai-ying) was one of the writers who wrote several books around the people's struggle against Japanese imperialism in Northeast China after the Mukden Incident. The novels *Life and Death, Ma Po-lo,* and *The History of the Hulan River* are among her works as well as some short stories, and some essays published under the pen-name of Chiao Yin.

Life and Death deals with the wretched life of the peasants in a village near Harbin. After the fall of Northeast China the Japanese invaders fall on them, killing and raping. In their flight from the village, which is made under conditions of great hardship, they come to realize that resistance is their only way out. Eventually all of them — kind-hearted and honest people, old women, young widows, an old man known for his "good conscience," and even Erh Li Pan, a peasant who knows little beyond tending his goat — brace themselves and join the war of national defence. In his preface to the book Lu Hsun says:

> This is of course only a series of sketches. Her descriptions of events and scenes are better than her delineations of character. But the description of the northern people's firm resolution in life and their struggle against death are really good and show the author's keen observation and unusual skill in handling her themes. It is this that gives beauty and

freshness to the story she writes. The spirit of her works is sound.[1]

In *Ma Po-lo* and *The History of the Hulan River,* her later works, there is less vigour in her writing: her fighting spirit gives way to melancholy. This was due partly to her narrow contact with life and partly to unsound petty-bourgeois thoughts and feelings which frequently pushed her into an abyss of despondency. Prolonged depression robbed her of her health. She died in Hongkong in 1942.

Section 3. Revolutionary Poetry and Drama Movements During the Period of the League of Left-Wing Writers

(1) Members of the China Poetry Society and Other Poets

In 1930, after the formation of the League of Left-Wing Writers the Proletarian Poetry Society was formed, with the promotion of revolutionary literature as its aim. In September 1932 the China Poetry Society was formed in Shanghai under the sponsorship of the League of Left-Wing Writers. Among its founders were Mu Mu-tien, Pu Feng, and Jen Chun. The aims of the society were set forth as follows:

In China, a semi-colonial country, everything is bathed in a rainstorm. A great deal of material for poems and songs is waiting to be gathered and ex-

[1] *Ibid.*, p. 325.

> pressed. But China's poetical circles are sunk in silence. Some of the poets clamour for Westernization while some are intoxicated by the beauty of poetry on such themes as balmy breezes, flowers, snow, and moonlight. . . . To write poems which have absolutely nothing to do with the life of the vast masses does not coincide with this great era of ours.[1]

The last two sentences were evidently directed at the decadent bourgeois poets, members of the Crescent and Modern groups. The China Poetry Society showed a militant spirit from the very beginning of its existence.

After its formation the China Poetry Society expanded rapidly. Apart from the central organization in Shanghai, which did everything to increase its membership, branch societies were formed in Canton, Peking, Tsingtao, and Amoy, each one with a large membership. Besides its own journal the society also edited supplements in newspapers. Later it even had a branch among the Chinese students in Japan, which published *Poetical Life* in Tokyo. In short, in promoting the movement of revolutionary poetry the China Poetry Society performed a useful service indeed.

The organ of the China Poetry Society was *New Poetry,* published every ten days. It made its first appearance in February 1933.

The aim of the society was to make poetry an art of the people. As writers of popular poetry always write from a revolutionary standpoint and follow the principle of realism the members of the society wrote with a clear purpose. They were not interested in such themes as light breezes, flowers, snow and moonlight. They were

---

[1] Jen Chun, "About the China Poetry Society."

interested in social conditions, in the life of the people. Poetry, to be popular, must be clear and easily understood. Its form should be one that is suited to its content. The test of the popular character of a poem is whether or not it can be easily recited and readily appreciated by the people. Accordingly members of the society adopted, though not without some reservations, the form of folk songs, ballads, and popular and nursery rhymes, using these forms to write many poems and songs on entirely new themes. The following are a few examples: Shih Ling's *The New Cowherd's Song*; the late Nieh Erh's *Song of the Longshoremen, Song of the Brick Makers,* and *Song of the Newsboy.* They also wrote many poems with a natural, flowing rhythm that is well suited to declamation. These poems have a style entirely different from that of the works of the Crescent and Modern groups. Poets of the China Poetry Society put forward the slogan: "Make poetry read like folk songs," and published a special number of "folk songs" in *New Poetry.* To increase the propagandist effect of the new poetry they paid special attention to the art of recitation.

In 1935, in line with the political situation of the time, the China Poetry Society put forward the slogan "Write national-defence poetry!" It published a big volume of "national-defence" poetry as well as *The Library of National-Defence Poetry* and many books on the principles and theory of such poetry.

Tsang Keh-chia was another poet of this period who aimed to expose the darker side of society in his poems though he was not a member of the China Poetry Society. His first collection of poems, *The Brand,* appeared in 1934. Other collections — *The Black Hand of Crime, Canal* and

My Own Portrait — soon followed. During the War of Resistance he published *Life in the Ranks, To the Motherland, Song of the Clay* and *Treasure.* Tsang Keh-chia was so revolted by the conditions of his time that he said he would use his poems to mirror the miserable conditions of the people which he saw with his own eyes. In this he succeeded. He wrote about the life and miseries of the colliers, ricksha pullers, workers and bondmaids. In *The Black Hand of Crime* he describes the miseries of the workers and the evils of religion, which the imperialists used as a tool of aggression. In *Villages, Lantern Festival,* and *Reply to a Guest* he describes the ruination of the countryside. In these poems he exposes and castigates the dark old society. His poems had a stimulating effect on the readers. But owing to the limitations of his mental horizcn he could not speak for the suffering people as if he were one of them. He wrote from the standpoint of a bystander. He showed sympathy but for them had no message — he could not tell them what to do. In his poems of rural life his thoughts linger in the realm of the past, on the countryside as it was in feudal times. He was unable to perceive the main conflict and struggle in the countryside, the conflict and struggle between the peasants and the landlords. There was a certain amount of hope expressed in his works but it was vague. He paid great attention to the form of poetry. The arrangement of the stanzas and the choice of words show that he spent much time in their perfection. Some of his lines have a slickness which shows that he was influenced by the poets of the Crescent group and by traditional Chinese poetry. The excessive attention he paid to the choice of words sometimes gave his poems an air of artificiality.

(2) The Left-Wing Drama Movement and the Movement of National Salvation Drama

In about 1930 Shen Tuan-hsien and Cheng Po-chi organized the Shanghai Art Drama Association under the auspices of the League of Left-Wing Writers. This was the first association to use drama in the cause of the revolution. It staged plays around the theme of the current political situation, for which tickets were sold to workers at reduced rates. The members of the association knew that a few big performances would not serve the purpose of bringing drama to the working people. Performances must be simpler and given regularly. They accordingly organized a mobile drama troupe, which performed to the workers of the power-house and the women textile workers. Meanwhile the Play-Writing Research Association was formed to help the playwrights. One of the plays that was written with this help was *Ah Chen* by Nai Chao and Ping Lu, which described the revolutionary movement in the countryside.

Under the impact of the rising revolutionary movement and guided by the League of Left-Wing Writers, the drama movement in Shanghai made greater progress than elsewhere. The revolutionary drama became the dominant force in dramatic circles and many plays were written reflecting social conditions. Tien Han, among others, wrote *Flood* and *Dance of Fire*. Hung Shen wrote the *Wu Kuei Bridge, Fragrant Rice,* and some others. Ou-yang Yu-chien wrote *Three Families Living Together* and other plays. Hsia Yen (the pen-name of Shen Tuan-hsien) wrote *Under the Eaves of Shanghai.* Besides these plays there were many others written on historical themes. The plays *Thunderstorm* and *Sunrise* by the realist playwright Tsao Yu also appeared at this time.

The League of Left-Wing Dramatists and Stage Workers was formed in 1931, shortly before the Mukden Incident. Members of the league were very active. Besides arranging performances for the workers they wrote many anti-Japanese plays which were staged in various places.

In about 1936, in line with the political situation, members of the dramatic circles took up the slogan "Write plays of national defence!" With an organized effort they wrote many plays having as their themes resistance to Japanese aggression, salvation of the nation, and opposition to the traitors. Members of the dramatic circles also launched a movement for collective work, organizing playwrights to work in collaboration with one another. Sometimes a theme would be proposed and put before interested playwrights who would then study it together. After having arrived at a common understanding of the theme they would then use this as a basis and produce the play by collective work, with one of them doing the actual writing. The achievements made through such collaboration may not have been very outstanding, though many plays were written in this way.

Section 4. The Rise of Reportage and Attempts at Producing Popular Literature

(1) Rise of Reportage Literature

After the formation of the League of Left-Wing Writers great efforts were made to promote reportage as a literary form. In a resolution on the new task of China's proletarian revolutionary literature passed by the Executive Committee of the League in November 1931 it was pointed out that writers "must study and adopt, with discretion, the methods of China's traditional popular literature, the reportage literature of Western Europe, propaganda technique, popular stories published in wall newspapers, and poems for recitation."

Under the patronage and guidance of the League of Left-Wing Writers and inspired by the needs of the revolution, a tremendous amount of reportage appeared which achieved immediate success.

The main characteristic of reportage is that it gives quick information on current events. It is highly journalistic in nature but is different from the news items of newspapers. A piece of reportage is more or less a feature article. It gives vivid word pictures of people and scenes which convey to the reader almost a visual picture of the event and enable him to understand the message the writer wants to put across. The chief aim of reportage is to give timely reflection as well as keen analysis of the constantly changing political and social scene.

Reportage is a versatile and militant form of literature. Readers are anxious to know what is happening here, there, and everywhere. It is the duty of writers to put the facts before them as speedily as possible of all the latest events and point out their significance. Progressive journals also like to publish reportage articles. Reportage literature therefore became immensely popular.

(2) A Wide Coverage

Ever since its formation the League of Left-Wing Writers had paid great attention to seeking out worker and peasant correspondents. They organized activities among workers, shop assistants, students, government employees and intellectuals in the rural areas, with the result that their circle of correspondents was widened to include people in many kinds of occupations. The writings of these correspondents naturally reflected the life of the people around them. Many of these writings were published in *Literary News,* the only literary journal of the time with journalistic leanings.

A year after the founding of the League of Left-Wing Writers the Mukden Incident occurred. This incident, which was a matter of great importance to the Chinese people, acted as a spur on the progress of reportage literature. At that time the patriotic movement of the workers of Shanghai and the students of various places was in full swing. This movement, which was really a struggle against imperialism, occupied a great deal of space in reportage literature. During the "January 28" Incident when the people of Shanghai resisted a Japanese attack many workers and writers came into the war effort. They visited the soldiers at the front, carried out propaganda, and canvassed for subscriptions. The events in this heroic struggle against imperialism demanded quick reporting to the broad reading public. The writers of that time did try to fulfil this task. Even people who did not specialize in literary writing — like Shen Tuan-hsien and Shih Yi — produced a great deal of reportage literature.

Although thanks to the compromising attitude of the reactionary Kuomintang regime China was defeated in the "January 28" battle, the anti-Japanese movement of the Chinese people, under the leadership of the Chinese Communist Party, expanded in both scope and influence among the masses. As a result reportage literature made similar progress. Although the works of reportage literature of this time did not deal directly with events in the battle-line they dealt with the conditions of life of the people in various places, reflecting the calamities brought to the Chinese people by the Japanese imperialists in their frenzied aggression as well as the Chinese people's resistance to and struggle against these calamities. On the whole the authors of these works faithfully described the life of the Chinese people at that time. Most of these works made their first appearance in magazines and newspapers, and were later published as a collection entitled *Living Records* edited by Sun Jui-yu.

In 1935 the reactionary Kuomintang regime and the Japanese imperialists signed the "Ho-Umezu Agreement." The agreement was nothing short of a betrayal of the interests of China, a deed of sale with regard to North China. In August of the same year the Chinese Communist Party published "An Appeal to All Countrymen for Resistance to Japan and Salvation of the Nation," which called upon the people of the whole country to stop the civil war and pool their efforts for resistance to Japanese aggression. This appeal won the immediate support of the people all over the country. In December the students of Peking launched the "December 9" patriotic movement which led to a burst of anti-Japanese activities throughout the country. At that time both the international and domestic situation was exceedingly precarious and marked by fast change. All the patriotic movements, the demand for resistance to Japanese aggression, and the criminal activities of the Japanese invaders and Chinese traitors were reflected in the reportage literature of that time which contained an immense amount of vivid material on these subjects. The articles were carried by magazines — *Popular Life, Life of Reading, Mid-Stream, Light* and the like. Progressive newspapers also devoted a good deal of space to them. Apart from a handful of professional writers most of the authors were students and young people engaged in various occupations.

Among the more popular reportage works of this period was *Bond Labour* by Hsia Yen. This book describes how the Japanese textile factory owners took advantage of the feudal conditions in China to create an inferno on earth. The writer wielded a powerful pen with which he roused his readers' hatred of Japanese imperialism and enhanced their fighting spirit. At the end of the book the writer says: "The coming of dawn is something which cannot be barred." To the readers these were no empty words but something which had real significance.

The *Trilogy of the Top of a Wall* by Pai Wei and *Spring in Taiyuan in 1936* by Sung Chih-ti were also notable works of the early days of reportage.

(3) Attempts at the Production of Popular Literature

The League of Left-Wing Writers also paid attention to the use of the traditional forms of folk literature, like ballads, chantefables, opera scripts and so on, with the idea of adapting them to new needs. The writers held that this was a correct method for revolutionary popular literature.

Quite a few works were produced on the lines of folk literature by members of the left-wing literary circles. The *Crossroads,* a fortnightly, carried many articles of this kind. Unfortunately, the writers of these articles were unable to gain first-hand experience of the life of the workers and peasants, and this reflected itself in their works. The use of the old form of folk literature was therefore never fully developed. This attempt, however, was not without historical importance to the promotion of popular literature or influence on later forms of popular literature.

Chu Chiu-pai and Lu Hsun were among the writers who tried their hand at works of this kind.

After the "January 28" Incident Chu Chiu-pai wrote a long song entitled *Japanese Troops on the March.* It was written in two versions, one in the Shanghai dialect and one in Mandarin, and was very popular at the time. Later he produced two more compositions, one entitled *The Hero's Wise Plan of Surrendering Shanghai,* and the other, *When Paramours Part Company with Each Other in Yangchow.* Both were written in Mandarin and in the chantefable style, and were directed against the reactionary generals of the Kuomintang who retreated from Shanghai without offering any resistance to the Japanese attack. Besides the above he also wrote "The Tune of May," "Sights Seen in the Battle of Shanghai," "The Disgusting X," and other works.

Lu Hsun wrote "Song of Good Things," "Song of the Course of Civics," "Folk Rhymes of Nanking," and some other works. All these pieces were carried by *Crossroads.* "Song of Good Things" describes the disreputable behaviour of the reactionary military officers and government officials of the Kuomintang. The "Song of the Course of Civics" was a satire on the reactionary warlord Ho Chien who issued an order commanding the schools to add to their curriculum a course on civics instilling servile ideas. The "Folk Rhymes of Nanking" caricatures the behaviour of the reactionary Kuomintang officials when they were paying their respects to Sun Yat-sen's Mausoleum.

More urgent tasks forbade Chu Chiu-pai and Lu Hsun to indulge in more of this form of literature. But from these few pieces it is clear that these two outstanding writers laid great emphasis on the importance of the traditional folk literature of China.

CHAPTER TEN

LITERARY WORKS ON THE WAR OF RESISTANCE

Section 1. Reportage, "Street Poetry," "Street Plays" and Popular Literary Works

(1) Reportage in Full Flourish

During the early period of the War of Resistance, reportage experienced a tremendous development. It became the most popular of all literary forms among both the writers and the broad reading public.

This unprecedented development showed itself not only in the number of works produced during this period but in their actual quality. First and foremost, they covered a wider scope of subjects than ever before. Practically all aspects of life were depicted — the heroism of the soldiers at the front; the selfless work of the people in the rear; the anguish and sufferings of the sick and wounded officers and soldiers; the sorrow and hardships of refugees; the sanguinary atrocities of the enemy; the heroic martyrdom and firm resistance of the people in enemy-occupied areas; the cowardice and covetousness of the backward section of the people in the war zones;

the heroism and courage of the progressive masses in the front-lines; the bitter struggles of the people behind the enemy lines; the birth and growth of the armed forces in the enemy's rear; the misrule and the crimes of the secret agents in the areas under Kuomintang control; the free, democratic, happy life, production and construction in the liberated areas; the death-bed struggle of the dregs of society; and the determined forward march of the new-born forces. In a word, all that should be recorded was written in black and white. In addition, reportage improved in presentation as it gained ground. At the outset of the war, reportage was marred by dull and monotonous narration, a documentary style and stereotyped generalizations. As the war continued, however, the writers, the richer for their deeper and wider contacts with life, gained a fuller and deeper understanding of things as they stood. It was on the basis of this understanding that more works flowed from their pens, works which tackled a wider sweep, were more vivid and picturesque.

From 1942 onwards, the reactionary fascist rule and the stalemate at the front combined to lessen the amount of reportage produced in the Kuomintang-controlled areas. It was not until 1944, when the various democratic movements swept the rear areas, that a spate of reportage reflecting these movements appeared.

(2) The "Street Poetry," Declamatory Poem and "Street Play"

Next to reportage, poetry had the most prolific output among the various branches of Chinese literature in this early period of the war. It was found the best form for agitational material to arouse the people's fighting spirit for the War of Resistance. But if poetry was to perform its best service in the course of the anti-aggression propaganda, it was not enough to rest content with quantitative abundance. Particular attention was therefore paid to the question of the popularization of poetry, a question which had come up time and again since the founding of the League of Left-Wing Writers. On the basis of previous researches, attempts were made to further solve the question through creative writing. It was in the course of these researches and writing that "street poetry" and declamatory verse were brought into being.

"Street poetry" originated in Yenan, the capital of the Communist-led Shensi-Kansu-Ningsia Border Region. Meant for the broad mass of people, the "street poetry" consisted of brief and terse verses which took a specific battle or political event as their theme and used straightforward colloquial language easily understandable to the people. In some ways they were similar to a poster but they went further, for they were more concrete and vivid than a poster while their rhyme and rhythm was easy to remember and recite. In short, they possessed all the special features and standards demanded of poetry.

In the Kuomintang-controlled areas the "street poetry," which was sometimes known as "wall poems" or "handbill poems," came up against all sorts of difficulties, with the result that the writers in these areas had to content themselves with merely discussing and studying it. Although some poems after this style did appear, the form, as such, failed to catch on to any great extent.

The declamatory poem, on the other hand, became fairly popular. It was initiated by the China Poetry

Society in 1934 and made further progress after the outbreak of the war. During and after the war, poems were often recited at mass rallies and evening parties. Many poetical bodies organized poetry-reciting meetings. The Northwest Front Service Corps even formed a poetry declamation group which was sent to the front to recite poems among the soldiers.

Poetry declamation, at bottom, was in line with aims of popularizing poetry. But in actual practice, it was far from satisfactory, as in most cases the poems were declaimed among the intellectuals instead of the broad masses of workers and peasants. This was because, apart from the limitations created by the objective conditions, the content, form and the language of these verses had little mass appeal.

The "street play" was a new move in the popularization of drama, which grew out of the "reportage play." The "reportage play" was created by the Chinese Workers' and Peasants' Red Army in Kiangsi Province during the agrarian revolution. It had filled an important role in arousing the Red Army fighters.

On the eve of the War of Resistance the "reportage play" developed into the "street play." After the war broke out, as its presentation was well suited to the taste of the workers and peasants, the "street play" was most extensively used by various front service corps, resistance propaganda groups, national salvation theatrical companies and itinerant theatrical troupes. Of these short plays, the best known was *Put Down Your Whip,* a portrayal of the cruelties of the Japanese imperialists and the sufferings and tribulations of the people in Northeast China which was occupied by the invaders before the outbreak of the War of Resistance in 1937. This play was widely staged on the eve of the War of Resistance. After the war broke out, it was produced on countless occasions, playing a big role in educating the people and rousing them to join the resistance movement.

In the rear areas, there were other dramatic forms akin to the "street play," such as the "tea-house play," "demonstration play" and the "lantern play."

(3) Popular Literary Works

In the early period of the war, a series of periodicals and magazines devoted to popular literary works were published. There were, to name a few, *The Weekly Magazine* and *The People's Magazine* in Hankow, and *Starlight* and *The Five-Day Gazette of Popular Art and Literature* in Chengtu.

During this period, most of the popular literary works took the old forms usually followed by classical operas, *kutze* (story-telling chanted to drum-beats), jingles or *shulaipao* (story-telling to the playing of castanets). Nevertheless, most of the authors failed to fully understand the essentials of popular literature or that the old forms should be accepted critically by making use of everything of value and discarding whatever was worthless. In their mechanical interpretation of the principle of "pouring new wine into old bottles," they simply modelled upon the old forms instead of using what they wanted from them. Some went so far as to write verses on the War of Resistance after the style of some indecent folk ballads, thus vulgarizing the principle of making use of the old forms. The popular literature during this period was, in the main, marked by insufficient depiction of reality, flimsy portrayal of characters and a tendency towards formulism. There were two reasons for this, apart from the lack of understanding of the essentials of popular literature as mentioned above. One was that some authors, thinking it fairly easy to write popular literary works, were not sufficiently conscientious in their approach and sometimes scamped them. The other was that among those who were engaged in the work of popular literature there was a general lack of political understanding and a failure to see the people as the principal motivating force in the War of Resistance. Hence they more often than not depicted China and her enemy through certain battles in a stereotyped, formulistic approach. Despite their shortcomings these literary works with their popular style played a useful part in the early period of the War of Resistance. As time passed, the shortcomings were gradually realized and overcome.

And it was in the course of practice that another question arose and found its solution — the role of local art and literature in promoting popular art and literature. The importance of this became increasingly clear and attracted general attention in the course of constant practice and the anti-Japanese propaganda activities. Mao Tun said:

> Many of my friends have now tried their hand at *kutze* and the repertoires of Peking, Hupeh and Hunan operas with the War of Resistance as their theme, and Kwangtung's debutant poets are also bent on writing

folk ballads in the Cantonese dialect. This is a piece of inspiring news. We should see that such activities spread like wild fire. Those who are engaged in research on folk art and literature should work out plans to turn these writers' efforts to good account, while artists of *kutze,* story-telling and Peking, Hunan, Hupeh and Kwangtung operas should keep in touch and co-operate closely with those writers who are engaged in writing after the old forms. Only when we have done something along these lines can we say we have worked for the War of Resistance.

Afraid that the spread of popular literature might rouse the people to more energetic action against the Japanese aggressors, the reactionary Kuomintang government tried by all means to prevent popular literature from developing, and even banned it. After the fall of Wuhan in 1938, the writing of popular literary works gradually lost ground in the Kuomintang-controlled areas.

Section 2. Literary Works on the Early Period of the War of Resistance

Poetry was in great vogue in the early period of the War of Resistance, when the poets, one and all, plunged themselves into the war with tremendous excitement and enthusiasm, sounding a clarion call for poetical works directed against the alien invaders. A dozen or more poetical magazines were published at that time. The first to appear were *Pioneer* and *Anti-Aircraft Gun* in

Shanghai and *Current Notes* and *Era of Poetry* in Wuhan, to be followed by *Chinese Poetry* in Changsha, *Battle Song* in Kunming, *Chinese Poetical World* and *Vertex* in Kweilin, and others. A spate of poems on the War of Resistance were written by such well-known poets as Kuo Mo-jo, Tsang Keh-chia, Hsiao San (Emi Siao), Ho Chi-fang, Tien Chien, Ke Chung-ping and Yuan Shui-pai, and many other young poets. Available data shows that from the beginning of the War of Resistance to June 1942 over a hundred collections of poetry were published in pamphlet form and a total of over half a million lines was written. Although this period enjoyed an abundance of poetical works, not many could be said to be outstanding. This was particularly true at the very beginning of the war, when by and large they were little more than an enthusiastic call raised on the impulse of the authors' emotions. As the poets lacked a profound experience and observation of life and their works were mostly turned out in a hurry, it is hardly surprising that the poems should be weak in artistic value. As the war went on, progressive poets gained a better understanding of the war and the strength of the people as the main force of the war, and they learned more about life. Calls based on pure enthusiasm no longer satisfied them and they turned out better works, though less in number.

In the field of fiction, very few works appeared in the early period of the war as most of the novelists had turned to reportage. Nevertheless, they also gained a better insight into the significance of the war as it continued, and learned to observe and study all phenomena and questions in the war, whose description called for a deeper form than reportage. By the end of the first year of the war an increasing number of novels on the war were appearing. They dealt with the battles at the front, the differences in outlook between the advanced and the backward, the influence of the War of Resistance on people with backward ideas in bringing about a change of views, and the seamy sides in the rear areas.

Drama registered its greatest achievements during the early period of the war with its one-act plays and "street plays." Most of these call upon the people to fight the invaders and are of an agitational character rather than a serious portrayal. In general, they are far from perfect artistically. With the progress of the war, agitation gave way to deeper reasoning in the field of drama, and multi-act plays appeared in large numbers. They depict the struggle of the soldiers and civilians in the War of Resistance, portray the struggle behind the enemy lines and expose the enemy and traitors in their true colours, and describe the darkness in the Kuomintang-ruled areas, and the progressive side in the War of Resistance. Some of them, based on historical stories, rouse the people to action against the Japanese invaders. Available data shows that 42 multi-act plays were published from the outbreak of the war to the spring of 1941.

Taken as a whole, socialist realism continued to be the main stream in creative writing in the field of poetry, fiction and drama during this period, although the methods employed varied in one way or another. Fired with enthusiasm by the War of Resistance, many middle-of-the-road writers also wrote a series of patriotic and realistic works. Many of these writers — namely Tien Chien and Ke Chung-ping, the poets, Tung Ping and Ai Wu, the novelists, and Hsia Yen, the playwright — registered notable achievements and exerted a relatively wide influence in the period under review.

(1) The Poems of Tien Chien and Ke Chung-ping

Tien Chien, with his vigorous and militant poems and unique style, was an outstanding figure in China's poetry circles between 1935 and 1936. This was on the eve of the War of Resistance, when the call-to-arms against Japanese aggression was resounding throughout the country and the entire nation had become caught up in the sole object of launching a revolutionary war for national liberation at the earliest possible date. With the exception of the works by members of the China Poetry Society and a few progressive poets, the poems of the time in general lagged behind the demands of the political situation and the anti-Japanese sentiments of the people. Tien Chien's poems, bursting with militancy and breaking through the old forms, came as a tremendous inspiration to the Chinese poetical world and aroused widespread interest.

From then on, Tien Chien published a series of collections of his poems under the titles of *Before Dawn, Chinese Pastoral, Stories of the Chinese Countryside, To the Fighters, Poems of the War of Resistance, Biography of a Cart Driver* and *Jung Kuan-hsiu.* From the very outset his poems were remarkable for their healthy sentiments, militancy and lack of ostentation. They cover a wide range of subjects, from the heroic struggle of the people and the farms and forests of the motherland in wartime to the atrocities of the enemy. His rural vignettes — lush fields of maize, golden cascades of rapeseed and turbulent rivers . . . provide a moving background to his picture of the motherland in plight.

His poems of the pre-war period and the early period of the war bear all the hallmarks of being the outcome of a volcanic outburst of emotion. Moreover, as the poet had failed to plumb life and social reality to their depths, the results are somewhat superficial. After the outbreak of the war, the poet went to the front and later to Yenan. During this period, his poems went a step further and showed that the poet had stepped out of his personal realm into the broad stream of life of the people. Characters of flesh and blood appeared in his poems — real people and real fighters.

But although the poet did step into the realm of the life of the people after his arrival in Yenan, he did not do so deeply enough. His handling of the various phenomena of life was inadequate and fragmentary, and there was still more than a vestige of his old way of presenting things on the impulse of the moment. This weakened his handling of his characters.

In spite of all this, it was always the poet's intention to integrate his poems with the tasks of the revolutionary struggle and, in fact, as shown by his "street poems," he acted up to it firmly. These poems were a real contribution to the movement. Furthermore, there is little trace in Tien Chien's poems of the sentimentality and melancholy peculiar to petty-bourgeois intellectuals. This is particularly praiseworthy when viewed against the circumstances of those days.

Now about Ke Chung-ping. During the later period of the Creation Society Ke Chung-ping wrote a series of poems, most of which appeared in the two collections, *The Mountains of Wind and Fire* and *Nocturnal Songs at the Seaside*. Then he laid down his pen for a long time, and only took it up again in Yenan after the outbreak of the war. This time, instead of giving vent to his personal feelings, his poems were brimful of confidence in the future of the revolution. This was the dominant characteristic of his poems in this period. Even *To My Lover* is filled with such an optimistic spirit.

In 1938, Ke Chung-ping turned out two full-length narrative poems, *The Self-Defence Corps in the Border Regions* and *The Railwaymen's Sabotage Team on the Peking-Hankow Line.* The first deals with the struggles against the traitors and Trotskyites waged by the militiamen in the border regions. The story, which to quote from the poet's preface to the poem, "was heard at the First Workers' Representative Conference of the Border Regions," centres around the daring deeds of Platoon Leader Li, the sentinel Han Wa and a few other militiamen. The high political vigilance of the people in the border regions and their fiery hatred of the traitors and Trotskyites are crystallized in these characters. The poem succeeds in conveying the impression that with such heroic militiamen the border regions could be an invulnerable fortress which neither the Japanese and puppet regime, nor the Kuomintang reactionaries could ever destroy no matter what plots or schemes they resorted to. They fortified the reader's determination and confidence in the defence of the border regions.

Originally the poet planned to write *The Railwaymen's Sabotage Team on the Peking-Hankow Line* in five parts, but somehow he finished only one and never completed the others. As it stands, the poem deserves high commendation as the first narrative poem to depict the organized struggle of workers, an attempt unprecedented in the history of Chinese poetry. The poet's sincere description of the workers and their political and ideological outlook adds lustre to the poem.

(2) The Novels of Tung Ping and Ai Wu

Tung Ping was the most successful of all the novelists whose works centred on the battle front during the early period of the war.

A native of Kwangtung Province, Tung Ping took part in the Uprising of Haifeng and Lufeng[1] while yet a child. Later he fled to Hongkong where he led a vagrant life, picking up odd jobs as a fisherman and street hawker. When the Japanese army made their surprise attack on Shanghai on January 28, 1932, he rushed to Shanghai to take part in the fight against the invaders. Later, he returned to Hongkong to participate in national-salvation activities, which involved making a trip to Japan. After the outbreak of the nation-wide War of Resistance, he joined the Communist-led New Fourth Army and died in action in northern Kiangsu in 1941. His works include *Night in Changhsia City, The Sorrowful Meileng City, Conflagration, The Giver, The Seventh Company, March Towards the Enemy's Rear* and *At the Foot of the Maoshan Mountains,* all collections of short stories.

Tung Ping began writing in about 1931. His first story, *The Messenger*, which was published in *Literature Monthly*, organ of the League of Left-Wing Writers, deals with the changes in the peasants' outlook during the agrarian struggle of the Uprising of Haifeng and Lufeng. It aroused great attention among the literary circles when it first came out for its straightforward style and powerful portrayal. He wrote some even more successful works

---

[1] This was a peasants' uprising in Haifeng and Lufeng Counties, Kwangtung Province, which began on October 30, 1927. It was led by the outstanding peasant leader Peng Pai (1895-1929), a member of the Chinese Communist Party.

after the outbreak of the War of Resistance, in which he created a group of anti-Japanese heroes. These stories, with their anti-Japanese sentiments and tang of life, convey the bursting vitality and determination of the author himself.

It is a pity that, gifted as he was, Tung Ping failed to see the anti-Japanese war in its true light. He did not see the broad mass of people led by the Chinese Communist Party as the factor making for the victory of the War of Resistance nor did he see the Kuomintang reactionaries' declarations of resistance as merely a matter of lip-service.

However, this weakness in his ideological outlook and perceptive faculties was not confined to him alone. It was one which was quite common among the writers of his day. Moreover, Tung Ping never failed to hold his reader's attention with his rich combat experience, his determination, vitality, homeliness, freshness and his superb combination of narrative and lyricism.

Of all those in the period under review who specialized in stories about the wartime life of the people in the rear areas, the most outstanding were Ai Wu and Sha Ting. A brief account of Sha Ting and his works will be given in the next section.

Prior to the war, Ai Wu published several collections of short stories under the titles of *A Night in South China*, *Travels in the South* and *Night Scene*. He first came into the public eye with his stories on the spontaneous struggle against imperialism waged by the Burmese people. He also wrote about peasants, soldiers and sedan-chair carriers. During the War of Resistance, he made bigger strides and wrote many short stories on the vast scene of life in the rear areas, two short novels entitled *Spring* and *Autumn Harvest,* and a full-length novel published after V-J Day under the title *A Mountain Region.*

Generally speaking, Ai Wu took a revolutionary stand in his writing and his themes and characters were analysed and handled from the revolutionary point of view.

(3) The Plays of Hsia Yen

Hsia Yen,[1] whose real name is Shen Tuan-hsien, came into the limelight on the eve of the War of Resistance with his plays *Sai Chin-hua, The Soul of Freedom* and *Under the Eaves of Shanghai.*

From the outbreak of the war to V-J Day, he turned out seven multi-act plays. Among these, *Within One Year, Li Li Tsao* and *Song of the Land of Rivers* describe various aspects of wartime life, including the struggle waged by the people against the Japanese; *Fortress of the Heart* deals with the unswerving struggle against the Japanese and their Chinese collaborators waged by the intellectuals behind the enemy lines; *City of Sorrow* lays bare the seamy sides in the Kuomintang-controlled areas and the areas behind the enemy lines, and *The Germ of Fascism* the incompatible contradictions between fascism and science; and *The Fragrant Grass and the End of the Horizon* is a portrayal of the progressive intellectuals and their love affairs in the rear areas.

These plays were in the main written against the background of the political struggles in the period under review and played a useful political role.

---

[1] Hsia Yen, born in Hangchow in 1900, is Vice-Minister of Culture.

Section 3. Literary Works Exposing the Kuomintang in the Later Period of the War and After V-J Day

During the latter part of the War of Resistance and after the surrender of the Japanese invaders, the Chiang Kai-shek reactionary government stepped up its fascist rule. White terror reigned in the areas under the Kuomintang control. Faced with this high-handed policy the writers and artists, with few exceptions, remained at their posts and stuck to the fight against the Japanese and for democracy.

Some of the writers carried on and enriched the tradition of the revolutionary literature, exposing the dark, fascist rule of the Kuomintang with the same enthusiasm with which they wrote about the War of Resistance during its early period. There were, for instance, *Rustic Songs* by Ma Fan-to, *Decay* and *Before and After the "Chingming" Festival* by Mao Tun, *Gold Rush, The Pent-Up Beasts* and *The Return* by Sha Ting, *Chu Yuan* by Kuo Mo-jo, and *The Picture of Promotion in Officialdom* by Chen Pai-chen.

Again, although some writers failed to fathom out the main contradictions or struggles of the time, they still adhered to the tradition of realism in their works on the War of Resistance and their historical stories. These works did to some extent reflect the political situation at that time or hold it up to ridicule, nevertheless they exerted less political influence than others. They include *Four Generations Live Together* by Lao Sheh, and a number of historical plays.

In general, in the latter part of the War of Resistance and after V-J Day the socialist trend was still the main stream in creative writing in the Kuomintang-controlled areas, though not all the works were written in the light of socialist realism. But these last represented only a minor tributary or even adverse currents, and had little influence.

(1) The Poems of Ma Fan-to

Rustic Songs by Ma Fan-to (the pen-name of Yuan Shui-pai) reflects the difficult life of the ordinary people in the Kuomintang-controlled areas from 1944 to the post-war period, and lashes out bitterly at the monstrous crimes committed by the Kuomintang government in selling out China and wreaking havoc among the people, and at the American imperialists for supporting the reactionary Kuomintang government's civil war and for invading China.

In 1944 the Japanese invaders penetrated deep into Kweichow Province in an all-out offensive, the Kuomintang troops were beating successive retreats, the fascist rule was being stepped up and the patriotic and democratic movement was soaring to new heights in the rear areas. Ma Fan-to's verses reflected the political situation of the day and voiced the people's joy and anger, love and hatred, and therefore won their immediate approval. They were passed from mouth to mouth in the Kuomintang-controlled areas.

The poet chose the title *Rustic Songs* because they were written after the style of folk ballads, children's songs and even popular rhymes of the day, and in colloquial language. They went over very well, whether read or sung, and gained wide circulation.

But the poet was after all a petty-bourgeois intellectual. Although he tried to keep in contact with the people and had in fact made certain achievements in this respect, still his contacts were too slight. He was never able to think and feel precisely as the man-in-the-street, or field, as the case may be. He did not have a thorough understanding of the reactionary character of the Kuomintang rule, nor did he fully estimate the revolutionary forces of the people.

(2) The Novels of Sha Ting and Mao Tun

Sha Ting began his writing career in 1931. By the eve of the anti-Japanese war he had published three collections of short stories entitled *The Navigation Line, Mud Cake* and *Difficulties,* which were followed by a series of stories written after the outbreak of the war, like *General H at the Front, Notes from the Enemy's Rear, The Magnet,*[1] *Strange Journey, Gold Rush, The Pent-Up Beasts* and *The Return.*

Sha Ting had a rich knowledge of China's rural areas, especially his native village in Szechuan Province where he lived for a long time. With few exceptions, his stories deal with rural life — the peasants, landlords and intellectuals of peasant origin, and the village officials, gentry and racketeers, and other representatives of the reactionary regime in the countryside.

Sha Ting's stories written before the war were on the whole handled from the revolutionary standpoint and in a realistic way. They painted a penetrating picture of

[1] An English version of this story was published in *Chinese Literature,* No. 2, 1957.

the tragic life of the man behind the plough and the cruelties of the landlords and bad gentry. No one could read his works without feeling the urge to rise and make short shrift of such a blood-thirsty system and such blood-suckers. He was, and still is, a conscientious and meticulous writer so that his stories of the pre-war period, though few in number, stand to this day.

During the period of the War of Resistance, Sha Ting won even greater successes. He still wrote of the countryside, but covered a broader scope of life and penetrated more deeply beneath the surface. His full-length novels *Gold Rush, The Pent-Up Beasts* and *The Return* and short stories "The Pastime of a Village Official" and "At the Fragrant Tea-House," with their well-knit structures, rank among the best works on the War of Resistance.

Gold Rush, The Pent-Up Beasts and *The Return* were the outcome of painstaking efforts during and after the war. Though in content and message these books may fall short of perfection, they are on the whole successful. Furthermore, they are handled with a delicate touch, penetratingly and conscientiously, in terse and expressive Szechuan dialect that adds to their colour.

During the War of Resistance Mao Tun turned out three full-length novels — *Stories of the First Stage, Frosted Leaves As Red As Flowers in Spring* and *Decay.* The second deals with the mentality and life of the gentry of a city during the early twenties, while the others are set against the background of the war.

The *Stories of the First Stage*, published in 1945, first appeared in instalments in the *Li Pao* of Hongkong, under the title of *Whither To?* In his postscript the author said that it was a popular novel written with an eye on the readers in Hongkong, and that he had tried to keep it popular in form, although he had fashioned the content to his own pattern. What he said of the content was true, but as to form, he maintained his intention in the first few sections, but swung back to his usual style as the story unfolded. In this story, Mao Tun attempted to depict the society of Shanghai in all its aspects during the three months following Japan's attack on the city on August 13, 1937. It was precisely because he attempted too wide a sweep and covered too many questions that his characters appear shallow and too loosely related to each other. In spite of this, the novel paints a fairly comprehensive canvas of a number of people in wartime Shanghai and can still be considered as an excellent work in terms of reportage.

Decay is an exposure of, and denunciation against, the sanguinary crimes of the secret agents — the backbone of the fascist rule of the Chiang Kai-shek clique. It shows how Chao Hui-ming, the heroine, because of a false step, falls into the abyss of a secret agents' organization, an experience which "none can suffer except the most ignoble, shameless and cruel." During the War of Resistance, the Chiang Kai-shek clique strengthened their rule of secret agents as never before. Through these secret agents they worked hand in glove with the Japanese and the puppet regime, in their attempt to surrender to the enemy. On the other hand, in dealing with the Communists and patriots, they resorted to all kinds of methods like trailing, spying, arrest, torture and murder. At the same time, they used the dirtiest methods of trapping young people into joining the secret organizations. Once entangled, one secret agent was always spied on by another who, in turn, was spied on by another, so that it was absolutely impossible for the victim to free himself from their toils. Chao Hui-ming was one of the many who were beguiled into becoming a secret agent, and through her the author gives a graphic and profound picture of the monstrous crimes of these bloodstained institutions, a hell on earth in the fullest sense of the phrase.

(3) The Plays of Kuo Mo-jo and Chen Pai-chen

Between 1941 and 1943, Kuo Mo-jo turned out five plays based on historical stories, namely *Chu Yuan,*[1] *Kao Chien-li, The Tiger Tally, The Peacock's Gall* and *Nan Kuan Tsao.*

Compared with his earlier works, Kuo Mo-jo's plays during this period showed a marked improvement both in message and method of writing. These works, in addition to inheriting the revolutionary romanticism of his earlier works, follow realism as their main trend, and this is particularly true of *Chu Yuan.* Chu Yuan, the central figure of the play, was the first patriotic poet in Chinese history. The play describes the great poet's struggle against the vicious ministers and traitors who attempt to sell out his motherland and his persistence in this struggle in the face of name-calling, mud-flinging and even banishment and attempted murder. Kuo Mo-jo's rich knowledge of Chinese history and his fervent love for the motherland stand him in good stead in bringing the character of the patriotic poet to life. The play had a remarkable effect as an educational and agitational work.

---

[1] An English version of this play was published by the Foreign Languages Press in 1955.

Chen Pai-chen,[1] who had tried his hand at writing plays prior to the War of Resistance, now came forward with more and better works. From the outbreak of the war to the post-war period, he turned out eight full-length plays in all — *The Den of Devils,* showing the Japanese and traitors in their true colours, *Wartime Men and Women* and *Wedding March,* exposing the seamy sides in the rear areas, *Autumn Harvest* (adapted from Ai Wu's novel of the same title), about the co-operation between the soldiers and civilians, *Spring Comes to the Earth*, about wartime industry, *Winter Scene*, a eulogy of the unbending spirit of a doctor and an exposure of the Kuomintang misrule, *The Picture of Promotion in Officialdom,* a satire against bureaucracy, and *Shih Ta-kai*, a historical play.

These plays show the playwright to be one who sees things through the eyes of the people and analyses and handles the characters and plots from a revolutionary viewpoint. His writings are fraught with healthy sentiments rather than melancholy and sentimentalism.

If we compare Chen Pai-chen's writings in the early period of the war with those of the later period we will see the development of his work as a literary realist. His earlier plays, *The Den of Devils* and *Wartime Men and Women,* which played some part in rousing the people to action against the enemy, show a certain lack of vitality, and the characters are not sufficiently typical. The weakness came from the author's lack of experience of life, and this also shows itself in their tinge of petty-

---

[1] Chen Pai-chen, born in Huaiyin, Kiangsu Province, in 1908, is now a member of the presidium of the Union of Chinese Dramatists and a secretary of the Union of Chinese Writers.

bourgeois romanticism and their adaptation to the tastes of small townsmen. Then the playwright underwent the difficulties of wartime life. It was an ordeal for him, but one which he faced courageously, and in the doing, steeled himself in the struggle. He became increasingly mature in outlook and, with a growing store of experience in life, turned out two excellent and realistic plays—*Winter Scene* and *The Picture of Promotion in Officialdom.*

(4) The Essay and Reportage

Since the May 4 Movement Lu Hsun had written a whole series of brief, terse political essays, of a very high literary order, which dealt timely and sharp attacks upon the feudal forces, imperialists, comprador-bureaucrats, warlords and racketeers and revealed a clear vision of a better future in store for the revolution.

During the early period of the League of Left-Wing Writers, Chu Chiu-pai also turned out a flood of pungent and militant essays which were spoken of as a match for Lu Hsun's.

After the outbreak of the War of Resistance, the essay attracted the attention of the writers as an effective weapon against the dregs of humanity in the anti-Japanese camp and the vileness of society. Nevertheless, as all the writers were focussing their attention on the war and many of them failed to gain a correct understanding of the united front, few tried their hand at the essay in spite of the efforts to advocate it. It was only after the fall of Shanghai that a number of progressive writers there combined to publish *Lu Hsun Feng* (Lu Hsun's style), a magazine devoted to essays against the Japanese and the puppet regime.

In 1944, a critical situation arose when the Japanese launched a new offensive and penetrated deep into Kweichow Province without meeting any resistance on the part of the Kuomintang troops. This was also the time when the reactionary Kuomintang government stepped up its fascist rule and the secret agents rode roughshod over the people. A new tide arose in the patriotic and democratic movement in the areas under the Kuomintang rule. Meanwhile, a large number of essay-writers emerged who ruthlessly exposed, ridiculed and tilted at the dark, fascist rule of the Kuomintang. During this period the essay came in for a rapid development, since its attacks fully conformed to the requirements of the broad mass of patriotic people in these areas.

In those times the literary pages of the newspapers throughout the country, with the exception of those run by the reactionaries, set aside a lot of space for essays. Among these the best known were the literary pages of the *Hsinhua Daily* and *Hsinshu Daily* in Chungking and the *Huahsi Evening Paper* in Chengtu. The magazine *Wild Grass* in Kweilin specialized in essays.

After the Japanese surrender, the reactionary Kuomintang government set going the civil war while strengthening its fascist rule of terror. During this period, despite the strict censorship of the reactionary government, the progressive essay-writers continued adroitly to expose and castigate the Chiang Kai-shek clique and the American imperialists with their pungent essays. In 1947, when the Chinese People's Liberation Army switched over to an all-out offensive, the Chinese people looked forward to their emancipation and the victory of the People's Liberation Army with boundless enthusiasm. The approaching doom of the reactionary Kuomintang regime posed before the entire Chinese people the question of how to help bring about its rapid and thorough collapse instead of merely exposing or ridiculing it. This was why the popularity of the essay dwindled in this period.

Reportage, which had seen its heyday in the early period of the war, and fallen away as the war entered a seesaw stage, took on a new lease of life in 1944, alongside the rise of the student movement and the movement for democracy in the Kuomintang-controlled areas. At that time, the progressive papers and magazines often carried reportage features on the developments of these movements and the efforts of the Chiang Kai-shek secret agents to undermine them. After the Japanese surrendered, the reportage-writers centred their efforts on exposing the plot of the Chiang Kai-shek clique in preparation for an anti-popular civil war, the terror-ridden fascist rule in all parts of the country and the atrocities committed by American soldiers in China. At the same time, they reported the students' demonstrations against violence, starvation, persecution and civil war; the workers', peasants' and townsfolks' heroic struggle against the reactionary rule; and the free, happy and democratic life in the liberated areas. Though less in number than the early period of the War of Resistance, these items of reportage played a useful role in pushing forward the people's democratic revolution, heightening the morale of the people in the Kuomintang-controlled areas in their fight against the Chiang Kai-shek clique and U.S. imperialism and fortifying them with greater confidence in the final victory.

Section 4. Literary Activities in the Shensi-Kansu-Ningsia Border Region and the Anti-Japanese Bases in the Enemy's Rear

(1) The Fine Tradition of the Literary Activities of the Workers' and Peasants' Red Army in the Soviet Areas

On the whole, the literary activities in the Soviet areas were characterized by their integration with the life of the worker, peasant and soldier. First and foremost, this showed itself in the vigorous growth of the artistic and literary activities in the army units. Fu Chung, now Vice-Director of the General Political Department of the Chinese People's Liberation Army, in recalling these activities, once said:

> At that time large numbers of excellent works appeared in the army units, ranging in form from pictures to drama, from the "reportage play" to dances and songs. Of these, the *Red Star Pictorial* in the central revolutionary base and the products of the Woodcut Printshop of the Fourth Front Army were the most popular among the soldiers. Such plays as *Down with Child Emperor Chiang Kai-shek, We Don't Want to Be the Slaves of the Japanese, Going to the Front in Arms* and *The Broken Straw-Sandals* (a satire against the enemy's unsuccessful attempt to pursue the Red Army and check its advance during the Long March) played a great part in heightening the morale of our army. As to songs, there was an even greater number of excellent ones, of which the *Three Disciplinary Rules and Eight Points for Attention* is still

sung today. At that time, even the men of the Kuomintang's Northeast Army learned to sing *Let Chinese Not Fight Chinese,* an agitational song exhorting the Kuomintang soldiers not to fight the civil war. There were also many "reportage plays" and dances created in the Red Army. A lot of space was devoted to literary works by the army newspapers. All forms of art and literature were widely used to describe the battles, extol the exemplary deeds of the combat heroes and encourage close relations between the army and the people. Although in such difficult conditions some of these works were far from perfect, nevertheless they exerted a great influence upon the soldiers and the broad mass of workers and peasants in the Soviet areas.

In those times, the struggle was a ruthless one. The Red Army was constantly exposed to the encirclements and attacks of the enemy; materials were in short supply; and there was a shortage of cultural personnel. To educate the rank and file and enhance their morale, to win the masses to the revolutionary side and to shatter the enemy, the Communist Party gave the lead for everyone — both officers and men — to use and enrich various forms of art and literature. Whether on the march or in battle, members of the propaganda teams in the Red Army used to start up their gramophones, shout slogans, sing songs or stage plays to inspire the men forward. When they set up camp, get-togethers were held between the men and the civilians with all sorts of entertainment.

During the Long March, art and literature also played a remarkable agitational role among the Red Army soldiers. Many a participant of the Long March still remembers how these propaganda teams helped the army on its way and how they looked forward to the literary and artistic activities. In his reminiscences *How We Crossed the Snow Mountains and Grasslands,* Pan Tze-li writes:

> Those young comrades of the theatrical troupes and propaganda teams, always full of spirit, were the most active on our way across the grasslands. While we rested, these young comrades, tired as they were, would give us a treat in the way of singing, dancing or staging plays. .Wherever they went, they were welcomed and well cared for by the men.

There is no end to such examples, which testify that art and literature were for the benefit of the Red Army soldiers, and were within their reach and integrated closely with their life.

Attention was also paid to drama. There was a very popular play entitled *Victory at All Costs* based on first-hand reports of the havoc wrought by the Kuomintang troops among the people in the areas around Kuangchang in Kiangsi Province. These materials were collected during the Kuomintang's fourth and fifth "encirclement and annihilation" campaigns. The play describes how a ten-year-old boy and his blind sister were murdered in cold blood by the Kuomintang troops when they refused to disclose the whereabouts of the Red Army. Wherever it was staged, the audiences used to shout, "Kill the White bandits!" It was highly praised as a successful play by Chu Chiu-pai at a meeting of the playwright, the director and the actors.

During this period, the revolutionary government organized the actors into sixty theatrical teams which fanned out to all the villages in the revolutionary bases and the front-lines. Almost all the plays and songs were written and composed by the members of the teams. Repertoires were constantly changed, particularly those of the "reportage play." These were rushed to completion and staged, giving a timely picture of current military and political events as well as economic and social questions and answering the problems which the peasants were not clear about. Drama played an especially useful role in the newly liberated area in reassuring the people, spreading revolutionary ideas and explaining the policies of the revolutionary government. When a Red Army unit arrived in Shansi, for instance, and the peasants heard there were actors in the army, they rushed to see them and asked them to put on a show.

The revolutionary government encouraged people to engage in creative writing. They attached great importance to the collection and use of folk songs. Some of the songs composed by the people in the revolutionary bases, or adapted by the propaganda teams of the army, were really first-rate, as these two from Hsinwu, Kiangsi Province will show:

> Without folk songs there is no fun,
> Without the Party there is no freedom.
> My love, you take the lead in joining the Red Army,
> And I'll take the lead in singing folk songs.
>
> — "No Freedom Without Revolution"

> It's the folk song that counts, not your voice . . .
> For they sing of the revolution.
> It's not how you look that counts,
> It's your courage in fighting the enemy.
>
> — "Give It to Them Hard!"

These two homely songs ring with the rural women's ardent love for the revolution.

The folk songs were popular among both the people and the commanders and men of the Red Army. During the "counter-encirclement and annihilation" campaigns, whenever the propaganda teams and the civilians' battle-front service teams gave performances, you would invariably hear these songs being sung by both soldiers and civilians. Literature and art were not only integrated with the life of the soldiers and peasants but became a medium of the friendship between them. Two in particular, *The Hsingkuo Folk Song* and *Pomegranate Blossoms,* which were written in the form of duologues on the close co-operation between the revolutionary masses and the Red Army, and overflowed with the spirit of collectivism, optimism and an unshakable conviction in the inevitable doom of the counter-revolutionary forces and the final victory of the revolution. These songs made a great contribution in arousing the people in the revolutionary areas.

(2) Further Development of the Literary Activities in the Border Regions and the Attempt at a New People's Literature

In 1935, the Red Army arrived in northern Shensi after its historic Long March. After the Sian Incident[1]

[1] Under the influence of the Chinese Red Army and the anti-Japanese mass movement, two Kuomintang armies, the North-eastern Army headed by Chang Hsueh-liang and the 17th Route Army headed by Yang Hu-cheng, supported in December 1937 the Communist proposal for an Anti-Japanese National United Front and urged Chiang Kai-shek to unite with the Communists

in 1936, a national anti-Japanese united front was formed, while many intellectuals flocked to northern Shensi from the Kuomintang-controlled areas. After the outbreak of the War of Resistance, an increasing number of writers and artists went to Yenan and other anti-Japanese bases where they, together with their colleagues already in these bases, worked for the revolution while carrying on literary and artistic activities under the guidance of the democratic government.

First and foremost, these activities carried on and enriched the fine tradition of those of the Workers' and Peasants' Red Army in the former Soviet areas — of bringing art and literature to the worker-peasant masses. Take the North China Liberated Area, the biggest of all the liberated areas at that time. In 1937, when the Eighth Route Army arrived in this area, wherever there were propaganda teams there were literary and artistic activities on a mass scale. Their militant songs, dances, short plays and "reportage plays" gave a dynamic impetus to the local literary and artistic activities. Once the peasants had gained their emancipation and their living standards and political consciousness had gone up as a result of the movement for reduction of land rent and loan interests, they demanded culture. With the help of the cultural institutions and literary and artistic organizations, a host of theatrical troupes sprang up in

---

and resist Japan. Chiang rejected their demands, prepared even more actively to "annihilate the Communists" and massacred a number of patriotic youths in Sian. Chang Hsueh-liang and Yang Hu-cheng thereupon arrested Chiang Kai-shek in Sian on December 12, 1937, and released him only on his promise to unite with the Communists and fight the Japanese invaders.

the North China villages, which employed the *yangko*[1] dance and other old artistic forms with new content to reflect the new life of the peasants. In Liaohsien County alone, over thirty rural theatrical troupes were organized in a month, and there were even more in the Peiyo Region and Central Hopei Region. Their performances won the warm approval of the peasants. By 1940 or so, these rural theatrical troupes had assumed a mass character. In the summer of 1940, the Taihang Region boasted a hundred permanent rural theatrical troupes. In May 1942, there were about 1,700 such troupes in the Central Hopei Region while the Peiyo Region came forward with over 1,400 theatrical troupes, *yangko* dance groups and propaganda teams. These troupes were particularly active during festivals or on memorial days or during the slack season. When the measures for carrying out the central task of a certain period were passed on to organizations at lower levels, they never failed to stage plays centring around the task. Small performances were staged even during battle. In the villages around the guerrilla areas they rehearsed and staged plays in the underground shelters, sometimes right under the nose of the enemy stationed in the fortresses. All this served the current struggle and played a remarkable role in agitation and education. In 1941, the Shansi-Chahar-Hopei Border Region formed scores of model rural theatrical troupes, which issued over 10,000 copies of songs and plays.

---

[1] *Yangko* used to be a popular song and dance form among the peasants in North China. Later, talking, singing and certain story plots were added to it, giving it the character of a play, which was further developed and improved by the art and literary workers in the liberated areas.

To push forward literary and artistic activities among the workers and peasants, many professional theatrical troupes and literary and artistic bodies were formed and an army of writers, artists and actors trained. Take, again, the North China Liberated Area. Up to 1942, there were in this area such professional theatrical troupes as the Taihangshan Theatrical Troupe, Resistance Theatrical Company, Central Hopei Frontline Troupe and the New Age Theatrical Company. In addition to performances, these troupes often ran short-term courses on drama for the peasants. In southeastern Shansi, there were the National Revolutionary Art School and Lu Hsun Art School, and in the Shansi-Chahar-Hopei Border Region, the Lienta Institute of Art and Literature, all of which turned out a great amount of literary and artistic talent for all parts of North China. In addition, there were the Rural Dramatic Workers' Association in the Taihang Region, the Society of Literature for National Salvation in the Shansi-Chahar-Hopei Border Region and the Cultural Construction Society in central Hopei, all of which specialized in guiding cultural work in the rural areas. Apart from carrying out their own activities these theatrical troupes, schools and organizations made a great contribution in helping and encouraging literary and artistic activities among the masses.

Literary and artistic activities were also vigorously carried out with a fair amount of success among the workers and peasants in the Shensi-Kansu-Ningsia Border Region, Shansi-Suiyuan Liberated Area and Shantung Liberated Area.

The activities of the professional actors, writers and producers were mostly concentrated in Yenan. At one time between 1938 and 1939, a literary evening was held almost every three days in Yenan. Anti-Japanese songs caught on well. The walls were decked with "street poems," literary bulletins and cartoons, a fascinating sight to behold!

In addition, this period also produced a string of literary works on the heroic deeds of the Eighth Route Army, and the land reclamation and happy life of the people in the border regions. A number of stories and reportages in this vein was turned out by Liu Pai-yu, Chou Erh-fu and other established writers, depicting the happy life of the soldiers and civilians in the border regions led by the Communist Party, their labour enthusiasm and their confidence in the War of Resistance, thus heightening the morale of the people in their fight for democracy.

Great importance was also attached to folk arts like story-telling and local operas in the liberated areas — a continuation of the fine tradition of the former Soviet areas.

During this period, the men of letters in the liberated areas spared no effort to find a road to a new people's literature. This was part of a process of the gradual transition to a new stage of development, which ended up with the successful solution to the question when Comrade Mao Tse-tung's *Talks at the Yenan Forum on Art and Literature* came out in 1942. This document of great historic significance marked a turning-point in modern Chinese literature. It brought about an enormous change in the art and literature in the liberated areas and advanced it to a new stage.

CHAPTER ELEVEN

LITERATURE IN THE LIBERATED AREAS ON THE PATH OF SOCIALIST REALISM

Section 1. Works Mirroring Mass Struggles and Productive Activities

Mao Tse-tung's *Talks at the Yenan Forum on Art and Literature* marked a turning-point for the writers and artists in the liberated areas. They intensified their study of Marxism-Leninism and Mao Tse-tung's theory of the Chinese revolution. By undergoing ideological remoulding and taking part in the various mass struggles and practical revolutionary work they came to understand from their own experience the policies of the Chinese Communist Party and the People's Government. This was the chief reason for the healthy growth of art and literature in the liberated areas.

New themes and new characters swept like a tidal wave into every form of literary and artistic creation. Chou Yang has made the following rough analysis of the subject matter of 177 works in the *Chinese People's Literature Series* which includes operas, plays, novels, reportage and narrative poetry:[1]

---

[1] Chou Yang, *China's New Literature and Art,* Foreign Languages Press, Peking, 1954, p. 53.

The War of Resistance to Japanese Aggression, the People's War of Liberation (including all forms of mass struggle against the enemy), and the People's Army (their discipline and relations with the people) — 101.

Land reform in the countryside and other anti-feudal struggles (including rent reduction, settling scores with landlords, struggles against superstition, and illiteracy, promotion of sanitation, and freedom of choice in marriage) — 41.

Industrial and agricultural production — 16.

The history of the revolution (mainly the agrarian revolution in northern Shensi) — 7.

Other topics (like the working style of cadres, and so on) — 12.

The above figures show the general scope of art and literature in the liberated areas. Of the content of the new art and literature, Chou Yang has this to say:

> The struggle for national liberation, the class struggle and productive activities are the predominant themes. As the workers, peasants and soldiers have become the masters in society, so have they become the central figures in the works of art and literature. Intellectuals are generally portrayed as cadres in all sorts of work for the cause of the people's liberation, as brain-workers working together with manual workers. Themes about intellectuals who take no part in the people's struggle, who live only within their own small circle and individualistic world, are obviously worthless and have no place in the literary and artistic works of the liberated areas.[1]

---

[1] *Ibid.*, pp. 53-54.

Among the representative works which reflect the War of Resistance, the People's War of Liberation, and the People's Army, some describe the heroic deeds of the peasants in their struggles against the Japanese aggressors, Kuomintang reactionaries and other adversaries, as for example such novels as Ma Feng and Hsi Jung's *Heroes of the Luliang Mountain*, Chao Shu-li's *Changes in Li Village*,[1] Yuan Ching and Kung Chueh's *Daughters and Sons*.[2]

Outstanding works reflecting the peasants' struggle, like Chao Shu-li's "Rhymes of Li Yu-tsai,"[3] and Chou Li-po's *Hurricane*,[4] depict the great rural movements for rent and interests reduction and land reform. *The White-Haired Girl*,[5] an opera by Ho Ching-chih and Ting Yi, Yuan Chang-ching's *The River of Scarlet Leaves* (opera) and stories like Chao Shu-li's "Hsiao Erh-hei's Marriage,"[6] present as their central characters women who have suffered severe oppression in the feudal society, show the bitterness of the rural struggle against feudalism and at the same time describe the new, happy life after liberation.

Among the works on industrial and agricultural production are *yangko* plays like *Brother and Sister Pioneers*

[1,2] These two novels were translated and published in English by the Foreign Languages Press of Peking in 1953 and 1958 respectively.

[3] Included in *Rhymes of Li Yu-tsai and Other Stories*, Foreign Languages Press, 1954.

[4] Translated and published in English by the Foreign Languages Press in 1955.

[5] Translated and published in English by the Foreign Languages Press in 1954.

[6] Included in *Rhymes of Li Yu-tsai and Other Stories*, Foreign Languages Press, 1954.

and *Get Mobilized!*, novels like Ouyang Shan's *Uncle Kao*,[1] Liu Ching's *Sowing* and Tsao Ming's *The Moving Force*, plays like *How an Artillery Shell Is Made* by Chen Chi-tung and *Song of the Red Flag* by Lu Mei and others, and the famous long poem *Wang Kuei and Li Hsiang-hsiang*[2] by Li Chi.

Spare-time literary and artistic activities were very popular among the workers, peasants and soldiers of the liberated areas. So apart from the works of the professional writers and artists, an astonishing amount of literary and artistic talent was thrown up in the areas as a whole. Many of the professional writers and artists made great efforts to promote these amateur activities. This was especially true of those working in the army units who took a direct part in the battles, living and fighting together with the soldiers, doing propaganda and giving performances in the trenches. Some shed their blood on the battlefield and some lost their lives. They are heroes who will live for ever in the history of modern Chinese literature.

(1) The Novels of Chao Shu-li

After the Yenan Forum all the writers in the liberated areas made resolute efforts to carry out Mao Tse-tung's principles on art and literature. Among them Chao Shu-li was one of the first to show the results in his work.

Chao Shu-li was a native of Chinshui County, Shansi Province. Born of a poor-peasant family, he suffered

[1] An English version of this novel was published by the Foreign Languages Press in 1957.

[2] Ditto, 1954.

all the miseries of the poor. While in secondary school, he joined the student movement and was put in prison. He always took a keen interest in peasant music and drama. During his student days he came into contact with the new literature. For many years he urged writers to write for the peasants and to create a popular form of literature.

After the outbreak of the War of Resistance his ideas made further progress as the result of Party education. After the rectification campaign he wrote of the great changes he had experienced in the villages and the lives of people he was familiar with. These included the "Rhymes of Li Yu-tsai," and "Hsiao Erh-hei's Marriage" written in 1943, *Changes in Li Village* in 1945 and some short stories which were published later.

In his article "On the Works of Chao Shu-li," written in 1946, Chou Yang points out:

> Great changes have been taking place in the wide rural areas that are already liberated. An intense and complex struggle has been going on between the peasants and the landlords. During the War of Resistance to Japanese Aggression, the Communist Party launched a movement in the countryside for the reduction of land rents and interest payments; this movement did much to improve the peasants' living standards. As a result it helped to organize the forces of the Chinese people for the struggle against imperialism. Since our victory over Japan, the fight for lower rents and interest payments has been continuing, combined with the mass struggle to punish traitors and rapacious landlords, a struggle that will end only when the remnant forces of feudalism in the countryside are eradi-

> cated and the peasants completely liberated. In the eight years of war against Japanese aggression, the peasants have become more united and class-conscious than ever before. They now recognize the actual causes of their poverty, and are determined to fight for the removal of these causes. . . . The boundless, and, therefore, irresistible revolutionary strength of the peasants is being brought into full play to effect elemental changes in the countryside, as well as in the rest of China; at the same time, the peasants themselves are being transformed in this upheaval. This is the greatest and most profound change in our country today — the change from an old to a new China.
>
> This tremendous change in the countryside demands expression in works of art and literature. The writings of Chao Shu-li meet this demand to a large extent.[1]

Although Chao Shu-li's works are about the villages and his characters are all peasants, there is an essential difference between his works and those of the realist writers of the past who also wrote about the villages and the peasants. Chao, in writing about the peasants, takes the proletarian-socialist standpoint rather than that of the ordinary peasant, or simply a democratic standpoint. He describes the peasants' revolutionary struggles led by the Chinese Communist Party, shows the important role played by the Communist cadres in these struggles, and forcefully explains the necessity of such leadership for the peasants' emancipation.

He extols the active and progressive aspects of the peasants and, at the same time, criticizes their passive

---

[1] Chou Yang, *op. cit.*, pp. 134-35.

and backward aspects. Moreover, he shows the process of the peasants' awakening to political consciousness as a result of the Party's education. The new bright things of life are always the dominant element in his works.

None of these characteristics had ever appeared in earlier works about the peasants and the countryside. Chao Shu-li's works, therefore, do not fall within the category of either peasant literature or classical realism but within the realm of socialist realism.

As regards the special features of his characterization Chou Yang has this to say:

> The first thing we notice in his characterization is that all the persons he describes play definite parts in the struggle, and develop in its course. Every psychological change is determined by the change of each character's position in the struggle and the change in relationships between him and others. The characters are never drawn as static or passive.
>
> . . . .
>
> Another good point in Chao Shu-li's characterization is that the people he describes show what they think and feel through their words and actions. He seldom gives lengthy descriptions of his characters, seldom introduces them himself, and seldom indulges in flowery descriptive passages. All characters are portrayed as they are. They are not "petty bourgeoisie dressed in the clothes of workers, peasants or soldiers." His peasants are real peasants. They act as peasants act, and speak as peasants speak. Everything about them is natural, simple and clear; there is nothing artificial or affected. Moreover, the peasants' real feelings are delineated with a minimum of actions and words.

. . . .

> Another feature of Chao Shu-li's characterization is the clear expression of a definite relationship between himself and his characters. He does not stand outside the struggle, but is right in the midst of it, among the peasants, as one of them. He does not observe and describe the peasants as if he were a bystander, or as if they were far beneath him.[1]

The main reason for these special features lies in the fact that Chao Shu-li takes a proletarian stand with all its sharp distinctions between love and hatred, and that he has become one with the peasants in thoughts and feelings.

His correct stand and viewpoint, his long years of living in the countryside and becoming one with the peasants, his liking for popular arts and long years of work along this line have brought about his unique style of writing and use of language.

His language is the living language of the people. He uses the vernacular not only in dialogue but also in general narration. This is an outstanding characteristic. Next, the language he uses is the refined spoken language of the people. Some writers pay attention only to local dialect, or colloquialisms. Not so Chao Shu-li, who uses ordinary everyday words suited to the mentality and social position of each of his characters. In this connection, Chou Yang comments: "His dialogues are vivid and beautiful. Words come alive when spoken by his characters; they acquire vigour and colour."[2]

---

[1] *Ibid.*, pp. 140, 144, 146.

[2] *Ibid.*, p. 148.

His style of writing, a new national form which is lively and vigorous, enjoys enormous popularity among the masses. Chao Shu-li knows well the Chinese national literary style. It can be clearly seen from his writings that he has critically absorbed such excellent traditions of the Chinese popular novels as the well-worked out plot, clear and simple sentences, and absence of long dull passages of narration or description. These merits are noticeable in his "Rhymes of Li Yu-tsai" and "Hsiao Erh-hei's Marriage." By absorbing and improving on these good points of the traditional novel he has created a new, national form which is naturally liked by the masses. As a result he has integrated artistry with popular appeal.

Thus the literary achievements of Chao Shu-li have tremendous significance in the history of modern Chinese literature, a significance that lies, first and foremost, in the fact that he put into practice the directives on art and literature given by Mao Tse-tung and scored success in a comparatively short time.

Naturally it does not mean that there are no shortcomings in his writings. The new characters in his novels are not worked out to the fullest degree so far as typicality is concerned, and to this extent his *Changes in Li Village* has not fully achieved its purpose. But these defects are minor points besides his remarkable achievements.

(2) The Novels of Chou Li-po

During the two years between 1946 and 1948 land reform was carried out in the liberated areas. This played a significant role in the Chinese revolution. During this tremendous change in the countryside the peasants who had suffered oppression for thousands of years followed the lead of the Chinese Communist Party and stood on their own feet. Through intense, tortuous and complex struggles they overthrew the feudal rule of the landlord class, redistributed the land, and, in the doing, steeled themselves and became the masters of the new villages. This was a world shaking change in which many new people, new peasant heroes, came to the fore. It was these heroes who, in pushing this change forward, also advanced the progress of history. *The Hurricane* precisely reflects this historic change.

Before the War of Resistance Chou Li-po had already done a little writing. After the outbreak of the war he went to Yenan. In the wake of the rectification campaign he began to get into close contact with the life and struggles of the workers, peasants and soldiers. In the winter of 1946 he went to Northeast China where he took part in the land reform and saw for himself the whole process of this great struggle. *The Hurricane* is based on his personal experience and understanding of this struggle.

The Hurricane covers the early stage of the land reform. The events described happened in Yuanmao Village in Sungkiang Province in Northeast China. In the words of the writer, the purpose of writing this novel was:

> . . . To use the lively and rich material I had collected in the land reform in the Northeast to describe how our Party, for more than twenty years, had been leading the people in the great and bitter struggle against imperialism and feudalism, and to depict the peasants' happiness and sorrows during this period, so

as to educate and inspire the revolutionary masses as a whole.[1]

Taking the novel as a whole, the writer has achieved his purpose fairly well.

Because of the writer's strong class sentiments, because he had become one with the peasants in thoughts and feelings, because he has more than a passing familiarity with the new peasant heroes and the ordinary working peasants, he has an ardent love for them. He writes with warm affection about their thoughts and feelings, their lives and families, the relationships between them as well as their humour and interests. He breathes this ardour into almost all his characters.

In *The Hurricane* the new peasant heroes hold a dominant position. The writer has successfully created their images. In Part One, for instance, the main character Chao Yu-lin, a poor peasant, has been so ruthlessly exploited by the landlord that he is nicknamed "Naked Chao." But he has a firm character, a fine personality; he never yields to difficulties and has a high degree of class solidarity. When his political consciousness awakens he is persistently courageous and resolute in the struggles with the enemy. After he is admitted into the Party he further displays his noble proletarian character. Eventually he sacrifices himself in the cause of the workers' and peasants' liberation. The writer has eulogized with burning class sentiments the significance of Chao's noble death in a way that has moved and inspired thousands of readers.

---

[1] Chou Li-po, *The Hurricane*, Foreign Languages Press, Peking, 1955, p. vi.

In Part Two the writer portrays the ingenuity, courage, righteousness and selflessness of his main character, Kuo Chuan-hai, also a peasant who has suffered all sorts of torture and misery. Following the completion of the land reform Kuo leaves his bride and enlists in the army to defend the land reform.

Such minor characters as Pai Yu-shan, Li Chang-yu, Old Sun, and Old Tien are also vividly portrayed. Then there are his new type of peasant women like Mrs. Chao, the wife of Chao Yu-lin, Mrs. Pai and Liu Kwei-lan. The noble image of Mrs. Chao as the widow of a martyr is unforgettable.

Another notable feature of this novel is its simplicity, clearness and vigour in plot as well as in the use of language. The writer seldom uses long dull narrative; every line is filled with the glow of life; the story is clear and in bold relief; the language is the simple, spoken language of the people. As a result the story is one that is easy to grasp and conveys an impression of reality. In short, it is a powerful novel.

But this simplicity has its shortcomings. It hampers the writer from making a more profound analysis of his characters and from recording his observations of the social changes more calmly. Consequently he falls short of giving the fullest expression to the class relations and the complications of the class struggle in the countryside. He has also oversimplified the mental conflicts and struggles of some of his characters.

Naturally few literary works are perfect. The significance of *The Hurricane* lies in its fairly full expression of the process of land reform, realistic portrayal of the appearance and psychology of the various classes in the villages and characterization of a new type of hero. This is a victory for socialist realism.

(3) The Novels of Liu Pai-yu

The war waged by the Chinese People's Liberation Army (the Eighth Route Army and the New Fourth Army in the period of the War of Resistance) was a genuine people's war unprecedented in Chinese history. It won the wholehearted support of the people all over the country. The officers and men of the Liberation Army are the emancipated armed peasants who, under the leadership of the Communist Party, have overcome the weak points of the peasantry. Some have become steeled vanguards of the proletariat. During the war they showed unmatched heroism and unlimited devotion to the cause of the revolution.

This great war and the heroic officers and men who directed the war have been vividly mirrored in the literature of the liberated areas. They are especially well reflected in Liu Pai-yu's works.

Liu Pai-yu began writing before the War of Resistance. During the war he went to Yenan. For some time he was with the army and wrote some stories on the War of Resistance, which were later published in *Happiness* and *Sketches at Lungyen Village*. After the outbreak of the People's War of Liberation, he was with the people's army once more, this time for a longer period. With his deeper experience of army life he produced several successful works.

His stories written in this period were compiled into the *Raging Fires of Battle*, a collection of ten short stories written between 1947 and 1948 (later published under the title *Six A.M. and Other Stories*[1] with some slight change of content). In 1949 he published his short novel *Flames Ahead.*[2]

These short stories were written at a time when the Chinese People's Liberation Army began to pass over to the offensive. The writer has faithfully described many important battles and reflected the historic features of the period. In fact the stories are so closely connected with this period that they can serve, to some extent, as a history of the war.

The writer pays particular attention to the class characteristics of the army units. On the one hand he portrays in bold relief the Party's leadership in the army, on the other, he writes about the officers and men themselves — most of them labouring people. Having suffered brutal oppression at the hands of the imperialists, bureaucrats and landlords, these people have a vehement hatred for these enemies. With Party education they are quick to raise their political consciousness, and to recognize the enemy of the People's Liberation Army as their own. The interests of the revolution become as one with their own and their relations with the revolution are as flesh and blood. It is in fact a life-and-death relationship. The meaning of revolution to them is concrete and personal, one that is easily understood.

This is the root of the splendid qualities of the People's Liberation Army that the writer has so forcibly

---

[1] Translated and published in English by the Foreign Languages Press in 1953.

[2] Ditto, 1954.

portrayed. Under his pen these new heroic people seem to actually live. They possess simple and bright characters without any of the complex mental contradictions of individualism. They are filled with bitter hatred for the class enemy and brotherly love for their comrades-in-arms. The single aim of their lives is to serve the revolutionary cause. Such characters are very common in Liu Pai-yu's stories. Revolutionary class consciousness, however, is not something that awakens overnight, and the writer describes at great lengths the Party's education and guidance as the source of these admirable qualities. His "Three Invincible Fighters" is a case in point. In addition, the author has dwelt upon some wrong tendencies such as negligence of tactics and slackness, and described the correction of these wrong ideas through resolute struggle and the correct leadership of the Party.

Flames Ahead, which describes the great historic event of the crossing of the Yangtse by the People's Liberation Army in 1949, contains some powerful descriptions of the scenes of the crossing, and some interesting characterizations of the higher commanders. Novels of this kind were seldom seen in the liberated areas. The story of the crossing of the Yangtse is a story of overcoming difficulties. The theme of the novel centres on the way the people's army units overcame unimaginable hardships through sheer grit and will-power and eventually won the war. The keynote of the novel is expressed in the words of the political commissar, Liang Pin:

> Did you think victory came as easily as taking a stroll after an evening meal? No. There were always

these obstacles, difficulties. Only after you overcome them can you talk about "victory."[1]

With joy and confidence the writer extols the victory and points out the still greater victory which is bound to come. His ardour and lyrical portrayal impart his joy and confidence to the reader and at the same time bring home the hardships involved in winning the war, thus enhancing the fruits of the revolution.

(4) The Novels of Liu Ching and Tsao Ming

During the War of Resistance the Communist Party of China temporarily suspended the policy of confiscating the landlords' land in order to rally all forces to win the war. It adopted, instead, the policy of reducing the land rents and interest payments. This was a correct decision suited to the concrete conditions at that time.

The reduction of land rents and interest payments stimulated the peasants to produce more. On this basis the governments of the Communist-led border regions made great efforts to help the peasants to organize on mutual aid lines, mainly into brigades for the mutual exchange of labour. This tremendously raised agricultural output. In organizing the peasants measures of compulsion were pronounced taboo. Persuasion and good examples were the decisive factor in drawing the peasants into mutual-aid teams for agricultural or handicraft production.

---

[1] Liu Pai-yu, *Flames Ahead,* Foreign Languages Press, Peking, 1954, p. 103.

This historical event found its expression in many literary works in the liberated areas. Among these, Liu Ching's *Sowing* presents the fullest picture of the movement for mutual aid and bigger outputs in agriculture after the reduction of land rents.

Liu Ching, a native of northern Shensi, wrote some short stories in the early stages of the War of Resistance. After the rectification campaign he completed *Sowing* in 1947, a novel of about 200,000 words. The story is set in Wangchiakou, Chingchien, northern Shensi, and describes in a realistic way the peasants' activities and struggles around the main theme of collective sowing of grains.

Tsao Ming also wrote some short stories during the War of Resistance which were later collected in *The Lost Smile*. Her famous novel *The Moving Force*[1] was completed in 1948.

The significance of *The Moving Force* is that it is the first novel to give a fairly full picture of the new life of the workers after liberation.

(5) The Poems of Li Chi and "The White-Haired Girl"

Li Chi, who worked for years in the liberated areas, is a native of Honan Province. Having a taste for literature, he used to write short stories, reportage and poems in his spare time. All these writings were based on his personal observations and most of them were published in the Yenan *Liberation Daily*. In 1944 he wrote his

---

[1] Translated and published in English by the Cultural Press in 1950.

famous long narrative poem — *Wang Kuei and Li Hsiang-hsiang.*

This is an outstanding poem, and the first to show the results of Mao Tse-tung's *Talks at the Yenan Forum on Art and Literature.* As a poem, it is a shining example of the results of the Yenan Forum. Commenting on its significance Lu Ting-yi said:

> I have read through *Wang Kuei and Li Hsiang-hsiang* with immense delight because this is a poem. After the Yenan *Talks* drama was the first to show the results . . . and then came woodcuts. . . . Novels and ballads followed suit. . . . Poetry was the last of all. *Wang Kuei and Li Hsiang-hsiang* is precisely such a new poem. It is written in rich popular diction, excellent in content and form.

Lu Ting-yi's comment well sums up the significance and value of this poem.

The impact of the Yenan *Talks* showed itself first in operas. Since the outbreak of the War of Resistance considerable attention had been paid to the study and promotion of popular opera in the liberated areas. When the direction for literature and art was clarified at the Yenan Forum it was natural that the results should begin to show. After the publication of the operetta *Brother and Sister Pioneers* in 1943, a number of successful dramas came to the fore, like those mentioned in the first sections of this chapter. Among these, *The White-Haired Girl* is the most outstanding.

The White-Haired Girl is a collective work of the Yenan Lu Hsun Academy of Literature and Art and written by Ho Ching-chih and Ting Yi. Together with *The Hurricane,* it was awarded the Stalin Prize in 1951. The story of *The White-Haired Girl* was originally a tale that went the rounds by word of mouth and enjoyed enormous popularity in the Shansi-Chahar-Hopei Border Region.

It is a tale of a few cadres who go to a village to work but find it difficult to make much headway among the villagers. When few people turn up to their meetings, they discover that most of them have gone to a nearby temple to offer sacrifices to a "White-Haired Goddess." The accounts of this "Goddess" and her mysterious appearances are so vivid that the cadres' suspicions are aroused. Scenting a trick on the part of the landlord to sabotage the meeting by taking advantage of the superstition of the peasants, they start up investigations.

While they are on watch one night, a white figure enters the temple and snatches the food from the altar. The cadres pursue her and finally track her down in a cave. The "Goddess" then pours out her story.

She is the daughter of a poor peasant. Prior to the War of Resistance, the landlord contrived to drive her father to suicide by his extortions, and seized her in lieu of the debt. Later he raped her and she found herself with child. When this happened, he decided to murder her. In bitterness and hatred she escaped to a mountain cave where she managed to keep herself alive for several years. Because she is seldom in the sun and has no salt in her diet her hair and skin have turned white. The cadres bring her out of the dark cave into the bright sunlight and she begins a new life in the liberated area.

As with all stories handed down orally it was amended, amplified and polished by numerous people and gradually it came near perfection. It was a work forged by the ardour of the millions of peasants who opposed the old social system and supported the new one. It carried the clear message that, in the words of the opera, "The old society changed men into ghosts, while the new society changes ghosts into men."

The opera is based on the folk story. It retains the central anti-feudal theme by contrasting the old and new societies through the characterization and the development of the struggle.

A few characters are superbly portrayed, especially in their relation to the class struggle. The first to appear on the stage is Yang Pai-lao, the old peasant, Hsi-erh's father. Driven out of his mind by the landlord's extortions, he shouts: "Magistrates, rich men — you tigers and wolves!" and "I'll have it out with them!" But he, like other peasants of the past, does not know how to fight. All he can do is to take passive resistance in the form of suicide.

Yang Pai-lao, however, is not the main character. His main role is to show the helplessness of the peasants of the last generation. The main characters are Hsi-erh, Uncle Chao and Ta-chun. Hsi-erh is only seventeen, but her life of suffering and privations has sharpened her class hatred. Commenting on her father's way of resistance, she says to Aunty Chang:

> . . . But I'm not like my father! Even a chicken will struggle when it's killed, and I'm a human being! Even if it kills me, Aunty, I'm going to speak my mind!

She struggles resolutely against the intolerable miseries forced on her by the landlord and her struggle is literally a life-and-death one, for the landlord wants to kill her. But she wants to go on living and this she does, courageously. Eventually she comes through it and sees the new society led by the Communist Party. The story of Hsi-erh aroused the hatred of thousands for the class enemy and at the same time strengthened their confidence in the victory of the revolution.

Through Uncle Chao and Ta-chun the authors show that the peasants cannot win their struggles against the landlords without the leadership of the Communist Party, and that the revolution led by the Party has in turn always been a source of encouragement and strength to the peasants' struggle. Uncle Chao has seen the Red Army help the poor win their emancipation years before, and it is an experience he has never forgotten. He tells Hsi-erh he is confident that the Red Army will come back again and it is this that gives Hsi-erh the strength to go on living. He disagrees with Yang Pai-lao's suicide and encourages all around him to go on living, cost what it may. "A day will come when power changes hands," he says. When Ta-chun lays into Mu Jen-chih, a lackey of landlord Huang Shih-jen, he advises him to make a quick get-away. "Go northwest, quickly!" Ta-chun flees to Shansi Province and joins the Eighth Route Army. Later he returns with the army to liberate his village. Landlord Huang is faced with his crimes, Hsi-erh is rescued and all the peasants emancipated. Through these characters and incidents the opera not only shows the class contradictions and struggle in the countryside, but also what measures the peasants should take to wipe out the class enemy — the landlords — and win the victory. This is the strongest point of this opera and the reason why it is classed as a work of socialist realism.

Apart from its socialist content, the opera is genuinely national in form. The story is a popular tale reflecting the life of the labouring folk. The language is the common language of the people. The songs, with their strong flavour of folk tunes, have a great variety of melody. The opera also bears some of the characteristics of the old Chinese opera which are familiar to and liked by the peasants. This strong national flavour has helped the opera to win its wide popularity among the people. It is also favourably received among people of other countries. This is another outstanding achievement of the opera.

Section 2. The Literary Activities Among the Workers, Peasants and Soldiers; the Reform of the Folk Arts

(1) Poems, Ballads and Drama in the Army Units

The Yenan Forum clearly defined the policy for literature as one reflecting the life and struggle of the workers, peasants and soldiers. So the Party and all those engaged in art and literature attached special attention to the literary efforts of the workers, peasants and soldiers and to training literary talent among them. In the liberated areas where political and economic reforms had led to the cultural emancipation of the people, the big bulk of workers, peasants and soldiers took an active part in artistic and literary activities and displayed immense powers of creation.

In the People's Liberation Army, the fine traditions of the Red Army period were continued. After the study of Mao Tse-tung's *Talks at the Yenan Forum on Art and Literature* the soldiers' ideological and artistic level was gradually raised. The literary activities led by the Party were within the reach of the rank-and-file fighters, were closely linked with the day-to-day struggles and served the needs of the war. The soldiers set up clubs, held propaganda rallies, published wall newspapers, distributed leaflets and pictorials and staged performances in the trenches. All these activities reflected the fighters' own lives and struggles. Here are a few examples.

During the Battle of Chinsi in Northeast China, when 25,000 copies of 71 ballads, poems and front-line propaganda leaflets, written by the soldiers of one column of the Fourth Field Army, were distributed in the trenches, the fighters scrambled to read them. Having read and digested them, they examined their own conduct, sent challenges to other units and competed in composing other poems and songs to educate the fighters and raise their morale.

In the Huai-Hai Campaign, members of the Second Field Army composed many poems and battlefield propaganda leaflets, of which twenty-nine were selected and printed. These poems and leaflets were usually well illustrated and became treasured possessions among the soldiers. One man of the 28th Regiment, after having seen a picture commending a hero, resolved to do something heroic so that he could also appear in the pictorial. When another fighter on the front-line had his uniform set alight by an incendiary bomb, he was for a moment nonplussed, until he suddenly remembered having seen in a pictorial a picture of a fighter in similar predicament who rolled on the ground and extinguished the flames. He did the same and was saved from serious burns. "It is that little pictorial that saved my life," he said.

Battlefield poems and pictures were likewise popular in the North, East and Northwest. Poems, articles and paintings ran into thousands and tens of thousands. The *Selected Book of Fighters' Poems* published in the Shensi-Kansu-Ningsia Border Region alone contained over a hundred good poems.

In addition to writing poems and ballads the soldiers also staged plays. These performances, usually small, were based on the stories of the company concerned, written up and acted by themselves.

In this way the literary and artistic activities of the army, led by the Party, and with the help of the Literary and Art Working Corps and the propaganda teams, touched every corner of the vast front. They uncovered rich talent among the fighters and led to the production of many excellent works. After the liberation of the whole country further progress was made. Many works of higher ideological and artistic level came to the fore, particularly from among the fighters themselves.

(2) Peasants' Songs and Poems

During the War of Resistance, when the border region governments carried out the policy for reduction of land rents and interest payments, the peasants' living standards went up, and so did their cultural level. Again, in 1947, when land reform was carried out in the liberated areas, and the broad masses of the peasants received land, their political consciousness was greatly raised. As a result the peasants' literary and artistic activities gathered momentum and gained tremendous influence. These activities centred mainly on poems and drama. The dramas, which were for the most part based on the traditional kinds, will be discussed on later pages.

Peasants in the liberated areas called their poetic compositions "emancipation poems." During the course of winning their emancipation their attention was concentrated on the landlords' past exploitation. The first thing they wrote about were their accusations against the landlords. These poems are filled with the sentiments of class hatred. The poem *Remove the Flag-Stone and Look* is a case in point.

> Chichen Kuan
> Is a fine place.
> Firs and pine trees grow in the stone courtyard.
> Remove the flag-stone and look,
> They are growing on the backs of the poor.

Following their emancipation the peasants felt deeply grateful to Chairman Mao and the Communist Party, whom they regarded as having saved their lives. They wrote many poems expressing their ardent love for the people's leader, as for example, the poem *When the Sun Comes Out It Glows Red*:

> When the sun comes out it glows red,
> The sun is like our Mao Tse-tung.
> Without the sun the grain won't grow,
> Without Mao Tse-tung the poor will ever be poor.

The popular song *The East in Red Glow*, which enjoys nation-wide popularity, was based on a poem by Li Tseng-cheng, a young peasant.

Another popular song, *The Sky-High Building Rises from the Ground*, was written by Sun Wan-fu, an old peasant hero of Chutzu County, northern Shensi.

There was a tremendous number of peasants' poems but no adequate collection has been made. Nevertheless, according to the editors' note in the anthology *There Appears in China Mao Tse-tung* edited by the China Popular Literature Research Association in 1951, over 500 poems in praise of Chairman Mao were already gathered, most of them written by peasants.

(3) Songs of the Workers

Owing to the absence of large cities in the liberated areas there was little literary and artistic activities among the workers. Since 1947, with the liberation of one big city after another, the workers have taken up literary and artistic activities. In Northeast China, for example, considerable achievements were made in Lushun, Talien and Harbin. In Harbin some workers took part in writing the drama *Trade Unions Are Good.* In Talien literary and artistic groups were formed in almost every factory and there was no end of stuff written. Chang Keng's report to the National Congress of Writers and Artists held in 1949 disclosed the following situation: "In the Lushun-Talien area alone during the two years from 1947 to 1949 there have been hundreds of dramas written and performed by workers." Following the liberation of Tsinan, in Shantung Province, dramatic and musical activities were organized in almost all large and medium factories, and some of the workers tried their hand at writing plays. In Tientsin, within six months after its liberation, there were about 40 recreation groups in the factories. Wall newspapers were published in most factories. About 5,000 industrial and managerial workers were taking part in literary and artistic activities. Some of them served as newspaper correspondents while others took up drawing. They began to show their creative talents.

It was not long before they were writing poems and other literary material. They first wrote of their joy and excitement in the liberation. *New Year Happiness,* a poem written by Tsui Keng-san, an old worker of the Electric Light Company at Shihchiachuang, bubbles over with the gaiety of the workers after liberation.

A Happy New Year!
A Happy New Year!
This is the best one yet!
Chiang Kai-shek
Is near his end,
And Truman
Can't lift a finger.
The democratic forces are forging ahead
As powerful as the Yellow River;
Nation-wide victory is in sight,
So how can I keep from singing!
Singing!
Singing!

The workers were well aware that it was Chairman Mao and the Communist Party who had brought them the happy life and transformed their jobs from drudgery to creative work. So they too expressed their gratitude and love for Chairman Mao and the Party. In his poem *Long for the Sun* Wang Yen-tien, a worker of the No. 2 Power Plant in northern Hopei, eulogizes the Communist Party with real feeling, as shown in the last stanza of his poem:

The Communist Party is like the sun,
Shining over the hearts of the people,

> The sun is warm and bright,
> When it comes out the people are overjoyed.
> It shines on the workers, peasants, soldiers, students
> and traders alike,
> Who fight Chiang Kai-shek as one man!

Following the liberation of the whole nation, the workers' literary and artistic activities have made further rapid progress. The writings of the workers have made tremendous headway and new talent has come to the fore time and again.

(4) Reform of the Folk Arts

Prior to Chairman Mao's *Talks at the Yenan Forum* the popularization of literary and artistic work already received great attention in the liberated areas. After the Yenan Forum this work was further stressed, with the reform of the folk arts ranking as the foremost task. In 1943 at the literary and educational congress held in the Shensi-Kansu-Ningsia Border Region, the problem of "launching an artistic and literary movement for the masses" was discussed. In his summary report to the congress Chou Yang pointed out:

> To lead the mass literary movement now under way is one of the primary tasks of the leading Party and government bodies at all levels. It must be realized that art and literature are the most lively and effective forms of social education, the best means for the Party's policies and government enactments to reach deep into the masses. Planned organization and concrete leadership must be provided for the mass artistic and literary movement. Minute attention and concern

must be extended to the artistic and literary associations and workers. Further improvement must be made in their political and material treatment. Various measures should be taken to stimulate their interest in writing and other creative work. The mobilization of the masses, the efforts made by the literary and artistic workers, and correct leadership are the guarantees to the successful carrying out of the literary and artistic movement in the border region.

First of all there was the drama movement in the countryside. Rural drama troupes were extensively formed, as the following examples from Shantung Province will show.

In Chiaotung region there were over 10,000 rural drama troupes and clubs in 1945 which made their influence widely felt. In central and south Shantung, there were 143 drama troupes in Chunan County and 110 in Yinan County, which has well over a third of the total number of villages of the county. Almost every village had a new *yangko* dance troupe.

The situation was practically the same in the North and the Northwest, in the Shansi-Suiyuan Region, and Northeast China. Dramas were written and performed by the peasants around the theme of the happenings in the villages. The characters in the plays were all peasants. Such plays produced by the peasants ran into thousands.

Peasants called the new *yangko* "struggle *yangko*," just as during the land reform they had called many plays "emancipation dramas." This was quite correct. Although most of these works used old folk forms, mainly the *yangko*, as a basis, they had been more or less adapted to their new content. Many literary and artistic works were created on the basis of laborious researches in the *yangko*. As a result of these researches the new plays were a further advance on the *yangko*. A comparison between the first *yangko* drama *Brother and Sister Pioneers* and the opera *The White-Haired Girl* will illustrate this process of development.

Next came the reform of story-telling and the reform and retraining of the folk artists. These two things are inseparable. First of all, the task was to contact, unite with, educate and remould the folk story-tellers; to encourage, guide and help them to compose and tell new stories and revise and tell the old. Through such training many new story-tellers came to the fore in the liberated areas. The folk stories *Liu Chiao's Reunion* and *Chang Yu-lan Goes to the Poll* composed by Han Chi-hsiang, for instance, attained a higher ideological and artistic level. Such story-tellers as Shih Wei-chun, Feng Ming-shan and Wang Tsun-san compiled new stories which went down very well with their audiences.

Finally came the reform of old Chinese operas. The primary measuring rod for the reform of the old operas in the liberated areas was whether or not they conformed with the interests of the people. All the old operas were sifted through. Those that were detrimental to the interests of the people were restricted. Those which were beneficial to the people were developed. At the same time new operas were written like *Escape to Liang Mountain* and *The Storming of Chu Village*. Similar principles were adopted towards the local dramas. Efforts were also made to unite with and remould the opera actors and singers. They were no longer despised and oppressed as they had been in the old society. Most of them were willing to remould and improve themselves. In the liberated areas, where the new and old artists formed a united front, the demarcation between the new and old gradually disappeared.

As to the relation between the literary and artistic activities of the workers, peasants and soldiers and the work of the professional writers and artists in the liberated areas, and the principles for its development, Chou Yang has made a profound analysis and clear explanation in his *The People's New Literature and Art*:

> The literary and artistic activities of workers, peasants and soldiers have given new blood and new life to the literature and art of the liberated areas. Their works and those of the professionals form the two integral parts of this literature and art. The workers, peasants and soldiers not only accept the new literature and art; they also take an active part in their creation. Once given a chance, the latent revolutionary vigour of our workers, peasants and soldiers will prove indeed inexhaustible. Similarly, they have shown unlimited vigour and ability in artistic creation. To popularize literature and art, the creative enthusiasm of the masses must be aroused. Professional writers and artists must direct the masses in their creative endeavours; they must also draw sustenance from such works to enrich their own. It is an error to take a contemptuous or indifferent attitude towards the creations of the masses. That kind of attitude was corrected in the main after Comrade Mao Tse-tung's *Talks at the Yenan Forum on Art and Literature*. Yet, while they give guidance to the masses in their literary and artistic activities, professional writers and artists

must remember that these activities are amateur in nature and should not interfere with work in factories and fields, nor with the military duty of the soldiers. Since our literature and art serve a political purpose, they must serve our struggle and our country's productive efforts; that means, they must expedite the former and not hinder the latter.

Thus, we must observe the seasonal nature of rural life and not lay too much stress on regular activities. In the factories, we must keep in mind, production is collective and highly organized; in the army, we must fit into combat conditions and characteristics. Some drama troupes in the villages and factories follow the correct rule that "dramatics must not interfere with work." Nothing too ambitious should be attempted, and the tendency to produce elaborate and costly dramas overcome. It must be remembered that the most important aims of popular literature and art are to educate the workers, peasants and soldiers, and to raise their political consciousness and enthusiasm for work and struggle. Popular literature and art must not be fostered for their own sake. Literature and art cannot be divorced from the current political tasks and the needs of the masses.[1]

[1] Chou Yang, *op. cit.*, pp. 71-72.

CHAPTER TWELVE

THE VICTORY OF MAO TSE-TUNG'S PRINCIPLES ON ART AND LITERATURE

Section 1. The Victory of the Chinese People's Revolution and the Convocation of the All-China Congress of Writers and Artists

In July 1946 Chiang Kai-shek, under the instigation and with the support of the U.S. imperialists, threw his entire army into an all-out attack on the liberated areas. To defeat this counter-revolutionary offensive, the Chinese Communist Party called upon and organized the entire people of the nation to wage a revolutionary civil war. This was the Third Revolutionary Civil War, also known as the People's War of Liberation.

In January 1949 with the peaceful liberation of Peking, a continuous stream of writers and artists came to Peking from the liberated areas as well as the Kuomintang-controlled areas. This led to the first nation-wide meeting of the Chinese writers and artists. On March 22 the North China Cultural and Art Working Committee and the North China Writers' Union held a tea party to entertain the writers and artists in Peking. At the party Kuo Mo-jo proposed that an all-China congress of writers and artists be held with the aim of forming a new national organization of writers and artists. This won the unanimous approval of all those present. A preparatory committee was then established, which after three months outlined the objectives of the forthcoming congress as being to sum up experience, exchange opinions, accept criticism, and encourage study so as to settle the principles and tasks for the art and literary work of the nation; to form a new national organization of writers and artists; and to work under the leadership of Chairman Mao to make the best use of art and literature as a weapon to encourage the revolutionary spirit and stimulate enthusiasm for production so as to bring about the speedy and complete defeat of imperialism, feudalism and bureaucrat-capitalism and attain nation-wide victory in the building of a new-democratic culture.

The congress, which opened on July 2, lasted eighteen days and ended on July 19. It was attended by 650 delegates.

The congress listened to and discussed Chou En-lai's political report, Kuo Mo-jo's general report on the people's art and literature of New China, Mao Tun's report on the revolutionary literature in the Kuomintang-controlled areas and Chou Yang's report on the art and literature of the liberated areas.

The congress unanimously approved these reports, adopted a resolution on the principles for future work and declared their intention to strive resolutely for its implementation.

The congress passed a declaration and sent messages of greetings to Chairman Mao, Commander-in-Chief Chu Teh and the entire body of officers and men of the People's Liberation Army; it founded the All-China Federation of Writers and Artists, drew up a set of rules for the federation and elected a national committee with Kuo Mo-jo as chairman and Mao Tun and Chou Yang as vice-chairmen.

After the congress, on July 23, the All-China Writers' Union was founded. Members of the national committee were elected with Mao Tun as chairman and Ke Chung-ping and others as vice-chairmen.

At the inaugural meeting of the congress Chu Teh, Commander-in-Chief of the Chinese People's Liberation Army, delivered a speech on behalf of the Central Committee of the Communist Party of China.

Section 2. The Realization of Mao Tse-tung's Principles on Art and Literature

This was the first nation-wide congress of writers and artists in the whole of the thirty years that had passed since the May 4 Movement in 1919, and it showed a degree of unity and solidarity among the writers and artists that had never been reached before.

Since the First Revolutionary Civil War the revolutionary writers and artists had worked in two separate areas — the revolutionary bases and Kuomintang-occupied areas. Although they had overcome all kinds of hardships and scored many victories they had never joined forces. Now, with the victory of the people's revolution led by the Chinese Communist Party and Mao Tse-tung these two contingents of writers and artists were able to come together. In short, without the victory of the people's revolution, the congress could never have been held.

The congress showed the broad scope and special features of the unity reached under the banner of new democracy, under Mao Tse-tung's principles on art and literature. It brought together the writers and artists of all circles. The unity was one not only between the Party writers and artists and the non-Party, but also between those of the old liberated areas and those of the new, those who belonged to the new school of art and literature and those who belonged to the old, and between the army, local and national minority writers and artists and those of the rest of the nation.

It was on the basis of this unity that representatives of the writers and artists of all circles exchanged views, summed up experience and pledged themselves as one man to fight for the implementation of Mao Tse-tung's principles on art and literature.

The complete correctness of Mao Tse-tung's talks at Yenan in 1942 was borne out by the reports of Chou En-lai, Kuo Mo-jo, Mao Tun and Chou Yang, by the special reports on each area as well as those of certain outstanding writers and artists. In the light of the history of the literary movement over the last thirty years and the personal experience of the writers, the congress unanimously supported the principle that art and literature should serve the people and, first of all, serve the workers, peasants and soldiers. Accordingly they passed the following resolution:

> Having heard Vice-Chairman Chou En-lai's political report and Kuo Mo-jo's general report on New China's art and literature, this congress unanimously agrees that the direction and tasks outlined in the above reports for Chinese writers and artists to carry out under

Comrade Mao Tse-tung's principles on art and literature are completely correct. We unanimously agree with these reports and accept them as the directive for our future work which we will make great efforts to carry out.

Since the congress, Mao Tse-tung's *Talks at the Yenan Forum on Art and Literature* has become the common programme of struggle for the literary movement of New China. The principles laid down in this work have been widely studied and have become a guide for action. Under such ideological guidance the people's literary and art movement of New China has entered a new stage, one in which the writers and artists of the whole nation follow Mao Tse-tung's principles on art and literature. Socialist realism will therefore make still greater headway and bring about even greater achievements in China's literature.

INDEX